PHOTOGRAPHY IN IRELAND

THE NINETEENTH CENTURY

Experimental Colour Transparencies
John Joly, Dublin, c1894

LANTERN SLIDES

PHOTOGRAPHY IN IRELAND

THE NINETEENTH CENTURY

Edward Chandler

DUBLIN 2001

First published in 2001 by Éamonn de Búrca for
EDMUND BURKE PUBLISHER
"Cloonagashel", 27 Priory Drive, Blackrock,Co. Dublin, Ireland

ISBN 0 946130 34 5
British Library Cataloguing in Publication Data
A catalogue for this book is available
from the British Library

*This publication has received support from The Heritage Council
under the 2001 Publications Grant Scheme.*

*We would also like to thank the National Library of Ireland
for their assistance.*

Design and photography by Edward Chandler

PRINTED BY BETAPRINT LTD, DUBLIN

Introduction

MANY OF THE BOOKS published in Ireland in recent years relating to early photography have been, what I call, subject orientated. That is the subject matter of the images has tended to take precedence over everything else, what the picture is "of" seems to be more important than other things which photo historians find important, such as image "quality" or the processes used to create it.

This approach can be ascertained by the provision, with the illustrations in these books, of voluminous captions explaining what the pictures are all about and virtually no information about the photographers who might be lucky in such cases to even get their names mentioned. The research necessary to establish this descriptive information is, no doubt, admirable. It is a pity, however, that a little more attention has not been paid to the men, or women, who stood in front of those views and captured them for posterity.

It is not really surprising that many people should look at photography like this, one of the most important functions of photography since it was invented has been the recording of everyday reality and I fully recognise this function. What I am objecting to is the use of subject matter as the only criterion for evaluating a photograph and ignoring other factors such as print quality, composition, general pictorial values and, most importantly, the creator of the image.

When planning this book I was determined that I would do proper justice to the hundreds of Irish photographers of the nineteenth century who, while wrestling with crude and cumbersome cameras, and using primitive techniques and processes – often injurious to health – never the less, very often produced images of great beauty.

The plate section is intended to show outstanding images by important Irish photographers or by those who, in my opinion, contributed greatly to the development of the medium in Ireland. The images have been carefully chosen, not only for their fine photographic qualities but also because of interesting subject matter. In this section of the book all images are printed in colour as it was felt that this was the only way by which all the various processes involved might be presented reasonably accurately. While most of these particular images have been reproduced from actual vintage prints or very good colour photographic copies, in some cases it has been necessary to use modern monochrome prints – mostly obtained from National institutions – made from old paper or glass negatives – or even prints from copy negatives. Modern computer technology has been used, where necessary, to adjust the colouration and tonalities of these to closely match what the originals would have looked like.

Old photographic images can carry many kinds of blemishes such as fading, stains, spots, tears and other surface abrasions. Where it can be ascertained that these "faults" may have been part of the original image from its creation they have been preserved, however, if they appear to have been acquired during the lifetime of the image – due to neglect or poor storage – they have been judiciously toned down or even removed. Some of the people who have loaned images have expressed a desire that their images should be reproduced as they are, blemishes and all, and in these cases their wishes have obviously been respected. The intention has been, at all times, to present images which look as close as possible to those which would have been presented by the original photographers.

The first edition of Helmut Gernsheim's monumental *History of Photography* was published in 1956. It rapidly became a guide book for photographic historians as to which early photographers were worthy of attention. In this respect it played an important part in stimulating further study and research. (It was also used by budding collectors as a guide to which photographers were worth collecting.) Very few Irish photographers were thought worthy of inclusion, one of the few was John Shaw Smith who is consequently one early Irish photographer who is known abroad.

I would like to think that the present work might serve a similar useful function in stimulating an interest in early photography among present day Irish students. The appendices at the back of the book have been included with that end in mind. Some of these have been extracted from sources based abroad and difficult of access and, as far as I know, are not available on the Net.

Several of the photographers dealt with are, in my opinion, world-class figures as far as the quality of their work is concerned. They are, however, almost unknown outside Ireland, and would amply repay further study and research. Virtually nothing has been written about individual Irish nineteenth century photographers, notable exceptions are the late Kieran Hickey's *Light of Other Days* on the Lawrence Collection and *Impressions of an Irish Countess* by David Davison about the Countess of Rosse.

I have tried to make the various index sections of the book as comprehensive as possible, these have been based on lists which I have collected over the years and on the lists published in Thom's and other streets directories between the 1840s and 1900. Because of the way some of these directories were prepared there are bound to be errors, mostly of ommission. I apologise in advance for the fact that there are most probably some photographers who accidentally may not be included.

I would like to acknowledge here the assistance of the The Heritage Council and the National Library of Ireland through the National Photographic Archive in the production and publication of this book.

Elsewhere on this page I acknowledge the help of many colleagues and friends who have helped to make this book much better than it would otherwise have been, however, I feel that I must mention two people who read my text, Gránnia MacLochlainn of the National Photographic Archive and Peter Walsh both of whom helped to make sure that my atrocious grammar and spelling were under control and that I was not in danger of making rash statements which I might regret later .

Finally I must give a special word of thanks to my friend Sean Sexton who has consistently encouraged me over the years to get my thoughts on photography down on paper.

Edward Chandler, September, 2001

Acknowledgements

Mr. John Benjafield; Mr. Joseph Collins; Mr. Stephen Coonan; Mr. David Davison; Éamonn and Vivien de Búrca; Dr. Patricia Donlon; Mr. John Duggan; G. A. Duncan; Mr. Eric Earle; The International Museum of Photography, George Eastman House, Rochester, N.Y.; The Fox Talbot Museum, Lacock Abbey, Wiltshire; The Gallery of Photography, Dublin; Ms. Meta Gale; Mr. Phillipe Garner, Sothebys, London; Mr. Tom Hayes; Mr. Robert Hershkovitz; The Irish Architectural Archive; Mr. Michael Jacob; Mr. Kenneth Jacobson; Dr. Noel Kissane, National Library of Ireland; Dr. Alf MacLochlainn; Ms. Gráinnia MacLochlainn, National Photographic Archive; Mr. Michael McCaughen, Ulster Folk and Transport Museum, Cultra; Mr. W, A. Maguire, Ulster Museum, Belfast; Ms. Jane Meadows; Ms. Pauline Moreau; Mr. George Morrison; Ms. Alison Morrison-Low, Royal Museums of Scotland; National Museum of Photography, Film and T.V., Bradford; Mrs Osborne, Newton Anner House; Mr. John Osman; Mr. Terence Pepper, National Portrait Gallery, London; Mr. Tom O'Flaherty, Photographic Society of Ireland; The National Archives, Dublin; The Public Record Office, London; The Religious Society of Friends; The Earl of Rosse; The Royal Irish Academy; The Royal Society of Antiquaries in Ireland; The Science and Social Picture Library, London; The Science Museum, London; Ms. Sonia Schorman; Mr. Sean Sexton; Mr. Jim Shiels; Mr. Peader Slattery; Ms. Jennifer Smith; Ms. Lindsey Stewart, Christies, London; Mr. Roger Taylor; Ms. Beryl Vosburgh; Mr. Peter Walsh; Ms. Elinor Wiltshire

Preface

GENERAL HISTORIES are among the most difficult of all to compile, and this is especially true of that ubiquitous, pervasive and intensely fragile thing we all take for granted – the photograph. While presenting excellent testimony to the appearance of people, objects, places and events over time, the photograph can at best only vaguely suggest the character traits of the sitter, or the richness of diversity in a settlement or landscape. Like any other historical document it presents us with only a trace of the actuality of the moment.

A photograph 'speaks' for itself through the language of vision, but in an entirely different way from any other graphic medium. Over the past 160 years photographs have become an integral part of the world of ideas, in the same way that objects are part of our perceptual world. But photographs become the stuff of history only when we provide expansion beyond the realms of picture storytelling by referencing written records and artefacts.

Eddie Chandler has been doing this for over thirty years, piecing together the lives and careers of largely forgotten men and women who pushed forward the boundaries of the visual world. From the very start, in 1839, and throughout the half-century under discussion in Chandler's synthesis, there was no mainstream movement in the art-science of shadow fixing. Irish photographers like their contemporaries elsewhere, not only sustained but also added to the predominant currents along photography's evolutionary path, both philosophically and technically. Their story is part of a larger one where patents bedevilled the progress of the calotype for years. Where commercial rivals struggled for survival, leisured amateurs compiled their albums, the slow and costly daguerreotype mirror went dark, and the difficult to manipulate wet plate collodion process triumphed in adversity until the plates turned dry.

Chandler's no-nonsense prose style, blending scholarship and an infectious passion for his subject, is always enjoyable to read. He is inquisitive, informative, insightful. As a photo-grapher he is a mature interpreter of landscape, water and stone – whether it be Venice stippled with light bouncing off the canals, or the gritty texture of graven stone angels blotched with lichen. The selection of plates here tells its own story of his feelings for pictorial photography. Over the years he has constantly sought recognition for Irish masterworks of the genre. His case for the restoration of the reputations of W. D. Hemphill and Augusta Crofton among the canon of high Victorian wet-plate pictorialists is, to say the least, compelling.

The historical narrative is refreshingly wide ranging, with a colourful cast of characters like Beatty the Belfast engraver, who played a key role in the development of early photography and who, although he lived into the 1890s, died a pauper and has left virtually no photographs behind. Intriguing also is the swarthy 'Turk', Leone Glukman, who held centre stage among studio portraitists in the 1840s and '50s. His most enduring image is that of John Mitchel, radical Nationalist, Young Irelander and editor of The United Irishman whose *Jail Journal*, first published in 1913 (usually including a lithographic version of Glukman's daguerreotype), is still in print.

Reprints, long overdue, allow some of the achievements of Coghill, Grubb and Joly to be appreciated at first hand among the useful appendices. These were some of the most important photographers of the nineteenth century and their work reflects the obsessions of early photographic pioneers not only in Ireland but everywhere. They dealt in complex factors of high artistic, cultural and scientific value, from the sometimes acrimonious debates about 'Art's youngest and fairest child', to significant technological achievements in optics and chemistry. Concerns which dominate thinking in photographic galleries and laboratories today.

Peter Walsh, Dublin, September 2001

Peter Walsh is an historian with particular interests in early photography, seventeenth century architecture and local history. From 1979 to 1999 he was Curator of the Guinness Museum.

THE DAGUERREOTYPE

Anonymous verse from *The Dublin University Journal* Vol. XXI, 1843

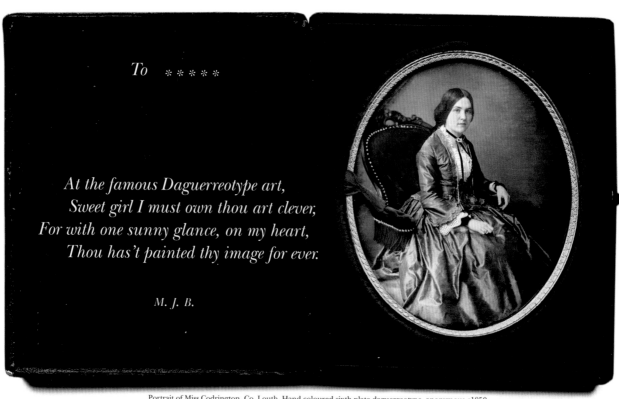

To　＊＊＊＊＊

At the famous Daguerreotype art,
　Sweet girl I must own thou art clever,
For with one sunny glance, on my heart,
　Thou has't painted thy image for ever.

M. J. B.

Portrait of Miss Codrington, Co. Louth. Hand coloured sixth plate daguerreotype, anonymous c1850

Contents

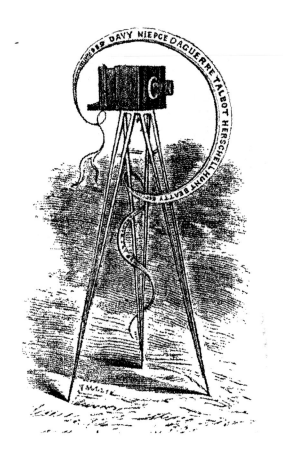

This device and the illustration of the camera on p.iv were used by
Francis Stewart Beatty in a series of articles on photography
published in *The Dublin Journal* in 1858.
They are wood engravings and were probably executed by himself.
(Interestingly he has added his own name at the end of the list of
illustrious photographic pioneers whose names appear on the scroll around the camera).

Picture Credits

Chandler Private Collection, Frontispiece, Plts 11, 16, 18, 27, 28, 29, 31, 32, 33, 35 ,36, 38, 39, pp. iv, 3, 14, 15, 18, 24, 32(left), 35,
38, 42, 43, 44, 45, 47, 51,55, 60, 61, 65, 66(bottom), 67, 69, 70(left), 71, 77, 80, 82, 83, 87, 88, 91, 92(bottom), 96(Coghill).
Christies South Kensington, Plt 5, pp. 48, 66(top). / County Museum, Clonmel, Plts. 22, 23, 24, pp. 38, 39.
David Davison, Plt. 12, p. 34, 68. / John Duggan, p. vii, 28(left). / Éamonn de Búrca, p 64(top left)
Phillipe Garner, pp. 19, 20. / Illustrated London News, pp. 27(left), 114(right). / Mason Technology, p. 63.
George Morrison, Plt. 9, p. 24. / National Museum of Photography, Film and T.V., Bradford, Plt. 1.
National Library of Ireland, Plts.17, 19, 20, 29, 37, 38, 39, 41, 43, 44, pp. ii, x, 7, 31, 36, 37, 59, 61, 62, 89, 90, 91, 114(left).
National Portrait Gallery, London, Plt. 2 / John Osman, Plt. 34.
Photographic Society of Ireland, Plts 7, 8, 10, 21, 40, 42, pp. 30(right), 31(left), 40, 84, 92(top), 96, 123.
Private Collections, Plts. 6, 13, 15, 23, 24, 26, pp. 22, 23, 24, 27(right),86.
Royal Soc. of Antiquaries of Ireland, p. 81. / Science Museum London, Plts. 3, 4, 10, pp. 9, 11, 30(left),
Shaws Illustrated Directory 1850, p. 97, 98. / Sean Sexton, Plts. 14, 25, p. 33, / Jim Shiels, p. 70.
The Society of Friends, p. 49. Talbot Collection, p. 24(bottom right).
Ulster Museum, Belfast, p. 5, / Peter Walsh, p. 22, 92(bottom).

While every effort has been made to locate sources and credit material, if there are cases where this has not been possible our apologies are extended.

List of Plates

A Cork street scene
John or Alphonsus Mott (?) 1840s
QUARTER PLATE DAGUERREOTYPE IN A CEDAR WOOD FRAME

PLATE 1

Maria Edgeworth, Novelist
Richard Beard, Polytechnic Studio, May 1841
NINTH PLATE DAGUERREOTYPE

PLATE 2

St. George's Church and Hardwick Street, Dublin
Anonymous, c1846
MODERN PRINT FROM A CALOTYPE NEGATIVE

PLATE 3

The Four Courts, Dublin
Anonymous, c1846
MODERN PRINT FROM CALOTYPE NEGATIVE

PLATE 4

Patrick Byrne, the blind Irish Harper
Hill and Adamson, Edinburgh, 1844
MODERN PRINT FROM A CALOTYPE NEGATIVE

PLATE 5

The Chess Players, Leone Glukman and William Constable
Attributed to William Constable, c1850
MODERN PRINT COPY FROM A DAGUERREOTYPE

PLATE 6

Pillars, The Temple of Karnac, Egypt
John Shaw Smith, 1850-51
SALT PRINT FROM A WAXED PAPER NEGATIVE

PLATE 7

St. Peter's and The Vatican, Rome
John Shaw Smith, 1850-51
PRINT C1895 FROM A CALOTYPE NEGATIVE

PLATE 8

Young Ireland leaders William Smith O'Brien and Thomas Francis Meagher in prison
Attributed to Leone Glukman, 1848
COPY PRINT FROM ORIGINAL DAGUERREOTYPE (?)

PLATE 9

Stonebreakers, Roscrea
Alfred Capel Cure, 1855
MODERN PRINT FROM A CALOTYPE NEGATIVE

PLATE 10

Unidentified French Chateau
Capt. Edward King-Tenison, Roscommon, c1854
SALT PRINT FROM A PAPER (CALOTYPE ?) NEGATIVE

PLATE 11

View of Birr Castle, Co. Offaly
Mary, Countess of Rosse, c1854
SALT PRINT FROM A CALOTYPE NEGATIVE

PLATE 12

Game, Hanging
Francis Edmund Currey, Lismore Castle, Co. Waterford, c1855
ALBUMEN PRINT FROM COLLODION NEGATIVE

PLATE 13

St. Patrick's Bridge, Cork, damaged in a flash flood, 1853
Humphrey Haines, Cork, 1857
ALBUMEN PRINT FROM A COLLODION NEGATIVE (STEREO)

PLATE 14

Reginald's Tower, The Mall, Waterford
Strangman Davis Goff, Waterford, c1855
ALBUMEN PRINT FROM A COLLODION NEGATIVE

PLATE 15

College Green, Dublin
Attributed to Thomas Grubb, Dublin, c1855
ALBUMEN PRINT FROM A COLLODION NEGATIVE

PLATE 16

Playing Chess
Edward Harding, Cork, c1858
HALF PLATE AMBROTYPE

PLATE 17

"Mr. Ffrench"
Augusta (Crofton) Dillon, Lady Clonbrock, Co. Galway, c1865
ALBUMEN PRINT FROM A COLLODION NEGATIVE

PLATE 18

Child portrait study
Hon. Luke Dillon or Lady Augusta (Crofton) Dillon, Co. Galway c1870
ALBUMEN PRINT FROM A COLLODION NEGATIVE

PLATE 19

Rockingham, Co. Roscommon
Robert, Earl of Kingston, Co. Roscommon, c1863
ALBUMEN PRINT FROM A COLLODION NEGATIVE

PLATE 20

Field Marshall, Viscount Hugh Gough
Sir Robert Shaw, Dublin, c1857
ALBUMEN PRINT FROM A COLLODION NEGATIVE

PLATE 21

Girl with a Mirror (Miss Osborne)
William Despard Hemphill, Clonmel, Co. Tipperary, c1866
ALBUMEN PRINT FROM A COLLODION NEGATIVE

PLATE 22

"Judith with the Head of Holefernes"
William Despard Hemphill, Clonmel, Co. Tipperary, c1865
ALBUMEN PRINT FROM A COLLODION NEGATIVE

PLATE 23

"Rachel and her Sisters"
William Despard Hemphill, Clonmel, Co. Tipperary, c1865
ALBUMEN PRINT FROM A COLLODION NEGATIVE

PLATE 24

Mr. Gillies, Grenadier Guards
Sir Robert Shaw, Dublin, c1860
ALBUMEN PRINT FROM A COLLODION NEGATIVE

PLATE 25

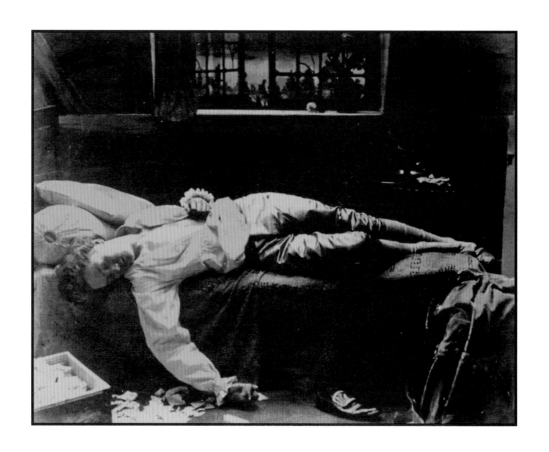

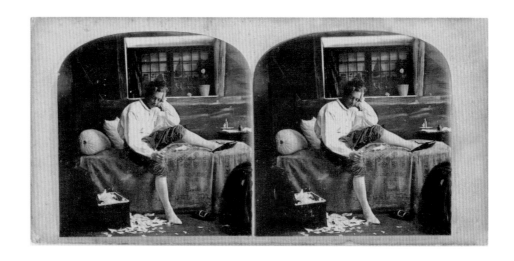

The Death of Chatterton
James Robinson, Dublin, 1857
SALT PRINT FROM A COLLODION (?) NEGATIVE

STEREO CARD VARIATION OF ORIGINAL COMPOSITION
HAND COLOURED ALBUMEN PRINTS FROM COLLODION NEGATIVES

PLATE 26

Castletownsend, Co. Cork
Sir John Joscelyn Coghill, Dublin, c1860
ALBUMEN PRINT FROM A COLLODION NEGATIVE

PLATE 27

The Nave, Dublin International Exhibition, Earlsfort Terrace
The London Stereoscopic and Photographic Company, 1865
ALBUMEN PRINT FROM A COLLODION NEGATIVE

PLATE 28

Punchestown Races
Anonymous, possibly Frederick Holland Mares, Dublin, c1864
MODERN PRINT FROM A STEREOSCOPIC COLLODION NEGATIVE

PLATE 29

The Dublin Photographic Society in the Dargle Valley (?)
The London Photographic and Stereoscopic Company, c1857
FROM A STEREO CARD, ALBUMEN PRINT
It is the writer's view that the gentlemen in this picture are members of the D.P.S.
The two men in the centre are undoubtedly Joseph Kirk and Thomas Bewley and the man seated on
the left might be Sir John J. Cognhill (see p.55)

PLATE 30

Glencar Waterfall, Co. Sligo
Frederick Holland Mares, Dublin, c1863
ALBUMEN PRINT FROM A COLLODION NEGATIVE

PLATE 31

In Glendalough. Co. Wicklow. 76.

Glendalough, Co. Wicklow
Frederick Holland Mares, Dublin, 1863
ALBUMEN PRINT FROM A COLLODION NEGATIVE

PLATE 32

Near Rostrevor
D. Welsh, Armagh, c1875
TWO PRINT PANORAMA (JOINED AT THE TREE)
ALBUMEN PRINTS FROM COLLODION NEGATIVES

PLATE 33

The Funeral of The Earl of Mayo, assassinated in India, Eden Quay, Dublin,
Attributed to Chancellor, 1878
ALBUMEN PRINT FROM A COLLODION NEGATIVE

PLATE 34

Elaborately framed coloured portrait of a lady
Thomas Cranfield, Dublin, c1860
HAND COLOURED ALBUMEN PRINT

PLATE 35

Rostrevor, Co. Down
T. Agmondisham Vesey, Rostrevor, 1878
ALBUMEN PRINT FROM A COLLODION NEGATIVE

PLATE 36

The "Great Eastern" in Dublin port, on her last voyage before being broken up.
Robert French for William Lawrence, Dublin, 1889
ALBUMEN PRINT FROM A DRY PLATE NEGATIVE

PLATE 37

Alexandra, Princess of Wales in Academic Dress – Hon. Doctor of Music
Lafayette, Dublin, c1885
ALBUMEN PRINT FROM A DRY PLATE NEGATIVE

PLATE 38

Double (trick) self-portrait
Victor Smyth, Dublin, c1893
MODERN PRINT FROM A DRY PLATE NEGATIVE

PLATE 39

Mammoth portrait of Miss Maud Gonne
Alfred Werner FRPS, Dublin, 1893
LARGE CONTACT PLATINUM PRINT APPROXIMATELY 1625MM X 1050MM

PLATE 40

From Roche's Hotel, Glengarriff, Co. Cork
Robert French for William Lawrence, Dublin, c1890
ALBUMEN PRINT FROM A DRY PLATE NEGATIVE

PLATE 41

"The Harvest Where the Wattles Grow"
Alfred Werner FRPS, Dublin, c1895
CARBON PRINT FROM A DRY PLATE NEGATIVE

PLATE 42

Lancers in College Green, Dublin
John Joseph Clarke, Dublin, c1900
MODERN PRINT FROM A DRY PLATE NEGATIVE

PLATE 43

Nassau Street, Dublin
John Joseph Clarke Dublin, c1900
MODERN PRINT FROM A DRY PLATE NEGATIVE

PLATE 44

CHAPTER I

"From today painting is dead"

THE ORIGINS of photography are to be found in the two sciences of chemistry and optics. The earliest photographic cameras were based on the camera obscura, this was a darkened chamber with originally a small hole in one wall and in which images of the external world could be observed projected on the opposite wall. Later a lens was used which greatly improved brightness and image quality. Cameras obscura took many forms, from large permanent buildings to small portable boxes which were carried by artists and travellers and used to trace the impressions of places visited.

The optical phenomenon of the formation of images in a darkened chamber had been known for a long time. The Chinese certainly were aware of it during the Middle Ages and the earliest mention of it outside China appeared nearly one thousand years ago in the writings of the Arabian scholar Alhazen:

"... If the image of the sun at the time of an eclipse – provided it is not a total one – passes through a small round hole on to a plane surface opposite, it will be crescent-shaped ... The image of the sun only shows this property when the hole is very small."[1]

The first published illustration of the use of a camera obscura to look at eclipses without damaging the eyes appeared in a work by the Dutch mathematician Frisius in 1545 *(see illustration p. 3)*. In 1558 Battista Della Porta, from Naples published a description of the instrument and for the first time suggested its use as an aid to drawing.

Cesare Cesariano, a pupil of Leonardo da Vinci, described in 1521 a camera obscura in which everything outside a room could be seen. Leonardo's notebooks contain several references to the instrument, these were not, however, published until the eighteenth century.

Sensational claims have been made by Lynn Picknett and Clive Prince in *Turin Shroud–In Whose Image?* (1994) that the Shroud was actually made in 1492 by Leonardo da Vinci using a crude form of photography with a camera obscura almost 350 years before photography's invention. The claim is also made that he actually used his own face as Christ! Leonardo was well known to have been involved in many arcane pursuits including the practice of alchemy and the two authors claim that a form of photography was known to alchemists for centuries before its official publication in 1839.

Experiments were carried out using materials and equipment which would have been available to Leonardo, producing results which appear very similar to the image on the Shroud. The book makes convincing reading, but it is difficult to believe that such a wonderful invention as photography could have been kept secret for so long and the absence of other early examples suggests that these claims have to be treated with caution[2].

William Molyneux, a Fellow of the Royal Society, published *Dioptrica Nova* in Dublin in 1692, in which he describes various optical devices including the telescope and the microscope. The camera obscura is not actually mentioned, but his familiarity with lenses, however, would suggest that he must have been aware of their image making properties. There is a copy of the book in Marsh's Library, Dublin.

Cameras obscura were extensively used by the "old master" painters of the sixteenth and seventeenth centuries. Their use may be deduced by looking at some of the interiors painted by the Dutch painters of that period. A number of church interiors display a kind of distortion which is today associated with extreme wide angle lenses and is an effect which is virtually impossible to see with the naked eye.

It is, however, unlikely that artists of this calibre would have needed to trace these images from the screen of the camera obscura, it is much more likely that the instrument would have been used to construct compositions which would then be sketched and painted. It should also be realised that the primitive lenses then available would have produced a very indistinct picture which would have been very difficult to trace.

The old alchemist's trick of causing certain substances to darken with exposure to light was also known for centuries, however the first published account of experiments with light sensitive chemicals, by Johann Schulze appeared in 1727. Further important work on the effects of sunlight on silver nitrate was done by Carl Wilhelm Scheele in the late eighteenth century.

He made the significant discovery that silver chloride – which could also be used for photography – becomes insoluble in ammonia when exposed to light, having been soluble before exposure. This was published in his book on chemistry, in German, in 1777. Scheele had, in fact, inadvertently solved a problem which prevented the introduction of a practical photographic process for nearly fifty years. This was the inability of early inventors to permanently fix their images. It appears amazing that all of the early photographic experimentors – some of them extremely eminent scientists of the time – failed to realise the significance of Scheele's discovery. A possible explanation might be that most early pioneers preferred the use of silver nitrate because of its greater sensitivity.

The earliest recorded attempts to capture the images of the camera obscura were by the well known potter, Thomas Wedgwood in England and date from the end of the eighteenth century[3]. He discovered however, that the sensitive materials available to him were too slow to allow their use in a camera obscura. Instead he formed images by placing opaque objects on sensitised sheets of paper or leather and exposing them to sunlight. He could not, however, fix these images permanently and no example of his work survives. During the early years of the nineteenth century Sir Humphrey Davy, the eminent English physicist, also carried out experiments. However, he also had the same problem – the inability to permanently fix the images. Davy, used silver chloride in his experiments instead of the more usual silver nitrate and it is inconceivable that a scientist of his calibre was not aware of Scheele's discovery.

The earliest surviving fixed photographs were made in France by Joseph Nicéphore Niépce of Chalon sur Saône. Several of the experimental pictures he made in the years 1825-27 still exist as faint images on pewter plates. These required long exposures in the camera obscura of up to eight hours.

Because Niépce used a totally different process, employing, instead of silver, a strange combination of bitumen and oil of lavender, he was able to fix his images. This process was a dead end as far as the future development of photography was concerned. It did however, lead indirectly to the development of the daguerreotype process.

The daguerreotype was the brain child of another French pioneer, Louis Jacques Mandé Daguerre of Paris, who had heard about Niépce's experiments and eventually formed a partnership with him which lasted until Niépce's death in 1833. Daguerre carried on alone, and over the next five years succeeded in inventing one of the first practical photographic processes which became known as the daguerreotype.

When Daguerre had perfected his process he wanted desperately to exploit it financially as he had worked on it for almost twenty years. The problem Daguerre faced in making details of his process public was the fact that the equipment and materials to practice it were commonly available. This meant that once details of the process were known anyone was free to practice it. Daguerre ran the risk of receiving nothing for his many years of research and work.

The problem was solved by the French government taking over and releasing the process to the world, and at the same time, paying Daguerre a pension for life. In return he was required to publish details of the process in a book and in a special presentation by the famous French physicist, Arago, at the Académie des Sciences on Monday 19th August, 1839.

While Daguerre was perfecting his process in France, across the channel in England, William Henry Fox Talbot had also been seeking a way of capturing camera obscura images. He first succeeded in making negative images on paper in 1834, from these he made positives, also on paper, by contact.

Initially Talbot used common salt to fix these images both negative and positive but this was not very effective. The permanent fixing of photographic images was not finally solved until the discovery of the chemical sodium thio-sulphate. In 1839 the first person to realise the potential of this substance as a "fixer" was Sir John Herschel the great English physicist, he called it "hypo" after the old name for it, sodium hypo-sulphate. Herschel is, incidently, also credited with coining the word "photography". "Hypo" is still, even today, an important constituent of modern fixing solutions.

At this time Talbot's process required very lengthy exposures, and could not, in all fairness, be said to compare with the daguerreotype process as far as image quality was concerned. Talbot called his process photogenic drawing.

Alarmed on hearing of the announcement of the daguerreotype in France, Talbot hurriedly issued details of his own process and took out a patent on it.

At the time of their introduction both processes shared the same basic drawback. The long exposure times required ruled out their use for portraiture. Both processes were, however, substantially improved within a short time of their announcement. In 1840 the speed of the daguerreotype was increased by a factor of ten by the use of bromine, a discovery of John Frederick Goddard. Joseph Petzval invented the first large-aperture lens for exclusive photographic use – up to this time telescope lenses were pressed into service – this was manufactured and introduced by Friedrich Voigtlander in 1840. The same year, in America, Wolcott invented a mirror camera working on the same principle as a reflector telescope or a modern mirror lens. All these developments contributed to the shortening of exposure times, so that by the beginning of 1841 the taking of portraits became possible.

Since its invention, photography has enjoyed an almost universal popularity. Visual images were traditionally created by the artist's hand and were therefore interpretive in character. The concept of a process which allowed the images of objects and scenes to actually inscribe themselves, without interpretation, was regarded as somehow miraculous. This property of photography was recognised from the start as being its most important asset. At last, it was thought, it had become possible to obtain a completely objective image (this, of course, was not completely true, as every photographer will know).

The established visual art world tended to regard photography with varying emotions ranging from outright horror that livelihood was being threatened, through admiration, to contempt. The idea that photography was going to put artists out of work was understandable, and in fact, a great many artists, particularly miniaturists, lost their livelihood or, of necessity, became photographers. Many others ended their days, sadly, as mere photographic colourists.

The disquiet felt by artists at the invention of photography was perhaps, most famously verbalised by Paul Delaroche, a member of the Académie des Beaux-Arts, who is reputed to have said, on first seeing a daguerreotype, "From today, painting is dead!"

The same Paul Delaroche, apparently after he had recovered from his shock, eagerly embraced the new invention realising that it presented not only incredible opportunities to artists as a reference medium, but also as a creative medium in itself.

He had as students at the Beaux-Arts in Paris during the 1840s men who were later to rank as some of the most important early pioneers of the new medium. Henri Le Secq, Gustave Le Gray, Charles Nègre, Camille Silvy and the Englishman Roger Fenton[4]. Also studying with Delaroche at this time was one of Daguerre's sons and a certain Louis Werner who was later, with his wife Augustine, to set up a photographic studio in Dublin and whose son Alfred was to become one of the most distinguished Irish photographers at the end of the nineteenth century[5].

Cameras obscura

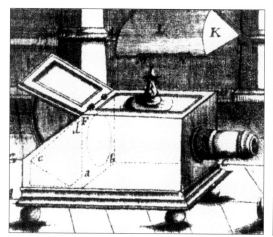

Portable reflex camera obscura, 1685, as used by travelling artists.

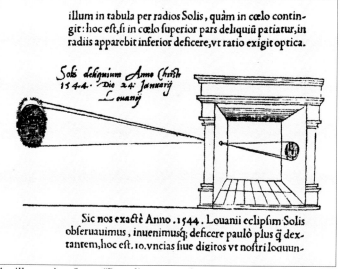

An illustration from *"De radio astronomico et geometrico liber"* 1545 showing the use of a camera obscura for observing eclipses without harming the eyes. This is the earliest illustration of the instrument.

CHAPTER II

Francis Stewart Beatty the first Irish photographer,

THE INVENTION of photography on silver plates in France by Daguerre and on paper negatives in England by Talbot, and the subsequent developments in both countries is generally considered to be photography's early mainstream history. It is quite likely, however, that at the same time many other people elsewhere, working in obscurity, were experimenting along similar lines. The so-called industrial revolution had created a climate in the early nineteenth century where the idea of performing tasks more efficiently by machine instead of laboriously by hand had become a popular concept. In this kind of climate it would be perfectly logical that some experimenters, possibly failed artists, might get the idea of creating pictures by machine.

The early literature of photography contains many intriguing reports of mysterious techniques and of anonymous men working to perfect them. Some of these reports actually pre-date the publication of the two principal processes in 1839 by many years. One such was the young man who visited the shop of the famous Parisian optician Chevalier in 1826 and who, when purchasing a cheap camera obscura, claimed he had devised a process for capturing the fleeting images of the instrument. Intrigued, Chevalier, knowing about Daguerre's then secret experiments, quizzed the young man further and was rewarded by receiving a small bottle containing a brown liquid which was supposed to contain the secret of the process. Chevalier, although a brilliant optician was no chemist and could not get the process to work. He eventually told Daguerre about the young man who then searched Paris in vain to find him.[6] He was never heard of again.

The use of light sensitive materials to copy drawings and engravings was described in *The Art of Engraving* a book published in 1839 and the technique appeared not to be a new innovation at the time.[7]

All the learned journals and most of the daily newspapers carried reports of the invention of photography during the early part of 1839. Fox Talbot's paper negative process was patented early in that year, thus preventing anyone wishing to use it. Even if it were possible for such a person to obtain technical details to do so, these were still kept secret.

The book written by Daguerre describing his process and published in 1839 ran to four editions in the English translation alone during the latter part of that year including one published in Dublin. As the materials required to practice the process were commonly available, and the manipulation required no more than average skill, it is most likely that there were Irish people attempting to take daguerreotypes during the years 1839 to 1841. One such person that we do know of was Francis Stewart Beatty, an engraver from Belfast who claimed, years later, in a long article published in 1879 in *The Photographic News*, to have been the earliest person in the "British Isles" to have successfully taken daguerreotypes independently of the inventor. He states, in a quotation from the article:[8]

"About this time, 1839, the scientific journals of all countries made the announcement that M. Daguerre of Paris had discovered a means by which the fleeting images of external objects depicted on the ground-glass of the camera obscura could be retained on a tablet of polished silver plate, and be permanently fixed thereon. Splendid

Virtually none of Francis Beatty's photographic images have survived, the image shown above is said to be from a daguerreotype

specimens were exhibited in Paris of its architectural buildings, bridges & c. The most distinguished and scientific men of that day were taken by surprise by the publication of so wonderful an invention, and intense anxiety was experienced by all awaiting the publication of the details. Although communicated to the Academy of Sciences on the 7th January, 1839, the process was not published until the 15th June by M. Arago to the French Chamber of Deputies on the occasion of the French Government awarding to M. Daguerre, in conjunction with M. Isidore Niépce each a pension for the discovery and publication of all details.

Ever watchful then, as now, to investigate into any new discovery that may be useful and beneficial to the advance of science or art, I resolved at once to exercise what ability I possessed to accomplish what M. Daguerre had discovered, and proceeded to work at the problem, being at the time an amateur optician, chemist and a careful manipulator (my profession being an engraver).

After many failures and uphill work, I was much surprised when I succeeded in my object to my entire satisfaction, as a letter of mine, dated 20th September 1839, published in the *Belfast News Letter* of that date will more fully show, which is annexed:

'THE DAGUERREOTYPE – *On this curious subject the following interesting letter has been addressed to us by Mr. Beatty, the well-known engraver of this town. We have also received the specimen to which he refers, and the effect noticed by him is extremely singular.*

TO THE EDITOR OF THE NEWS LETTER
Sir – Being occasionally engaged since the announcement of M. Daguerre's extraordinary invention of fixing on silver, plated on copper, the minute images of external objects, produced by means of the camera obscura, after a number of experiments, I was somewhat surprised to find, that in using silver *(on)* paper, the effect was different from silver plated on copper, although treated in a similar manner. Silver plated on copper gives the true effect of light and shade – while silver *(on)* paper gives the opposite – namely, the light parts of the subject are dull, and the dark shades are, in a proportionate degree, light. *(Negative image)* In order to convince you of the fact I send you a specimen; but our days of late having been cloudy, you cannot expect it to be as perfect as I would wish. I hope before your next publication to be able to submit to you a specimen upon silver plated on copper, and silver on paper, in order that you may more completely understand the difference; Hoping that this communication may have the effect of promoting inquiry on the subject, I remain, your obedient servant.'

FRANCIS S. BEATTY."

The wording of this letter is ambiguous and difficult to understand if one is ignorant of the basic knowledge of how photography works, as we can safely assume most of the *News Letter* readers of the day were. Some interesting points do however emerge from it regarding Beatty's working methods. Little of the technical information essential to the successful operation of either Daguerre's or Talbot's processes had been officially released prior to September 1839, yet Beatty had apparently successfully achieved results in both. He continues in his article:-

"It is only now after the lapse of nearly forty years in which I have had experience of many vicissitudes of fortune intermingled with pleasure for the love of our beautiful art, and which entailed upon me endless expense of time and money in endeavouring to promote its interest, and at a time when there could be no reasonable prospect of a return for the outlay. However, I can never divest myself of the pride I possess in having taken an active part in the infancy of this invention, and by my humble abilities aiding to bring it forward to its present state of perfection. *I question whether there is any record of the successful accomplishment of a Daguerreotype picture in Great Britain at so early a date, September 20th, 1839, three months after its first publication of June 15th, 1839".* [9] (author's italics)

This last statement might be inclined to cause raised eyebrows in certain quarters, but when one remembers that the first English language edition of Daguerre's book did not appear until September 13th, Beatty's achievement begins to appear remarkable. It does not seem rash to claim that he was, if not actually the first, he certainly must have been one of the very first native people of these islands to successfully take daguerreotypes. The examples which he sent to the *Newsletter* would appear to establish and date his achievement rather neatly, however, it is most unlikely that the editor of that publication would have known at that time what an actual daguerreotype looked like.

The writer has endeavoured unsuccessfully to locate an earlier practitioner in Britain. According to Helmut Gernsheim the earliest recorded demonstration in London was presented by a visiting Frenchman, M. de St. Croix on September 13, exactly a week before Francis Beatty's letter appeared in the *News Letter.* Beatty's article continues:

"In the latter part of 1839, and continued in 1840, Belfast, my native place, its architectural buildings, old long bridge, spanning the River Lagan, was delineated by the daguerreotype executed by me, and were much admired by the nobility and gentry of the town and neighbourhood, and noted in the most flattering terms by the local newspapers of that day.

In June, 1840 Mr. Richard Beard patented in Great Britain the concave silvered mirror for the production of Daguerreotype portraits, being a communication from Mr. Wolcott,[10] an American photographer; and being desirous of giving this method a trial, I immediately set to work to grind and polish a concave mirror of short focus in speculum metal, having previously polished them for reflecting telescopes.

After considerable delay I accomplished my object, and in 1841 was enabled to produce portraits. Having communicated my success to Mr. Beard, he invited me over to London, and the October of that year found me in the Polytechnic Institution, when I was introduced to Messrs. Cooper[11] and Goddard[12]. At this time Mr. Beard was establishing a similar institution in Southampton; he, therefore, desired me to take my part as an operator until he would come home. In the meantime he would examine my specimens, which he took with him.

On the arrival of Mr. Beard from Southampton he mentioned to me his intention of establishing a Daguerreotype portrait gallery in Dublin, and that if I would accept of the operative management he would pay me a percentage of the work done. Having been in pretty good circumstances at the time, his terms did not meet with my approval, and I therefore declined the offer.

In 1842, in connection with another, we built a gallery for Daguerreotype portraiture in a central situation in Belfast, which we carried on for a considerable time. However, the expense of a Daguerreotype portrait being above the means of the general public, we had to abandon the undertaking".

This studio is almost certainly that which is known to have been in operation in Castle Street, Belfast during the early 1840s. The

6

following appeared in *The Banner of Ulster* in 1842: [13]

"It is not so generally known among our citizens as native merit demands that it should be, that the first person who introduced this new and beautiful art of imitating nature into Great Britain was Mr. Francis S. Beatty of Castle Street, a gentleman whose talents in several branches of the arts are as varied as they are creditable. We have seen both portraits and architectural views produced by Mr. Beatty, which in our opinion, could not be surpassed, either for accuracy of copy (which, however, is inseparable from the art), or for the skill with which the most minute details had been "fixed". His skim(?) to public patronage is supported by abilities of which his fellow-classmen ought to be proud, independently of the credit due to him for his successful prosecution of the photographic art".

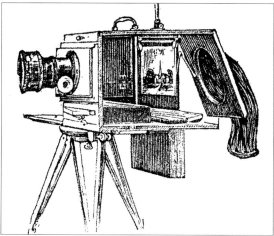

Francis Stewart Beatty's Collodion Wet Plate Field Camera, 1858, this had developing facilities built in, and removed the necessity of carrying a portable dark room for photography outdoors.

With the failure of the Castle Street studio, Beatty presumably continued to practice his profession as engraver. During the mid 1850s after the introduction of the wet-plate process he again took up photography and moved to Dublin where he opened a studio in College Green. As well as practising photography he also advertised engraving as part of his business.

The Dublin Journal published a series of six articles, in 1858 on "The Science of Photography"[14]. They were basically a brief history of photography up to that time. They go into great technical detail which suggests that they were written by someone with an intimate knowledge of the various processes then in use.

The fact that Beatty's name is mentioned several times in the articles would suggest that he had a hand in their writing. As well as this the articles contain certain details which only he would know. His appearance on the Dublin scene at about the same time is further proof of his possible authorship.

The articles are illustrated by wood engravings, possibly executed by himself, and showing various pieces of photographic equipment. Included is one of "Beatty's Wet Collodion Field Camera"*(see illustration)* which had, presumably, been invented by himself. One of the problems in using the collodion process was the fact that a portable darkroom was necessary if using it away from a studio. Beatty's camera avoided this by having all the processing steps taking place in the camera itself. This obviously was a great convenience and could only have been conceived by someone with much practical experience.

In 1859 he published *The National Photographic Almanac* as a wall chart. He also appears to have been one of the earliest experimenters in photo-lithography, taking out a patent in conjunction with Dr. Thomas Alexander of Killester in 1860.

His interest in photography was wide ranging, as the letter (beautifully written in copperplate script) congratulating Fox Talbot on his Photoglyphic process, sent to William Crookes of the *Photographic News* in 1859 shows. This was found in the archives of Lacock Abbey.

Francis Beatty's name continued to appear in the Dublin street directories at various addresses, Bachelors Walk, Capel Street, Benburb Street. During the 1880s he listed patent agent as part of his activities.

He never married, and at the advanced age of 83 he was admitted to the North Dublin Union, a workhouse, in 1890, dying there the following year.[15] He was buried in an unmarked grave in Mount Jerome Cemetery.[16] None of his early daguerreotype experiments appear to have survived.

CHAPTER III

The Calotype in Ireland

THE EVOLUTION of photography in Ireland, was influenced by events and developments which occurred elsewhere, particularly in England and France. One of the most important of these was Fox Talbot's decision to patent his "talbotype" process or "calotype" as it was later called. This restricted its use to those obtaining licences from the inventor, it was particularly prohibited to practice the process for commercial purposes. A peculiarity of the patent was that as far as the "British Isles" were concerned, it only applied in England and Wales and the border town of Berwick on Tweed, but not in Ireland or Scotland.

Daguerre's reaction to the patent was to take out a patent of his own on the daguerreotype in England and Wales, but again not in Ireland and Scotland. [17]

The daguerreotype was practised mostly by professional portraitists. Because of the complex manipulation required and the noxious chemicals employed it did not appeal to the amateur photographers of the day. These almost exclusively came from the landed gentry who had the time and resources to practice such a pastime. They favoured the calotype, and because Fox Talbot himself was of this class in society those interested tended to have no problems in being granted permission to practice the new process.

The fact that the restrictions in the use of both processes did not apply in Ireland would appear, in theory at least, to mean that more early photographers should have emerged in Ireland than in the sister island. In practice, however, the smaller population and the generally run down condition of the country at the time ensured that not many people were in a position to take up photography. A small number of Irish landed gentlemen did, however, practice the calotype.

By the middle 1840s daguerreotype studios were operating in Dublin, Belfast and Cork, the rest of the country was being served by various itinerant daguerreotypists travelling around in caravans and setting up shop wherever required. Individual Irish photographers of this period will be dealt with in later chapters.

In Scotland, the situation was somewhat different, some of the most famous names to be associated with the calotype were working there. The University of St. Andrews had as its Principal the famous Sir David Brewster. He was a personal friend of Fox Talbot and is credited with the introduction of the calotype process into Scotland. From 1840 he was the nucleus of a very important group experimenting with the process at St. Andrews.[18] This group included Robert Adamson, who later, in partnership with David Octavius Hill, produced a series of calotype portraits some of which are considered to be among the finest portraits ever taken by photography. Of Irish interest here is the several portraits made of the blind harpist Patrick Byrne who was visiting Edinburgh in 1843. He was photographed in various poses, *(see plate 5)* including one which was described as "in Ossianic Garb" complete with a laurel wreath on his brow!

Also in the St. Andrews group was William Holland Furlong of Dublin, assistant to the professor of chemistry at the university. However, not much is known about him and little survives by him, several prints are in the Scottish National Portrait Gallery in Edinburgh and a couple more are in albums in the J. Paul Getty Collection at Malibu, California. Another Irish photographer active in the St. Andrews circle at this time was Michael Packenham Edgeworth, a younger half-brother of the novelist Maria Edgeworth, who incidently carried on a long running intimate correspondance with Sir David himself. Seven of Packenham Edgeworth's images are also included in the album preserved in the Getty Collection[19] which, interestingly, also includes several views of Buttevant, Co. Cork taken in 1842 by Sir David Brewster's son while stationed there in the army. [20]

Furlong arrived at St. Andrews in 1840 or 1841, he was mentioned in a letter to Talbot from Brewster in October 1841, ". . .our Chemical Professor's assistant is now at work and successful . . Mr. Furlong, the gentleman *(to whom)* I allude executed an admirable portrait of a relative in

Thomas Moore by Henry Fox Talbot, early1840s   Thomas Moore with members of Fox Talbot's family, c1841

Ireland which I have seen." In another letter Brewster remarks "I enclose a negative, done in Ireland, by Mr. Furlong who has now begun the art here." [21] In March 1842 Furlong himself wrote to Talbot:

> "Sir, Though personally unknown to you, I take the liberty of addressing a few lines to you on the subject of your beautiful discovery of the calotype. Sir David Brewster some months ago sent you a negative which I made in the County of Wicklow and which you were kind enough to positive for me. I have never been able to preserve the positives without making them a disagreeable red colour, very unlike the beautiful lilac of your positive pictures. Will you be kind enough to let me know how you prepare and preserve your chloride pictures, what strength of nitrate of silver solution and what strength of the preserving solution.
>
> I am, Sir, Your Obedient Servant,
>
> W. H. Furlong"[22]

Furlong appears to have returned to Dublin during the late 1840s, his name does not appear, however, in any of the Dublin streets directories of the time. Bearing in mind his chemical interests he may have had some connection with the Thomas Furlong who practised as an apothecary at 17 Merrion Row during the late 1840s.

In a letter to *The Journal of the Photographic Society of London* in 1855, Furlong claimed to have discovered a method of preparing iodised paper by a single wash in 1841. This was in response to a previous letter from a Mr. Jordan who claimed that he had made a similar discovery in 1848.

The great advantage which the calotype had over the daguerreotype was the possibility of making any number of prints from the paper negative. Each daguerreotype on the other hand was unique and could only be duplicated with great difficulty. As far as photographic image quality and definition was concerned, however, the daguerreotype was far superior, and this was the main reason why it was preferred by professional portraitists.

A neighbour of Fox Talbot at Lacock Abbey in Wiltshire was the Irish poet Thomas Moore, whose house, Sloperton, was located nearby. The two men were friends and an extract from Moore's diaries, dated 18 August 1841, reads:

> "Having arranged with Hume to take a short trip to Ireland, (*I*) started for Lacock Abbey on my way to town. The day was beautiful, and I found grouped in full sunshine upon the grass before the house, Kit Talbot, Lady E. Fielding, Lady Charlotte and Mrs Talbot for the purpose of being photogenised by Henry Talbot who was busy preparing his apparatus. Walked alone for a while about the gardens, and then rejoined the party to see the result of the operation. But the portrait did not turn out satisfactorily, nor oddly enough were they at all like *(the subjects)*; whereas a dead likeness is, in general, the sure though frightful result of the Daguerre process". [23]

The latter statement is probably an example of Moore being loyal to his friend, who took at least two portraits of Moore, one of which shows him posing with members of the Talbot family. Of interest is the fact that it shows him to be considerably under average height, a disability which did not prevent him being accepted into the highest circles in the land, and which does not seem to have been taken into account when the statue of him in College Street, Dublin was being made.

Talbot's famous book, *Pencil of Nature,* was begun in 1844 and thereafter was published in six parts. A copy of the first part was sent to Thomas Moore and on 6 August he wrote to Talbot:

"Though the drawings *(calotypes)* were familiar to us, we were delighted to get your beautiful book and to read (which I did aloud for both) your simply written and interesting prefaces. As I could not please myself in any of the trials I made to pen something for the book, I am most glad that I did not send you anything at all for, to have been in partnership with Sol *(the sun)* without doing anything worthy of the connection would never have done for the poet – or rather would have done for me entirely" [24]

Talbot then suggested that Moore should transcribe two of his Irish Melodies for possible inclusion in a later part of the book. This was received by Moore with enthusiasm, however he later mentions a problem:

"On sitting down yesterday evening to copy the melodies for you, I came to a full stop owing to the shape of the paper, which taken in its oblong form would not contain such lines as: 'Dear harp of my Country in Darkness I found Thee' and turned the other way will not suit the shape of your book. So I must wait until you enlighten – or should I say photogenise me – on the shape of your book".

At Lacock Abbey, still preserved, is a manuscript in Moore's handwriting of two stanzas of *"Dear harp of my Country"* with a negative and a contemporary print copied in horizontal form. Talbot however, did not include this with any of the 24 subjects illustrated in *Pencil of Nature.* [25]

A search of Thomas Moore's library, now housed at the Royal Irish Academy in Dublin has failed to locate his copy of this now extremely rare and valuable book.

Henry Fox Talbot's achievement was the invention of the negative/positive process. The daguerreotype was a one-off process,

somewhat like modern colour transparencies, if copies were required they had to be taken in the camera. Copying original daguerreotypes was very difficult because of the highly reflective surface.

Talbot's process was originally called "photogenic drawing" and was extremely slow and limited in its application, improvements made to it over its first few years greatly increased its speed. It later was called the talbotype or calotype.

A sheet of good quality writing paper was made sensitive to light by coating one side of it with a silver nitrate solution by candle light. When dry it was placed in the camera obscura and an exposure, usually of several minutes, was made. Unlike modern films and photographic papers, an image would have been visible after exposure, no development being necessary. Fixation was accomplished originally by the use of a common salt solution and later by a solution of sodium thiosulphate or "hypo". The fixed negative was finally washed in running water and dried.

The negative was usually printed on "salt paper", this was made by soaking a sheet of writing paper in a solution of common salt, when dry it was coated on one side with a silver nitrate solution.

Printing was accomplished by contacting the negative with a sheet of salt paper in a pressure frame and exposing to the light of the sun. After exposure, fixing was again accomplished in a hypo or salt solution.

Calotypes taken in Ireland during the first ten years of photography are extremely rare, the process was notorious for fading and most of the work produced has probably literally faded away.

In the Fox Talbot Collection at the Science Museum in London are preserved, paper negatives exposed in Dublin. Thought at one time to have been taken by Talbot himself [26], they are now considered by many historians to have been taken by an associate of his, the Rev. Calvert Jones. The reason for this change of attribution is the fact that no record exists of Talbot ever visiting Ireland during the period of his photographic activity.

There are good views probably taken in the mid to late 1840s of the Black Church, St. George's Church, the Customs House, Amiens Street Station, the Four Courts, Trinity College, the guard at the Castle, Powerscourt, Co. Wicklow and several other locations.

The negatives fall into at least two groups. There is a large number which have been

A selection of the "Dublin" calotypes at the Science Museum, London

Estimated to have been taken during the mid 1840s, they are, clockwise:

The Rutland Fountain, Merrion Square, Dublin

Conciliation Hall, Burgh Quay, Dublin
(later Tivoli Theatre and Irish Press offices)

The Bank of Ireland, College Green, Dublin

clearly taken by the same group of three photographers. Each view has standing in the foreground two figures of the three men involved, the third in each case presumably is behind the camera. It is worth noting here that none of the figures appear to resemble either Fox Talbot or Calvert Jones.

The tallest of the three figures might be William Holland Furlong, the only existing photograph of him is a rather indistinct salt print in the previously mentioned Getty album. He would appear to have been extremely tall. Some of the Dublin views are clearly not by this group as no foreground figures are included and appear to have been taken on different sized cameras.

The Dublin negatives are part of the huge Fox Talbot Collection presented to the museum in 1937 by Miss Matilda Talbot, grand daughter of the inventor. Originally all of this material was considered to be the work of the inventor himself.

A curious fact about these negatives is that they vary greatly in size and shape, and appear to have been taken on many different cameras. Early cameras of this period were made of wood, and while calotype negatives might nominally be considered to be whole plate, half plate or other standard sizes, they could in practice vary slightly in size. This was due to the fact that each camera was individually made, sometimes by the local carpenter and a brass bound lens – purchased from a specialist maker like Ross, Voigtlander, Chevalier or Grubb – fitted to it.

The most likely, and obvious, explanation of the size variation in the "Fox Talbot" negatives is that they are not all the work of one photographer. This theory is further supported by the fact that different visual styles are apparent and the negatives display a variety of colourations which was probably due to variations in the chemistry used.

It was assumed that they were the work of Henry Fox Talbot or of some of his close associates such as the Rev. Calvert Jones, the

Rev. G. W. Bridges or Nicolaas Henneman who played important roles during the early development of the process. This assumption rests on the fact that they were found at Lacock Abbey. Making this kind of assumption becomes very dubious if one looks at the chaotic conditions which pertained at the time of The Science Museum's acquisition of this material, when the collection was divided arbitrarily among several institutions on the basis of subject matter (ie. many photographs of ships being allocated to the National Maritime Museum at Greenwich).

Fox Talbot, although very particular about those whom he permitted to use his process, did allow a select few to do so. In Ireland those wishing to use it, strictly speaking, did not require Fox Talbot's permission. However, because of possible technical difficulties which might arise, it was desirable to be on good terms with the inventor in case one needed to seek advice. Fox Talbot set up a commercial printing establishment at Reading where calotype photographers could send negatives to have salt prints made from them.

There is a lot of evidence in the form of correspondence in the archives at Lacock to prove that this service was much availed of. It would be perfectly natural that such negatives be retained at Reading for possible future reprints and for them to have accumulated there over time. The total number of negatives concerned is in excess of six thousand. Bearing in mind the slow speed of the calotype process, the amount of failures which must have taken place and the weather pertaining in these islands when photography would have been impossible for a great deal of the year, it seems unlikely that the gentlemen concerned could have amassed such a vast quantity of negatives in the ten years or so when the calotype process was in most use.

Blanket attribution of vast numbers of images to individual well known photographers has been attractive to some academic historians when writing about early photography. Lack of practical knowledge of the complexities of early processes and of the time required when compared with modern photography is probably responsible for this. A situation exists in relation to the large numbers of negatives in the Lawrence Collection at the National Photographic Archive which have, on occasions, been attributed to Robert French. (see Chap. VI)

The present writer's opinion is that the Science Museum material does actually contain a great many negatives by Fox Talbot and the associates mentioned above (many are actually signed by one or other of them), but also, much of it was accumulated at Reading and represents negative material sent there by many photographers to be printed. If this theory is correct it would be reasonable to assume that at least some of the Dublin negatives might have been taken by Irish photographers, who sent them to Reading to have prints made from them. Letters from Irish photographers, notably William Holland Furlong and Francis Stewart Beatty, have been found among the Fox Talbot archives at Lacock Abbey. One letter from Furlong, mentioned earlier, actually refers to negatives which he had enclosed for printing.

The Reading establishment ceased to function in 1847[27] and when the calotype process became obsolete the accumulated negative material was probably transferred to Lacock.

Obviously much research remains to be carried out on this vast and important collection, as it would appear to contain much of Irish interest. Because of the numbers, the fragility of the material and the difficulty of identifying subjects from 150 year old delicate paper negative images this will be a long term project. The few Irish researchers who have gained access to the collection have made important discoveries. Irish views were discovered, which had been either unidentified or wrongly identified. The Sackville Street and Henry Street/Earl Street crossing with Nelson Pillar in the centre was actually catalogued by the museum as The Place Vendome, Paris!

On May 12th, 1845 a paper was read to the Royal Irish Academy on the "catalystype process" by its inventor, a Dr. Thomas Woods of Parsonstown (Birr). It was claimed to be an improved version of the calotype, and as such was stated by Dr. Woods to be of sufficient difference to that process not to be covered by Fox Talbot's patent.[28] A hectic correspondence ensued between the Royal Irish Academy in Dublin and Fox Talbot who claimed that there was no material difference between the two processes and that the whole episode was merely a dastardly attempt to get around the restrictions of the patent. Be that as it may, it is only necessary to add that, the "catalystype process" never appears to have been very widely used.

CHAPTER IV

The Daguerreotype in Ireland

THE DAGUERREOTYPE process utilised thin silver or silver on copper plates. The most common sizes were whole plate (6.5 x 8.5 inches), half plate, quarter plate, sixth plate and ninth plate. The surface of the plate was highly polished to resemble a mirror. It was then exposed to the fumes of heated iodine crystals, this rendered the surface of the plate sensitive to light. It was placed in the camera and exposed in the usual way.

The plate was then exposed to the fumes of heated mercury. This had the effect of producing a white opaque (negative image) coating as the high light areas of the picture. The uncoated silver areas represented the shadow areas. In practice a finely detailed positive image was seen when the polished silver areas reflected a dark background. It is impossible to adequately reproduce a daguerreotype in print and although it is one of the oldest types of photograph the daguerreotype image, in the writer's opinion, is still one of the most beautiful.

The noxious chemicals and fumes used in the daguerreotype process must have made it a most unhealthy activity, bearing in mind the small unventilated darkrooms in which it was usually practised. There are no records of photographers dying as a result of their using it. The relatively short period – about ten years – in which it was in use may have prevented it from being lethal on a large scale. There are however records of some of its practitioners living to ripe old ages, like Albert Sands Southworth in America who – using the process for most of his life – lived to be over ninety, and the Irish photographer Beatty who practiced it in his youth and died at the age of 84.

From 1840 onwards instruction in the daguerreotype process was available at the Dublin Mechanics Institute, Lower Abbey Street, [29] and as it was quite easy to obtain the necessary materials to practice it, it is highly likely that it was being used in Dublin during the early 1840s. As already mentioned, Daguerre's patent did not apply in Ireland and this would, of course, have encouraged potential Irish users of the process. It is a pity that so few examples have survived from this early date. The most likely reason for this is the fact that daguerreotypes are so easily damaged, well intentioned attempts to clean them can result in their complete destruction unless the correct procedure is employed. One of the earliest surviving Irish daguerreotype views is of a street in Cork. It is preserved in the Kodak Collection at the National Museum of Photography, Film and Television at Bradford. The photographer was a certain John or Alphonsus (?) Mott.*(see plate 1)*

The Natural Philosophy Committee of the Royal Dublin Society decided in 1840 to purchase a daguerreotype outfit as the following extracts from their minute book show:[29]

18 June 1840
Resolved:
That Dr. Kane be authorised to obtain a complete set of daguerriotype *(sic)* apparatus at an expense not to exceed £15.

Tues. 18 August 1840
Resolved:
That the following bill be recommended for payment,
Soleil's account for Daguerrieotype and parallel mirror camera, £15.

Unfortunately the present whereabouts of Mon. Soleil's camera are unknown[30].

One of the effects of Fox Talbot's patent was to force those who wished to become professional portrait photographers to use the daguerreotype. This was possible in England and Wales if the right arrangements were made with Miles Berry, Daguerre's Patent Agent in Britain. Richard Beard, a London coal merchant and speculator paid £800 and acquired the entire daguerreotype concession for England and Wales in 1841. He opened the first portrait studio in London, and in fact Europe, in March of that year. [31]

A cartoon by Cruikshank from *Punch* showing Beard's London studio of 1841 which was similar to the first Dublin studio at the Rotunda and which opened the same year.

The daguerreotype process at this time was still rather slow, so it was essential that maximum use could be made of the available daylight. For this reason early studios or galleries tended to be located on the upper floors of tall buildings with extra large windows. These were often fitted with blue tinted glass. The daguerreotype process was mainly sensitive to blue light and by filtering out the red end of the spectrum of sunlight the overall strength of the light falling on the faces of the unfortunate sitters was reduced without reducing its actinic value as far as the daguerreotype plate was concerned. Exposure times at this period were usually measured in minutes.

Richard Beard's first London studio was a temporary timber and glass structure erected on the roof of the Royal Polytechnic Institution in Regent Street. This was the studio at which Francis Stewart Beatty worked in 1841. There was, almost immediately, a very great demand for portraits. Beatty described the situation as it existed in 1841:

"So great was the excitement created in London amongst the nobility, gentry and moneyed classes at this new species of portraiture which was then being produced at the Polytechnic, that during my stay the average amount of money taken each day, amounted to, I was told £150. However this included expensive cases, frames and jewellery. In the waiting rooms of this establishment you would see, awaiting their turn to enter the blue-glass roofed operating rooms, the noble dames and daughters of England's aristocracy, accommodating each other as well as their limited space would allow, awaiting for hours together before their desires were accomplished."

This quotation has been extracted from Beatty's previously mentioned article in the *Photographic News* of 1879, and it is a remarkable fact that almost everything that we know about the operating methods of this very important early studio has been culled from this single article by Beatty. [32]

An amusing description of what an experience it was to be daguerreotyped at the Regent Street Gallery has been left by another Irish observer, the famous novelist Maria Edgeworth:

"It is a wonderful mysterious operation. You are taken from one room into another upstairs and down and you see various people whispering and hear them in neighbouring passages and rooms unseen and the whole apparatus and stool on a high platform under a glass dome casting a snapdragon blue light making all look spectres and the men in black gliding about like 8 (?) etc. I have not, time to tell you more . . ." [33]

This description, one of the earliest of being daguerreotyped, was written on May 25 1841, approximately two months after the Polytechnic studio had opened. Remarkably the actual daguerreotype portrait has survived and is preserved at the National Portrait Gallery in London (*see plate 2*).

The enthusiasm with which photographic

Far left: The first Dublin daguerreotype studio. A temporary wooden structure, built over the entrance to the Rotunda in Upper Sackville Street, it opened in November 1841, and was possibly a branch of Richard Beard's London studio

Left: Glukman's first premises on the top floor of 13 Lower Sackville Street, 1845. Artist's impression using the illustration of Lower Sackville Street from *Shaw's Illustrated Directory of Dublin* of 1850 as a reference guide.

portraiture was received was not confined to London, in fact, most major European cities had daguerreotype galleries by the early part of 1842.

The first commercial photographic studio in Ireland was at the Rotunda in Dublin. It was opened in October 1841 and was a similar timber and glass structure to the Polytechnic studio in London, built over the main entrances into the Rotunda at the top of Sackville Street. The first newspaper advertisement for the new venture appeared in the *Freeman's Journal* of October 16:

> NOW OPEN
> Under Her Majesty's
> Royal Letters Patent
> Daguerreotype Portraits at the
> ROTUNDA
> The Proprietors have the honour to inform the Nobility, Gentry and citizens of Dublin, that their rooms ARE NOW OPEN for the taking of portraits and groups of figures. By their process they are enabled in a few seconds to fix the portraits and render them so durable that they will not be affected by any change of climate, but have all the appearance and character of a finely etched engraving. The Proprietors can with safety guarantee a perfect likeness, as it is the reflected image of the sitter that is retained on the plate by their process. Having devoted much of their time to this service and being the first artists who produced a miniature by this process; they feel assured that persons favouring them with a sitting will be perfectly satisfied with the correctness of the likeness. The price of

each portrait including a frame will be £1.1s. The Proprietors beg to say that the portraits can be taken equally well in any description of weather as if the sun was shining.

The proprietors' names are not given, Helmut Gernsheim in his general history of photography names Professor Leone Glukman as the first Dublin photographer in 1842 at 13 Lower Sackville Street. No record can be found of Glukman's presence in Dublin before 1844 when he advertised in the Dublin newspapers from the above address.

However, the above advertisement leaves no doubt about the Rotunda studio being in operation in 1841, the question remains as to whether Glukman was one of the proprietors. He is, however, known to have been working at Brighton with the daguerreotypist William Constable during the early 1840s.

A possible clue to the identity of the first Dublin photographer may be found in the fact that Richard Beard of London opened and operated branch studios in various British provincial cities such as Liverpool, Southampton, Brighton, Norwich and Manchester. Most of these were opened during the months of October and November 1841 and it would be perfectly natural that Dublin should be selected as a location for a possible branch. Francis Beatty, who was working for Beard at the time, does, in fact, state that he was asked to supervise the opening of such a studio. He was not interested however, his possible reason for refusing the offer will be discussed later.

The actual wording of the advertisement contains several points which would help to reinforce the Beard theory, including the reference to "Her Majesty's Royal Letters Patent". This was held by Beard and was not necessary to operate in Ireland (or Scotland), but might be mentioned by him for prestige purposes. Reference is made to the fact that the proprietors were the first to produce miniatures by the daguerreotype process. This would not be strictly true in relation to Beard. He might however, make such a statement being the first person to use the daguerreotype process commercially, taking miniature portraits. The plural proprietors mentioned might well represent Beard as the principal proprietor (in London) and the operator on the spot in Dublin, whoever that may have been.

The press advertisement for the studio continued to appear unchanged from time to time until February 1842 and then on April 23 a significant change occurs:

DAGUERREOTYPE
PORTRAIT ROOMS
ROTUNDA
LE CHEVALIER DOUSSIN DUBREUIL
has the honour to inform the public that he is now enabled in a few seconds to produce PORTRAITS much superior to any which have been hitherto made. Having availed himself of the latest improvements in the art, he is enabled to impart colour to the productions of this surprising discovery accomplishing the greatest *disiderature* and removing all previous objections to these portraits. He is now enabled to take full length groups of three or four persons and portraits of the same dimensions, also miniatures so small as to be put in rings, lockets, brooches and bracelets. The public are respectfully requested to visit the establishment and inspect the specimens. Open from 10 to 5 daily.

If the theory about the Rotunda being opened by Beard is correct, this change could be explained by the fact that, in all cases, shortly after their opening, he sold off his branches, complete with licences to operate, to the operators working at them. This would suggest that Dubreuil was working as manager while the first advertisement was appearing and on his acquiring the studio licence was free to put his own name in the new advertisement.

Curiously enough, details of this advertisement suggest that Dubreuil might have had some connection with Claudet, the other London daguerreotypist operating at this time. References to colour (hand applied) and the taking of full length groups, which were both offered in London by Claudet before Beard. Dubreuil also mentions, in another advertisement, the use of painted backgrounds, suggesting pastoral scenes. These were also introduced in London by Claudet. In a later advertisement he offers to replace old daguerreotypes which had faded with newly taken ones, this was also done by Claudet. Antoine Francois Jean Claudet had learned the daguerreotype process directly from Daguerre himself in Paris and, claiming he had been using it in Britain prior to Beard's arrangement with Daguerre, vehemently refused to purchase a licence. He was, as a daguerreotypist working in London, in a rather unique situation.

Francis Beatty's refusal to come to Dublin to open a branch on behalf of Beard might be explained by the fact, that as an Irishman he very likely knew that the daguerreotype process was free of patent in Ireland. One of the conditions of Beard's offer would have been the obligation on the new proprietor to purchase a licence to operate. Beatty would hardly be interested in such an offer. Doussin Dubreuil on the other hand was probably French and therefore may not have known about the conditions of Daguerre's patent when taking up Beard's offer to come to Dublin.

Some writers on Irish photographic history suggest that a certain Thomas Millard was involved in the setting-up of the Rotunda studio.[35] Millard was an English cabinet maker who had come to Dublin in 1838 and was employed on several building projects in the city including St. Anne's Clontarf.

He appears to have become quite wealthy and was involved, probably financially, in various enterprises including a number of photographic studios during the 1850s and 1860s. Simonton and Millard (with photographer James Simonton) and Millard and Robinson (with J. V. Robinson) were two such partnerships where Millard probably provided the funding.

It is quite possible that Millard was involved financially with the Rotunda with

Dubreuil providing the photographic expertise. The order for the studio bankruptcy which occurred in 1844 was taken out against Dubreuil alone. If Millard had been a financial partner, one would have expected his name to have been included, unless, of course he had wisely departed the enterprise by then.

An old drawing which was made from a daguerreotype, now lost, survives to show what the exterior of the studio looked like *(see illustration)*. This daguerreotype was displayed on the stand of Millard & Robinson at the Irish International Exhibition of 1865, which tends to give some credence to Thomas Millard having been involved in some way.

The Rotunda studio was open daily initially from 10 a.m. to 5 p.m. and those desiring a short sitting were advised to come early. Exposures varied, depending on the weather, between a few seconds to perhaps several minutes. In fine weather the glasshouse was dispensed with and the portraits were taken on the roof, with a painted background to simulate an interior, this obviously helped to shorten exposure times and reduce the sitters' ordeal.

The Rotunda, opening in October 1841, did not have a monopoly for long; on Thursday November 1 the following advertisement appeared in the Dublin papers:

IMPROVED DAGUERREOTYPE
PORTRAITS TAKEN
at No. 12 Sackville Street Lower
Mr. Treffry begs respectfully to inform the Nobility, Gentry and the citizens of Dublin that he has effected important improvements in the Daguerreotype process of taking likenesses having – by considerable study and application brought the extraordinary art to a degree of perfection – that could scarcely be contemplated by the original inventor. Portraits produced by Mr. Treffry's improved process are not only most accurate as likenesses, but are free from the indistinctness and contingency hitherto so objectionable in the Photographic impressions. The different colours (in ladies' dresses for instance) are so finely marked as to render them almost distinguishable; and a pleasing brightness and a prominence are thus given to the 'tout ensemble' of the picture. Mr. Treffry's portraits are taken in a DRAWING ROOM, his improvements have superseded the glass-house and

fitting-up effect of which is artificial in its operation and unpleasant to the sitter.
The charge for a portrait and frame is £1. 1s.

Not a lot is known about Mr. Treffry, he may have been the same Richard Treffry who took out a patent some years earlier for preserving animal and vegetable substances from decay. It should be realised that many of the people who took up photography at this time, were speculators who recognised the novelty which ordinary members of the public felt in having their likenesses captured, and eagerly exploited the opportunity offered for getting rich quickly.

Before the invention of photography only the wealthiest in society could afford to have their portraits painted or drawn. The new process, offering the potential of providing portraits – if not exactly to the masses – to large numbers of people who previously could not have afforded such a luxury. The fact that most of these people were quite uncritical, made it easy for the speculators to survive. Many of these early photographers had been originally second or third rate portrait and miniature painters who, driven out of business by the advent of the new medium, had taken up photography. The reason why so many of these new photographers were not Irish born was due, of course, to the necessity of their needing a licence to operate in England, it was much easier to set up shop as a daguerreotypist in Ireland (and Scotland) provided one could find the customers.

This latter condition may have been the reason why Mr. Treffry did not last very long in Dublin. The following year, 1842, a daguerreotypist of the same name began operating in Glasgow, his disappearance from the Dublin scene at about the same time makes it fairly safe to assume it was the same man.

He made some extravagant claims in his advertisement, some of which, like dispensing with the glasshouse and the taking of daguerreotypes in ordinary rooms, would make one doubt his ability. 'Glasshouses' or glass roofed studios continued to be used by photographers until the early twentieth century. [36]
Dubreuil at the Rotunda continued to advertise during 1842 and 1843, making new offers in almost every advertisement; such as the returning of old daguerreotypes to be coloured; in December 1842 he offered fixed (?) daguerreotypes; the use of antique furniture as props; and, probably the most

unusual of all offers from a professional daguerreotypist, the supply of materials to amateurs.

In June 1843 'The New Daguerreotype Rooms' were opened at 43 Grafton Street by a former miniature painter sporting the unlikely name of Horatio Nelson.[37] He was offering daguerreotypes 'in all the colours of nature' taken in one minute. Nelson, had graduated from the Dublin School of Art and began

AUCTIONS.

BY THE HIGH SHERIFF OF THE CITY OF DUBLIN.

Carolin a. Du Brenil

SALE BY AUCTION, on TO-MORROW (Thursday), 4th day of July, 1844, at the RO-TUNDO, by virtue of her Majesty's writ of *fieri facias* in this Cause, all the Defendant's Goods and Chattels, comprising a Wooden Building, now occupied by the Defendant over the grand entrance leading into the Rotundo in Sackville street, as also the Apparatus used by him in the Daguerreotypes, with some articles of Household Furniture, Specimens, &c.
JAMES BENJAMIN BALL, Esq , Sheriff.
Exempt from Auction Duty. Sale at Twelve o'Clock.
THOMAS FERRALL, Auctioneer, 10, Lower Ormond-quay.

Notice of Rotunda studio bankruptcy, July 1844

practising in 1836 at 10 College Green. He actually claimed to have introduced the daguerreotype process into Ireland; be that as it may, the present writer can find no reference to his photographic activities prior to 1843. In his advertisements, his main selling point was that he was an artist and that all the other daguerreotypists – there was only one other – were mere mechanics. He appears to have continued to paint miniatures, exhibiting them at the R.H.A. until 1845. One of the few surviving daguerreotypes which may be attributed to him with reasonable certainty is the circular portrait of the artist Sir Frederick Burton, preserved in the National Gallery of Ireland. Burton had been a fellow student of Nelson at the R.D.S. School of Art.

Dubreuil replied to Nelson's advertisement in one of his own:

". . . Mons. Dubreuil is the only one capable of offering daguerreotypes in colour, the others being merely paintings on ivory (?)".

A vicious price war began between the two rival studios over the following months, each endeavouring to outdo the other in ever more extravagant offers and price reductions

until eventually Dubreuil appears to have become bankrupt; his 'goods and chattels' were sold by public auction in July 1844. Horatio Nelson's Grafton Street studio then remained as the only permanent establishment in the city.

The bankruptcy ended the Rotunda's short period as a photographic studio. It was not, however, the end of Dubreuil's career in Dublin, the following advertisement appeared in *Saunder's News Letter* on April 5, 1845:

"The old established and photographic rooms of the Rotunda will be again open in a few days at Messrs P. & T. M'Anaspies, 31 Great Brunswick (*Pearse*) Street, under the direction of Mon. Dubreuil who has just returned from Paris and has the honour to inform the nobility and gentry and all his numerous friends and judges of this art that they will find at this establishment the real photography in all its perfection.
Portraits, Views etc. taken on silver plates, ditto on paper, photographic engravings etc"

And the following on May 24:

"DAGUERREOTYPE
DAGUERREOTYPE
DAGUERREOTYPE
Portrait rooms at the Queen's Royal Galleries of Arts and Manufactures, 31 Great Brunswick Street. Portraits taken from 5/- upwards, in a new and improved style and free from that ghastly effect produced by other 'Professors' giving character, dignity and expression to them. Groups, Landscapes and architectural drawings copied to any size at P. & T. M'Anaspie's, Figures and Patent Asphalt flagging works and Cement factory. Fronts of houses fitted up in a new and architectural style".

It should be remembered that, as well as the daguerreotypists based in Dublin, other itinerant daguerreotypists were at work in the country at large and from time to time would come into the city. One such was a certain M. Champeaux who, in 1842, came over from the Adelaide Gallery which had been established in London the previous year by Antoine Claudet. Champeaux stayed in Dublin for some weeks in 1842, not only taking daguerreotypes but selling quality cameras by Lerebours and other equipment.[38]

18

"Professor" Leone Glukman, photographed during a visit to Brighton by his friend William Constable. Modern print from a collodion wet plate negative, c1855.

in the mid 1840s, he called himself 'Professor High-school'. The term Natural Philosophy was used to describe various subjects like the study of Mechanics, Optics, Heat, Light, Air and the natural sciences.

Throughout his stay in Dublin Glukman's name is seen to be spelt in several different ways, Gluckman, Glukmann and Glukman, the latter, being the most usual will therefore be the one used here.

Before coming to Dublin he appears to have had a very close relationship with William Constable of Brighton and his family. Constable's role in the early history of the daguerreotype in Britain is very important. He was one of the very first people to purchase a licence in 1841 to practice the daguerreotype. He opened the first commercial studio in Brighton and was responsible for taking the earliest photograph of Prince Albert.

Glukman appears to have met him at Beard's London studio where both men were probably learning the process. Glukman and the Constable family carried on an extensive correspondence over a period of nearly forty years in which many other names were mentioned who were probably also involved in photography. One name mentioned several times was "Fonce" or Alphonses Mott who may have been the mysterious "Mr. Mott" who took the daguerreotype of a Cork street *(see elsewhere and plate 1)*. The actual timing of Glukman's arrival in Dublin is a matter of conjecture, he would appear to have been still with Constable during the latter part of 1844. Daguerreotypes depicting both of them together survive and one of these supposedly showing a communion *(see below)* has been dated to that year, however, its appearance might suggest a later date. It portrays a clean shaven Glukman, most other pictures of him show him bearded (unfortunately we do not know when he grew his beard!) A letter from Constable to Glukman dated December 1844 suggests that he may have been in Ireland somewhat earlier. Glukman apparently paid numerous visits to Constable during the 1840s and the daguerreotype could have been taken on one of these occasions.

This daguerreotype has been traditionally entitled "The Communion" and is supposed to represent a priest or clergyman, in the person of Glukman, giving communion to a seated gentleman, William Constable. The principal objection to this description in the writer's view – apart from the fact that neither man appears to have been overly religious – is the fact that Constable is seated, normally a person receiving communion would be kneeling. It is more likely

Probably Dubreuil's greatest claim to fame, while he was in Dublin, was his photographing Daniel O'Connell in prison during the latter part of 1844 *(see later)*.

Unfortunately his new studio did not last long either, closing after only a few months of operation. The following year, 1846 Dubreuil is seen to be still in business, this time from an address at 57 Upper Dorset Street. However, this is the last reference to his photographic activities in Ireland which can be found and he probably left the country shortly after this.

Probably the most interesting of all these early pioneer daguerreotypists in Dublin was "Professor" Leone Glukman. Long thought to have been the first Dublin professional photographer, he does not appear to have begun advertising under his own name until 1845. He called himself a Professor of Natural Philosophy, apparently without any academic justification. He occasionally used the distinction M.S.O.P. (Member of the Society of Oil Painters) after his name. Many early daguerreotypists assumed the title 'professor', another Dublin example was 'Professor' Blume who worked some years later in the city. Perhaps the most bizarre title to be adopted by a photographer, was that of John Jabez Mayall, an American who settled in London

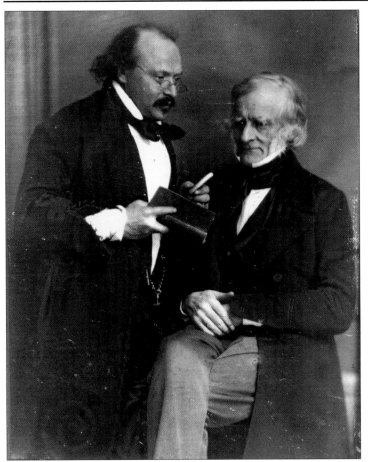

Leone Glukman and William Constable, c1844. A quarter plate daguerreotype supposedly showing the "enactment of a communion"

standing in the photographic world of the time. Constable remarked to Glukman, that he thought the reason for Dubreuil's request was that as he, Glukman, had recently acquired such a camera Dubreuil felt that he also should have one. This suggests that Dubreuil, recently bankrupt, was obviously feeling insecure and worried about the potential competition he was about to experience with Glukman's appearance on the scene. Now he would have to deal with two formidable competitors.

Very little is known of Leone Glukman's private life. One of the few definite facts we do have is that he was married to a widow, Mary Ann Whitley at the old St. Thomas's Church, Dublin on August 14, 1845.[39] Her address on the marriage certificate is 16 Lower Sackville Street, however, it is possible that she may have come to Ireland with Leone.

Another letter from Constable is also of interest, dated 22 October 1845, it would appear to have been written to Glukman shortly after a visit he had made to Brighton. It refers to an accident he (Glukman) had suffered in Brighton, transporting chemicals, suggesting that he was importing photographic materials at this time. Although early photographic processes used chemicals which were not particularly exotic they may not necessarily have been easily available in, what was after all, a provincial city like Dublin. Even today, it is sometimes difficult to obtain certain photographic products in areas away from the main distribution centres. The present writer on many occasions, even today, has had to obtain specialist photographic items from the U.K. and occasionally certain Kodak items from the U.S.A.

In those early days it was obviously advantagious for daguerreotypists to have some contact with a source of advice in case of technical problems. In England, the licenced patent holder, Richard Beard, was obliged to supply this. However, queries from Ireland – where no patent applied and from where no licence fees would have been received – would not have been very sympathetically dealt with. It follows from this that Glukman's friendly relationship with Constable – one of the most respected daguerreotypists in England – would have been of great value as a means of obtaining technical assistance from Beard, if required.

Fox Talbot's establishment at Reading has already been mentioned as a similar source of assistance and advice for those practising the calotype process.

Constable also refers, in this letter, to

that the picture represents an artist, Glukman, sketching a seated gentleman, in the person of Constable. As both of these men had been painters before they were photographers it would be perfectly natural that they would portray themselves in an artistic situation. The crayon which appears to be held by Glukman in his left hand is in reality in his right hand bearing in mind that a daguerreotype was normally a reversed mirror image.

Another daguerreotype – probably taken later in the 1850s, as it shows a bearded Glukman and a rather elderly Constable – is in the Smithsonian Institution in Washington, and is attributed to Constable (it might also, just as easily be attributed to Glukman). It shows Glukman and Constable playing chess with a lady – identified as a niece of Constable – looking on (*see plate 6*).

After he arrived in Dublin Glukman continued corresponding regularly with William Constable and later after Constable's death in 1861 with his nephew, Clair Grece. In his letter to Glukman, dated December 1844, Constable states that he had been approached by Dubreuil, from Dublin, asking where he might purchase a mirror camera. The fact that such a request should be made of Constable is an indication of Constable's experiments he was conducting with lenses he had acquired from Beard and that he was endeavouring to make gold chloride. He finally congratulates Glukman on his marriage and makes an intriguing statement:

> ". . . Mr. Barclay Phillips congratulates you and thinks one wife in Europe and a score in Asia ought to make you a very happy man and I trust and hope you are so."

This was obviously some kind of in joke between the two men and it brings up the question of Glukman's nationality; his name might suggest that he had originated somewhere in Central Europe, an old tradition suggests he was Hungarian. He might also have been German, as he sometimes called himself "Herr" Glukman in press advertisements. In one of these he mentions that he had just returned from Berlin with the latest developments in the photographic art. The above quotation about wives has suggested to some researchers that he may have been Turkish,[40] or of some other Middle Eastern origin, as a photograph exists of him in Middle Eastern garb.

Leone Glukman's first press advertisement in Dublin appeared in *Saunder's News Letter* on Saturday, February 1, 1845:

DAGUERREOTYPE
PORTRAIT ROOMS
13 Lower Sackville Street
Herr Glukman M.S.O.P. begs to acquaint the Public that he has after many experiments discovered a chemical process which enables him to give a natural life-like appearance in Colour and Shadow to the Daguerreotype pictures. TWELVE SHILLINGS AND SIXPENCE for a portrait of the most usual dimensions being such as till the present time has been uniformly charged a guinea. Extra sizes from £1. 1s. to £5 each picture. An additional fee, of 10/- *(50p)* for every additional portrait into the group and a 2nd copy at a discount of 4/- *(20p)* on every 5/- *(25p)* of original charge.

The claims to have discovered new developments have to be taken with considerable pinches of salt. It was quite usual for advertisers of all types in the middle of the nineteenth century to make extravagant claims. Virtually every daguerreotypist at one

time or another made the claim of having discovered some exclusive process which gave him an edge over his competitors. Perhaps the most interesting statement in the advertisement is the price, twelve shillings and sixpence *(62.5p)*, this was a considerable reduction on the usual price of the day which was one guinea *(£1. 5p.)*

The reaction of the competition, in the person of Horatio Nelson, was predictable. Within a week he began advertising again in his usual derogatory style. After his protracted encounter with Dubreuil resulting in the closure of the Rotunda, he was probably enjoying his monopoly, only to find he now had another fight on his hands. He was soon to discover, however, that his new adversary was not going to be so easily disposed of.

Glukman's wise response to Nelson's denigration was not to be drawn into a war of price-cutting and special offers, his attitude is best illustrated by an advertisement he placed in *Saunder's News Letter* in November 1845:

PHOTOGENIC OR
DAGUERREOTYPE PORTRAITS
13 Lower Sackville Street

HERR GLUKMAN invites the Public to inspect the results of his late improvements in the science of PHOTOGRAPHY.
He does not profess to give daguerreotype pictures on ivory or on silver plates or do impossibilities, but he has spared neither trouble nor expenditure in making improvements which enable him to give such pictures as cannot be equalled. No deposit required, or payment either, if the picture be not approved of, N.B. Professor Glukman gives instructions in the science of Photography and his late visit to Germany and France enables him to supply all necessary apparatus and chemicals.
An apprentice required.

The apprentice taken on by Glukman in response to this advertisement may have been William Andrews. Andrews, when opening his own studio in 1858, mentioned he had been long in Professor Glukman's employ.

Glukman's studio at 13 Lower Sackville Street was on the top floor, it can be seen in the illustration in *Shaw's Illustrated Directory* of 1850. The enlarged studio window with the word 'daguerreotypes' under it is clearly visible. In 1850, of course, Glukman was no longer occupying it, he had moved out in 1848 and it was subsequently used by other daguerreotypists, first by the former watchmaker Joseph Pinkney and later, in 1850, by 'Professor' Blume .

Glukman moved up the street to larger accommodation at 24 Upper Sackville Street, where he occupied the complete premises.

Glukman would appear to have always lived at his studio premises as no other addresses are ever given in the Dublin street directories published during his stay in the city, approximately 1844 to 1867.

Helmut Gernsheim, the photographic historian gives details of daguerreotypes being taken by Beard of Daniel O'Connell and others in Richmond Bridewell between May and September 1844. According to Gernsheim this was the first instance of photographs being taken in prison. Another source links Glukman's name with this event, if so it must have been one of his first activities on arriving in Dublin.

The following advertisement appeared in various Irish newspapers shortly after O'Connel's death in 1847:

"PORTRAIT OF DANIEL O'CONNELL
    Daguerreotype copies of an inimitable Daguerreotype of the late Liberator with which is presented gratuitously a lithographic portrait of a large size by an eminent Artist, being a facsimile of the Daguerreotype, may be had through Mr. Cranfield, Printseller, 23 Westmoreland Street and Mr. T. Delaney, 44 Lr. Ormond Quay, or direct from Mr. Beard, Patentee of the Daguerreotype, 85 King Street, London on receipt of Post Office order, at the following prices:
(There follows a range of sizes available at various prices)
    10% of any profits derived from the sale of O'Connell portraits will be appropriated to the Funds of the Relief Committee".

There is no record of Richard Beard visiting Dublin. O'Connell may have sat for him at the Polytechnic earlier in March 1844 during a visit to London.

A version of the advertisement appeared in *The Nation* on June 19, 1847. It carried the assertion that . . .

Lithographic copy of a daguerreotype of Daniel O'Connell, allegedly by Richard Beard, c1844. It may have been taken by Doussin Doubreuil at the Richmond Bridewell, Dublin while O'Connell was held there in 1844. *(see below)*

". . .this faithful photographic likeness is the only one for which he sat"

This drew a reply from T. M. Ray, antiquarian and Secretary of the Repeal Association, who was a great admirer of O'Connell. He stated that the Beard portrait was "distorted" (possibly because it clearly portrayed the great man as wearing a wig!) and that it was not the only O'Connell daguerreotype portrait. Ray claimed to have:

". . . a Daguerreotype portrait and a really fine one for which he (O'Connell) sat in Richmond Bridewell – it is taken by Mons. Dubreil (sic)" [41]

This is most probably true, as T. M. Ray had been a fellow prisoner with O'Connell, he was also photographed and was most likely a witness to the O'Connell portrait being taken. Dubreuil would have taken the prison portrait just before the bankruptcy at the Rotunda and before he set up his new studio at McAnaspies in Brunswick Street. His possible connection with Richard Beard at the setting up of the Rotunda studio in 1841, might explain Gernsheim's confusion over the name of the photographer. If we examine the wording of the advertisement, it does not actually state that the daguerreotype was by Beard.

A recently discovered daguerreotype (*far left, detail*) has been identified by some historians as Thomas Davis.

The suggestion is that it was used by Frederick Burton RHA as the model for the well known engraving of the patriot (*left*)

Taking into account artistic licence and the possible desire to idealise Davis there are similarities. As he died in September 1845 the daguerreotype would obviously have to have been taken in that year or earlier.

It has been attributed to Leone Glukman, or Horatio Nelson.

If it is Davis it is possibly the only photograph in existence of him.

Perhaps the O'Connell daguerreotype may have become the property of Beard at the time of the bankruptcy, possibly as a payment of outstanding debts. It is highly likely that, even though Dubreuil had taken over the proprietorship of the Rotunda in 1842, he would have had to rely on Beard to supply him with necessary materials.

Probably the best known portrait of the patriot Thomas Davis is the well known engraving by Frederick Burton. A quarter plate daguerreotype has recently been discovered of a seated man, the head and face of which bear a striking resemblance to the engraving suggesting that it might have been used by Burton as a model.[42] If it is Davis it must have been taken early in 1845 (he died in September of that year). He was one of the proprietors of the *Nation* newspaper, the offices of which were in Middle Abbey Street close to Lower Sackville Street, where Glukman had his studio, so it is likely that he could have been the photographer responsible. Glukman's later involvement with the Young Irelanders, and his general sympathy for the nationalist cause, also suggest this likelihood. There is also the possibility that Horatio Nelson might have been responsible, bearing in mind his possible association with Burton at the Dublin School of Art.

Leone Glukman's interests would appear to have been much wider than the taking of photographs. His marriage certificate lists 'gentleman' as his occupation. He seems to have been something of a showman who never missed an opportunity of promoting himself or his activities. He was a keen exhibitor at the various exhibitions of Arts and Manufactures organised by the Royal Dublin Society during the 1840s, winning a silver medal in 1847 for daguerreotypes. At this same exhibition George Yeates of Grafton Street showed equipment, including a camera obscura and slides for dissolving views to be used in a magic lantern.

In connection with these exhibitions held at the R. D. S. it is worth mentioning a public meeting which was held in July 1849 to discuss the possibility of allowing English manufacturers to exhibit at them. Prior to this only Irish exhibitors were eligible, Glukman along with other former exhibitors were present.

The following is an extract from the *Freeman's Journal* of July 28:

"Mr Glukman thought it would be no benefit to Irish manufacturers to have English manufacturers poking their noses in among them (hear hear). He himself was a foreigner but he nevertheless did not hesitate to state his conviction (hear hear). It appeared to him that there was no occasion to throw open the exhibition as if they went into every shop in Sackville Street, they would find there nothing but an exhibition of English manufacturers (cheers and laughter)"

Unfortunately Glukman and the others opposed to the inclusion of non Irish exhibitors were defeated and subsequent R. D. S. exhibitions were open to all.

The year 1848 was one of considerable political unrest in Ireland, as well as the rest of Europe, and this was responsible for the imprisonment and sentencing to death of William Smith O'Brien and other leaders of the Young Ireland movement at Kilmainham and other jails. Leone Glukman, good business man that he was, realised that there would be a ready sale for portraits of the condemned men. He published lithographically reproduced portraits of most of the imprisoned leaders, each stating that they were "from the daguerreotype by Professor Glukman". As it

Glukman's Young Ireland Lithographs

Left: Leone Glukman's lithographic portrait of William Smith O'Brien, published in 1848. One of the series of the Young Ireland leaders produced by him shortly after their arrest and imprisonment and drawn by the well known artist Henry O'Neill. All are stated to be "from a daguerreotype by Professor Glukman".

The O'Brien portrait bears a striking similarity to the well known anonymous prison photograph *(see plate 9)* and it is possible that this is by Glukman and was used by the artist as a reference for the lithograph.

The original prison photograph is reversed left to right, (the men's jackets appear to be buttoned wrongly). This would indicate that it was originally a daguerreotype. A detail is reproduced here *(below left)* reversed in order to make the comparison easier.

The inscription on the O'Brien lithograph, and on those of the other leaders, positively identifies Glukman as the photographer.

Below right: A salt print found at Lacock Abbey and attributed to an associate of Fox Talbot, Nicholaas Henneman. The subject has been identified as Thomas Francis Meagher.

Its similarity to Glukman's lithograph *(below centre)* from his daguerreotype, suggests that it is a calotype copy of the same daguerreotype. It was probably made to facilitate the drawing of the daguerreotype by the lithographic artist.

LITHOGRAPHED BY H. O'NEILL, FROM A DAGUERREOTYPE BY PROFESSOR GLUKMAN.

WHETHER ON THE SCAFFOLD HIGH, OR IN THE BATTLE'S VAN,

William S. O'Brien

THE FITTEST PLACE WHERE MAN CAN DIE, IS, WHERE HE DIES FOR MAN.

Kilmainham Gaol

Aug 31. 1848,

PUBLISHED BY PROFESSOR GLUKMAN, 24, UPPER SACKVILLE ST. DUBLIN.

was then practically impossible to reproduce daguerreotypes photographically, he had to resort to having them drawn on to lithographic stones by the well known artist Henry O'Neill from which they were printed. Although they are drawn portraits, O'Neill has managed to retain their essential photographic quality. Portraits of O'Brien, Charles Gavan Duffy, John Mitchell, Thomas F. Meagher, John Martin, Richard O'Gorman and Patrick O'Donohue all appeared towards the end of 1848. The portraits carried facsimile signatures and other messages from the condemned men, some of which suggest that the daguerreotypes had been actually taken in prison.

The publication of lithographic copies or engravings made from daguerreotypes was quite a common practice during the late 1840s. An advertisement appeared in 1848 for the firm of Lesage in Sackville Street stating that they were exhibiting a daguerreotype portrait of the famous Swedish singer Jenny Lind, who was visiting Ireland at the time, Lesage was offering engraved copies of the portrait adding that it was the only authentic portrait approved by Madame Lind herself. This might have been the beautiful coloured whole plate daguerreotype of the famous singer which is now preserved in the Science Museum, London.

In an advertisement for Glukman in *Shaw's Illustrated Directory of Dublin* for 1850 he lists the engraving and publishing of portraits from daguerreotypes as an important part of his business. A number of other examples of Glukman publishing exist, notably Sir William Wilde and Rev. Mortimer Sullivan D.D. Unfortunately none of the actual Glukman daguerreotypes of the celebrities mentioned above would appear to have survived.

Another prison photograph however, has survived, this portrays William Smith O'Brien and Thomas Francis Meagher together with a soldier and a jailer. It is said to have been taken just after the two men had been sentenced to be "hung, drawn and quartered". The generally relaxed atmosphere of the photograph would hardly suggest that it could have been taken on that occasion. Later the death sentence was commuted to transportation to Van Dieman's Land (Tasmania) and for several months prior to their leaving Ireland, they were held, in the Richmond Bridewell, Dublin. This would seem, at first sight, to be a more likely time and place for the photograph to have been taken. Several

places have, in fact, been suggested as the location of the photograph, Kilmainham Gaol, Richmond Bridewell, Clonmel Gaol and even Tasmania, on one occasion, has been mentioned.

However a letter, found among the fascinating collection of letters and other material regarding the incarceration of these prisoners preserved in the National Archives, casts other light on the matter. It is from the Governer of the Kilmainham Gaol, dated 19th October, 1848 and describes the precautions he had been ordered to take in guarding the prisoners:

Kilmainham Gaol
                                    19th Oct. 1848
     Sir,
     Agreeable to your direction, I beg to state, that early on the morning of the 6th. August last Mr. W. S. O'Brien was brought to this prison. I lodged him in a room appropriated to the Turnkeys to sleep in at night, having met with the *appropriation* of the High Sherrif and Board of Superintendance. Which room he continued to occupy – Mr. Meagher occupied a room next to it. *I had a Turnkey with them both by day and night, and a Military Sentinel* (Author's italics) outside their rooms. No visitors were allowed to see them except by an order from Mr. Riddington. No allowance of spirits were admitted, nor did they wish it; all the rest of the State Prisoners were under the same restrictions.
I am Sir,
Your most obedient servant,
Edward Allison,
Governor

The August 6 date suggests that this was before their trial and therefore, before they had been sentenced. The words in italics are interesting, as both a "Turnkey" and a "Military Sentinel" appear in the photograph with the two men. This would appear to be possible evidence in favour of the photograph being taken at Kilmainham some time either before or during the trial period.

However, it may well be that it was standard practice to guard such prisoners in this way ie. with a "Turnkey" and a "Sentinel". This would mean that the photograph could still have been taken at any of the various places where the two men had been held.

The collection at the Archives also contains several letters applying for permission to visit the prisoners. Requests of this nature were rarely granted, except perhaps to family members, unfortunately no application to take photographs survives, if in fact it ever existed.

Bearing in mind the strict controls in force on mere visitors to the accused, it seems incredible that a photographer was actually allowed to take his equipment into the gaol. The photographer responsible for this photograph is unknown, but, assuming the original was a daguerreotype this reduces the number of photographers in Dublin capable of taking it, In 1848 there were only about three or four practising daguerreotypists in the city.

A case could be made for it to have been taken by Leone Glukman, there is an intriguing similarity in the head and shoulders of O'Brien in this photograph to Glukman's published lithographic portrait, bearing in mind that a daguerreotype is usually reversed, left to right, due to a characteristic of the process. The prison photograph is clearly reversed, note the men's jackets and waistcoats which appear to be buttoned wrongly. The fact that Glukman later published his portraits of the Young Irelanders, and his support for exclusive Irish exhibitions at the R.D.S. suggests a sympathy for the Irish Nationalist cause. Also many of the activities he was involved in, while he was in Dublin, were characterised by a certain originality of mind. It would be entirely in character that he might be inclined to "pull strings" in order to gain access to the prisoners.

Obviously another candidate photographer could have been Dubreuil, as he had probably daguerreotyped O'Connell in prison in 1844, however all indications would suggest that he had departed the Irish scene well before 1848.

A puzzling feature of the prison photograph is the fact that surviving prints are on albumen paper, this did not come into use until the 1850s. A possible explanation might be that the original was a daguerreotype and that at some later date was copied in order to duplicate it and have prints made. The rather poor quality of the surviving prints does suggest that perhaps a copying procedure was involved.

Of further interest is the fact that an apparently faked version of the photograph exists, this has been unsuspectingly reproduced several times as the original, most notably in the first edition of Helmut Gernsheim's *History of Photography* in 1956. It is an obvious fake using actors or models in more or less the same poses as the original. O'Brien and Meagher are known physically from other sources and the actors used in the fake bear only superficial resemblances to them. The person responsible for it remains a mystery, it could have been taken in 1864 in order to cash in on the wave of popularity generated by O'Brien's death which occurred in that year. Gernsheim claims that the O'Brien/Meagher photograph is, in fact, the earliest known group photograph to have been taken in prison.

The Governor of Kilmainham, Mr. Allison's statement in his letter that the other state prisoners were also held at that location suggests the added possibility that they might also have been photographed by Glukman at this time. Most of these men figured in his series of published lithographs.

Another of Glukman's interests was the use of electricity for lighting.[43] This may seem surprising at such an early date, but it should be remembered that electrical experiments had been taking place in Britain and elsewhere since early in the century. One of the the principal pioneers in this work was Monsignor Nicholas Callan, who was Professor of Natural Philosophy at Maynooth College. Among other things, he invented an electrical battery which was known as the "Maynooth" battery. Callan and Glukman apparently knew each other, a portrait of Callan by Glukman exists and Glukman used some of Callan's batteries for his electrical experiments. The light was produced by carbon arc, (the invention of the incandescent lamp by Edison being many years in the future). Queen Victoria paid a state visit to Ireland in 1849 and one of the features of such visits were the "illuminations". This was the custom of mounting various types of display lighting on the fronts of buildings. It could take the form of welcoming messages, versions of the royal arms and other patriotic devices. During the 1840s they would normally have been produced using oil lanterns, fireworks or gas lighting.

As part of these celebrations Glukman typically decided to go one better than everyone else, he contrived to present an exhibition of electric light from the top of Nelson Pillar. The plan was to locate the very large and heavy batteries in the basement of the monument. Wirings from them were taken

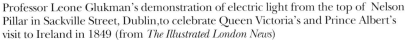

Professor Leone Glukman's demonstration of electric light from the top of Nelson Pillar in Sackville Street, Dublin,to celebrate Queen Victoria's and Prince Albert's visit to Ireland in 1849 (from *The Illustrated London News*)

Oscar Wilde as a child, an ambrotype attributed to Leone Glukman, c1861

up the column to the platform at the top of the monument where sets of carbon arc devices were mounted. In order to intensify the light he used large reflectors and lenses which were from lighthouses, and were borrowed from the Ballast Board.

The *Illustrated London News* published an amusing wood engraving showing a view of Sackville Street, with Nelson Pillar prominent in the centre with two great beams of white light streaming from the top of the monument and the street below thronged with eager sightseers. The same publication reported:

"The most attractive feature of the illuminations was the electric light, by Professor Glukman, from the top of Nelson's Pillar. It was the most perfect and powerful display of this beautiful light that has ever been produced in Dublin and much credit is due to the Professor for the time, labour and money expended on its production to do honour to the auspicious occasion. The trustees of this monument gave the Professor permission to exhibit the light which he did by means of a galvanic battery consisting of one hundred and eighty five cells of Callan's battery, in the most perfect working order".

This was was how it was officially re-ported, reality was, however, somewhat different. It rained, and the electric light was not what it should have been due to faulty connections. Undaunted, the Professor repeated the demonstration the following week from the top of the Rotunda, further up the street, and this time everything went according to plan. Assisting Glukman at the Rotunda on this occasion were several officers from the Royal Engineers as well as scientific gentlemen including William Lover, the famous surgeon and writer who was later a member of the Dublin Photographic Society.

The number of daguerreotype studios in England and Wales during the 1840s was strictly controlled by the vigilant attentions of Richard Beard's agents. Only those holding licences from him were permitted to practice. However, as has already been mentioned, no such control existed in Ireland and Scotland. This meant, in theory at least, that the number of daguerreotypists operating in Dublin during this period might have equalled those in London, in practice the determining factor was the amount of business available to sustain them.

As well as those already described, others were in business from time to time. When Leone Glukman vacated his premises at 13 Lower Sackville Street in 1848 they were taken over by Joseph H. Pinkney. Pinkney, an Englishman, had been a watchmaker who became bankrupt in 1844 and was probably trying his luck in a new and different field. In 1850 he exhibited at the R.D.S. exhibition, where 5" x 4" daguerreotype views of Killiney Castle and the GPO in Sackville Street by him were much admired. At the same exhibition, Barrett and Stanley of 90 Grafton Street were showing "miniatures on silver and painted

A ninth-plate daguerreotype *(left)* of Vere Foster [44] by Richard Beard, most probably taken at the Polytechnic Gallery in London during the early 1840s

Abandoning a diplomatic career to devote himself to the relief of suffering caused by the Famine, Vere Foster initiated a scheme of assisted emigration to America.
He devised an ingenious way of reassuring relatives back in Ireland that their kin folk in America were thriving. He organised the taking of daguerreo-types, and later ambrotypes, of the emigrants and had them sent home. These occasionally turn up in Ireland sometimes by famous American photo-graphers such as Matthew Brady and others *(right c1850)*

photographs". Geary Brothers were another firm of daguerreotypists operating from Grafton Street and Francis Martin a former miniature painter worked as a daguerreotypist at 46 Lower Sackville Street from the early 1850s to about 1860.

The daguerreotypists of Dublin have been treated here in some detail, the reason for this is twofold, firstly there were more of them operating in that city than elsewhere and secondly there is more information available about them. This is not to imply that other cities and towns were without their resident photographers during this period.

Francis S. Beatty has been mentioned in connection with the first studio to open in Belfast in 1842; this unfortunately did not survive very long due to lack of demand. In 1850 a daguerreotypist named A. Tulloch began operating. In the same year J. S. Stanton opened his "Photographic and Daguerreotype Portrait Gallery" and Emile Orange opened a studio at Castle Buildings. Some years later another firm of photographers, Hamill and Hughes were operating from an address in Castle Place. Photographers with the unusual name, Silo Modesto & Son were at 6 Donegall Place. Samuel Glyde, a former miniature painter, was operating from 12 Bridge Street by the mid 1850s.

One of the few surviving daguerreotype views taken in Ireland is of a street in Cork, The photographer's name was Mott and may have been the same Alphonsus Mott mentioned in William Constable's letters to Leone Glukman on a visit to Ireland. The earliest recorded daguerreotype studio to be founded in Cork was opened by Edward Harding at 4 South Mall, probably during the late 1840s or early 1850s.

Almost certainly by the mid 1850s most of the larger towns of the country would have had their resident photographer, and if not, would have been visited from time to time by one of the various itinerant operators circulating at that time. Not surprisingly, little survives in the way of doc-umentary information about these men, however the following advertisement appeared in the *Westmeath Independent* in October 1847:

"Mr. D. Lewis Davis Professor of the Daguerreotype, begs to appraise the inhabitants of this town *(Athlone)* and its Vicinity, that he intends devoting a part of his time for the purpose of taking Portraits, Mr. Davis having devoted his attention to this Art form from its invention by the celebrated French Artist Du Guer *(sic)*, and having studied under the best masters in France and Germany, flatters himself that his experience, together with some recent discoveries which he has made, will enable him to produce the most finished Portraits, combining depth of expression, with perfect fidelity of likeness. These Portraits are finished in a few minutes. Portrait on Silver Plate with frame 12/6 *(62.5p)* each. For further Particulars, Specimens etc. apply at the Royal Parisian Bazaar and Fancy Fair, now open at George Gray's Hotel, Athlone".

Professor Blume, previously mentioned in connection with Leone Glukman's former studio at 13 Lower Sackville Street in Dublin, also operated as an itinerant up until the 1860s *(see later)*. Another enterprising Irish daguerreotypist named Robert McGee made periodic trips into the North of England with his wagon, where he operated quite openly under the nose of the agent of the official patentee, Richard Beard. McGee had previously operated from a studio in Derry.

CHAPTER V

The Gentlemen Amateurs

URING THE FIRST fifteen or so years of photographic history the daguerreotype and the calotype could be said to have competed for public favour. Because of the patent restrictions imposed on the use of the calotype, the daguerreotype was by far the process most widely used by professionals, however, because of its simpler technique and its use of less expensive materials, the calotype was, on the whole, preferred by amateurs.

The first amateurs came, almost exclusively, from the upper classes of society. This is not surprising considering the time and expense required for the successful practice of photography. It was practised at many of the great houses in Ireland, particularly during and after the 1850s.

Michael Packenham Edgeworth and William Holland Furlong have already been referred to in relation to their activities with the Brewster group at St. Andrews in Scotland. They are probably some of the earliest Irish people to have practised the calotype process legitimately as it were. Sir David Brewster as a personal friend of Fox Talbot received permission to use the process and with it, very importantly, the necessary technical details. He in turn passed it on to the various young men in his small group at St. Andrews University which included, not only the two Irishmen mentioned, but the Scot, Robert Adamson, who was to become one of the most important figures in the early history of photography.

Photography has to be learned practically, and although text books were available, only a certain amount of expertise could be obtained from them. To become really proficient actual hands on experience was required. This is just as true today as it was in the nineteenth century. For the photographic historian, being able to trace where an otherwise isolated photographer had received his technical knowledge can sometimes be very important.

As far as Packenham Edgeworth was concerned he was a botanist who, from 1831, spent the greater part of his life in the Indian Civil Service. His interest in photography was kindled, while home on extended leave, by Henry Craigie Brewster, one of Sir David's sons. His entire photographic career at St. Andrews appears to have lasted only from 1842 to 1846.[45] He is said to have also experimented with the daguerreotype process which was unusual for an amateur.[46] No records seem to exist of any photographic activities during his time in India, which would appear to have been for the rest of his life.

As already mentioned William Holland Furlong appears to have returned to Dublin and may have been one of the three men involved in the so-called "Dublin" calotypes in the Science Museum Collection which date from the 1845-47 period. Apart from a letter to Fox Talbot in the Lacock Abbey archives, no further reference to him, photographic or otherwise, has been found.

Calotype views of the Roscrea area of Tipperary were taken about 1853 by Alfred Capel-Cure who was an English army officer stationed at the local barracks. Some of his paper negatives are also preserved in the Science Museum London and have only recently been identified. Several of his photographs feature portraits of some of the local people, most notably one of two "stonebreakers"*(see plate 10)*. They are probably among the very few true records existing of what the ordinary people of the country looked like in the immediate post-famine years.

Photography was practised widely by army

Soldiers at Roscrea Barracks, Co. Tipperary, one of a series of photographs taken by Alfred Capel-Cure, 1855

Powerscourt Waterfall, Co. Wicklow, by John Shaw Smith, c1855. Print c1895 from a calotype negative. One of the few Shaw Smith photographs of an Irish subject to have survived.

officers, it was obviously a useful accomplishment for men who travelled. Captain C. Wells of Mullingar, may also have been visiting with the army when he showed talbotypes at the Great Irish Exhibition of 1853, unfortunately no other details about him are known.

Many of these early photographers were men whose interests were mainly scientific or archaeological, rather than artistic, and these interests were reflected in their work, which could broadly be described as documentary. They were working when photography had not yet come under the influence of the older art of painting, and for this reason photographs from this early period are direct, and appeal very much to our modern eyes.

Some members of the landed gentry who were taking up photography at this time would have had a classical education and had possibly studied art. When they began taking photographs the inclination was to create pictures rather than to merely record views of nature.

Probably, the most important of all these Irish gentlemen calotype photographers was John Shaw Smith of Clonmult, Co. Cork. He was very interested in archaeology and was present at some of the early excavations at Pompeii and in Egypt.[47]

He appears to have been quite wealthy, as well as the estate at Clonmult he also owned 67 Fitzwilliam Square, Dublin and a villa, "Fairyhill" at Carysfort Avenue, Blackrock, Co. Dublin.

He did the "Grand Tour" during the winter of 1850–51. Travelling with his wife, he visited Italy, Greece, Egypt and other Middle East countries. His itinerary in Egypt was quite extensive, having taken a boat on the Nile, which appears in at least one of his photographs. He brought back over three hundred calotype views and at one time was thought to have been the first photographer to have visited Petra. This assumption has now, alas, been proved incorrect as Dr. George Keith of Edinburgh is known to have taken daguerreotypes at Petra in 1844.[48]

Shaw Smith used the waxed paper process. Waxing the negative made it more transparent which improved its definition. The waxed paper process was a variation of the calotype invented by the Frenchman, Gustave Le Gray. The image detail on prints was finer because of the greater transparency of the waxed paper negative.

John Shaw Smith also chemically altered the calotype process for its use in hot climates and achieved notably better results than others who were visiting the same places at that time. This modification in technique was the subject of a lecture which he presented to the Dublin Photographic Society in 1858.[49]

The collection of the Photographic Society of Ireland contains a large number of salt prints from calotypes by him, as well as a fascinating two volume set of albums on Egypt

Above: John Shaw Smith's "villa" at Carysfort
Avenue, Blackrock, Co. Dublin, c1850.
Modern print from a calotype negative.
Right: Captain Edward King Tenison (standing left)
with his wife Lady Louisa and other family members
at Kilronan Castle Co Roscommon, c1860.
Albumen print from a collodion negative.

with descriptions of the pictures written on
facing pages in a neat copperplate hand.

Disappointingly, virtually none of Shaw
Smith's surviving photographs are of Irish
subjects. In common with many other upper
class practitioners, he appears to have
abandoned photography by the late 1850s,
when the calotype process had become
obsolete. His end was tragic, he committed
suicide by shooting himself in the head in
1873, on being told he would have to submit
to being operated on for gall bladder trouble
without an anaesthetic, he was known to have
been dreading this ordeal.[50]

Edward King-Tenison of Kilronan Castle,
Co. Roscommon was also an early Irish
pioneer in the use of the calotype. He was
another landed gentleman who appears to
have spent much time on the continent
touring in France (*see plate 11*) and Spain with
his wife, Lady Louisa Anson who wrote of their
travels in *"In Castile and Andalucia"* (1853):

"The greatest annoyance in Spain, is
the constant opening of the luggage; on
arrival at any great town, all the boxes
are inspected; but if the traveller will
only make up his mind to bear it
patiently, he will find it a mere matter of
form . . . We invariably escaped very well,
and the immense quantity of luggage we
were tormented with, from the size of
Mr. Tenison's Talbotype apparatus,
rendered us very suspicious-looking

personages. In fact, it made us the
general subject of attention wherever we
went, and attracted an immense crowd
in the streets wherever the mysterious-
looking machine was put up. Many were
the remarks that were made upon it in
the different towns through which we
passed, and much of it excited the
wonder of the admiring crowd, who
could not imagine its object. 'Es
Musica?' asked one little urchin; some
more curious than the rest would offer
as much as threepence to be allowed to
have one peep; and our servant only
allayed their curiosity by informing them
it was a new machine for roasting
chestnuts! Sometimes Mr. Tenison would
let them peep through the ground glass,
after the picture was removed; but they
were intensely disgusted at not seeing
anything but the objects before them
turned upside down."[51]

In 1854 King-Tenison's name appears in
the catalogue of the London exhibition of the
"Photographic Society" held at the gallery of
the "Society of British Artists" in Pall Mall.
This was the first exhibition to be held by that
body and one of the first public photographic
exhibitions to be held anywhere. He showed
four prints of views of France from waxed
paper negatives. The following year he was
represented by ten views of Spain.

Some examples of King-Tenison's work
that have survived are from calotype negatives

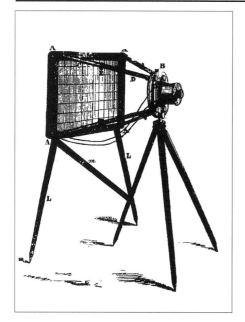

Far left: Portable wet plate camera designed and patented by Thomas Grubb in 1858.

Left: The Campanile, TCD, one of a series of large stereo views by Thomas Grubb, c1853. Modern print from a waxed Calotype negative.

printed by the Blanquardt-Evrard process. Louis Desiré Blanquardt-Evrard introduced this process in Paris in 1851 and offered a printing service for wealthy amateurs who were either not capable or not interested in printing their own work, however he also published some of the prints made by the process in limited editions.

The Blanquardt-Evrard process was almost exclusively used by the members of the Societé Francaise de Photographie in Paris and King-Tenison's use of it could mean that he was possibly a member of this Society during his sojourn in France. Prints produced by this process can be readily recognised by their purple-grey colour in contrast to the usual red brown of the normal calotype image.

Blanquart-Evrard was responsible for introducing the calotype process into France in 1844. He drew the attention of French artists like Charles Negrè, Henri Le Secq and Gustave Le Gray to the aesthetic possibilities of the process. Whereas in Britain and Ireland the calotype was practised largely by wealthy amateurs who were content to produce prints of whole plate size or smaller. In France, the process in the hands of professional artists – who on the whole were ignoring Talbot's patent – was greatly improved both in image quality and in the size of prints produced.

A very interesting album is preserved in the National Photographic Archive containing examples of King-Tenison's work, many signed by him. Interestingly a number of the images in this album have been copyrighted by King-Tenison's cousin, Sir Robert King, Earl of Kingston, of Rockingham House, near Boyle, Co. Roscommon

who, apparently was also a photographer. This was a necessary precaution for professional photographers who wished to be protected from piracy, but was unusual for an amateur.

Another early Irish calotypist who was probably working from the late 1840s was Thomas Grubb. Grubb was a member of an old Quaker family and at this time he appears in the Dublin Streets directories as an engineer with the Bank of Ireland, however he later became much more well known as a manufacturer of telescopes and other optical instruments. He became world famous for the design and construction of astronomical telescopes; his factory at Rathmines (Observatory Lane) was responsible for supplying a massive instrument to the observatory at Melbourne in Australia. He also supplied telescopes to the observatories at Glasgow and Dunsink near Dublin. He turned his professional attention to the design and manufacture of camera lenses, taking out many patents. In 1858 he patented a portable wet plate camera of an unusual design comprising a collapsible framework of rods which was covered by a light-tight cloth material. It looks like such a good idea, that it is surprising that it never appears to have been put into production. The usual portable camera of those days required a small suitcase to transport it! [52]

The only surviving photographic material by Thomas Grubb, which may be safely attributed, is a collection of waxed paper negatives of various locations including one of his house in Leinster Square, Rathmines. There are 74 negatives each measuring approximately 220mm square, and

"The Lismore Crozier" found hidden in a wall of the castle. Photographed by Francis Edmund Currey, hand tinted albumen print from a collodion negative, early 1860s.

"The Egg Lady" photographed by Francis Edmund Currey at Lismore Castle, 1853 Salt print from a calotype negative.

representing 37 images. These range from architectural views to landscapes and initially when discovered were something of a mystery because of the duplication. When slight differences were discovered between each pair of images it was realised that they were actually stereoscopic. [53]

These are amongst the earliest stereoscopic material to be discovered in Ireland, dating them was relatively easy, as one of the images shows the building of the campanile in Trinity College

Dublin, which was completed in 1853. The size of the above negatives might suggest that they were designed to produce prints to be viewed on a Wheatstone reflecting stereoscope or something similar. It is interesting to surmise that Grubb, with his interests in the optical field, might have had contacts with Charles Wheatstone the inventor of this type of instrument.

Francis Edmund Currey was the land steward of the Duke of Devonshire at Lismore Castle, County Waterford. Currey appears to have had a very free hand in his management of the estate as apparently Devonshire seldom lived in Ireland. This meant that Currey could virtually live as the lord of the manor, and was treated as such by the tenants and local inhabitants.

Currey appears to have had friends who also worked at Lismore, probably sharing his dark-room. John Gregory Crace was one of these who seems to have visited Lismore in 1853. Prints by him are in some of the albums which Currey compiled while at Lismore. The glasshouse studio

"Glasshouse" photographic studio/dark-room at Lismore Castle used by Francis Edmund Currey. Photographed by Alexander Shaw, c1855

Mary, Countess of Rosse, seated, examining stereoscopic photographs. c1860

at the castle was photographed by another friend, Alexander Shaw in about 1855. Unfortunately nothing more is known of Shaw.

Currey practised photography from the late 1840s, first using the calotype process and later in the mid 1850s changing to the collodion process.

The surviving albums of his work reveal a keen interest in the people, traditions and landscapes of the area surrounding Lismore and further afield. [54]

He was also interested in the artistic side of photography, being a member of the prestigious Amateur Photographic Association in company with some of the most famous photographers of the day, such as Roger Fenton and William Despard Hemphill.

The restrictions of Talbot's patent, played a large part in retarding the development of photography during the vital first ten years of its existence. Many approaches had been made to Talbot to relax his patent rights, all to no avail, until finally in 1851 he yielded to the joint persuasion of the president of the Royal Academy, Sir Charles Eastlake and the Earl of Rosse. [55]

It was a limited relaxation, however, as he retained the rights to the taking of portraits for profit, anyone wishing to practice other types of photography, for profit or otherwise, were free to do so. He realised of course, that most professionals would only be interested in the taking of portraits.

Mary, Countess of Rosse, wife of the above mentioned Earl, practised photography at Birr Castle from the 1850s. The third Earl of Rosse was an astronomer who became famous for constructing, during the 1840s, the largest telescope in the world. The Countess had a darkroom built in one of the towers of the castle which, after her death in 1885, remained untouched for almost a hundred years. This has been researched by David Davison who has written a fascinating book about Lady Rosse's photographic activities. The darkroom is a veritable treasure house of early photography. [56]

The Countess initially practised the calotype,[56] winning a silver medal for the best paper negative in competition at the Dublin Photographic Society in 1859. Talbot's relinquishing of his patent rights did have at least one beneficial effect. It left the way open for amateurs to use his process without the risk of being prosecuted.

By the late 1840s many of those, who were later active using the collodion wet plate process, during the 1850s as members of the Dublin Photographic Society, had probably taken up photography, but no calotype examples of their work survive, probably due to the instability of the process.

One problem all of the various negative processes which used paper as a base had, was that the fibres and textures of the paper interfered with the photograph's resolution. In practice this produced the characteristic atmospheric calotype image which, from the earliest days of photography, had always been compared unfavourably with the much better quality definition of the daguerreotype.

In 1851 Frederick Scott-Archer in London evolved his wet plate or collodion process. He coated glass plates with silver salts on collodion. After exposure and while still wet, the image was developed and used as a negative from which prints were made on albumen paper. This was the first process to use glass as a negative base and was a giant step forward as far as image resolution was concerned.

This much greater resolving power and the higher speed of the new process were largely responsible for its rendering both the daguerreotype and the calotype obsolete. Added to this was the fact that its use was completely unrestricted as far as patents or licences were concerned.

Within a short time most professional photographers had adopted the new process to produce paper prints, and for those who still preferred daguerreotype style portraits, ambrotypes, which superficially resembled daguerreotypes but were much easier, and cheaper, to produce. The method was to mount glass negatives with black backings in pinch-beck and leather cases, this had the effect of turning them into positive images. They were also known as collodion positives.

The preferred type of printing paper for the new process was albumen paper and was the first real "glossy" printing paper. As the name suggests was made by applying a sensitive coating containing albumen to paper. An industry soon developed to manufacture the new paper, and as, in those days, the only known source of albumen was the whites of eggs, large numbers of young girls were employed to break and separate eggs. This was a seasonal type of work as it was usually done at the time of year when eggs were plentiful and cheap.

Initially photographers made their own paper and a problem was what to do with the unused egg yolks. Photographic journals carried recipes designed to make use of them, one such was called "Photographer's Cheesecake", the recipe for which was published in the *British Journal of Photography* in 1861:

"A HINT TO ALBUMENISERS"
Dissolve a pound of butter in a basin placed on the hob, stir in a quarter of a pound of pounded lump sugar, and beat well together , then add the yolks of three eggs that have previously been well beaten; beat up all together thoroughly; throw in half a grated nutmeg and a pinch of salt, stir, and lastly add the juice of two fine-flavoured lemons and the rind of one lemon that has been peeled very thin; beat up all thoroughly, and pour into a dish lined with puff-pastry, bake for about twenty minutes.

Amateur photographers, on the whole, however, still preferred the calotype, they

Two stereo cards by the Cork amateur photographer Humphrey Haines, top a view at Castletownroche, Co. Cork, and below a view of part of the quays, Cork City. Albumen prints fron collodion negatives, c1855.

found it the easier process in spite of the longer exposure times and the inferior image quality. Taking wet plate photographs out of doors entailed the use of a portable darkroom for coating and developing the plates. Few amateurs relished the inconvenience of transporting such a device on their travels.

In Cork, Humphrey Haines an apothecary

Portable wet plate darkroom parked beside the statue of William III in College Green, a detail from a stereo card by Frederick Holland Mares, c1862.

Photography at Clonbrock House: Drinking group, probably by Lady Augusta (Crofton) Dillon, c1867. Modern print from a wet plate negative

Augusta Crofton with her camera, probably taken before her marriage, c1862

Above left: Group study; Luke Gerald Dillon later 4th Baron Clonbrock, his eldest son, Robin and his sister Georgina. Taken outside the "Photograph House" by Lady Augusta (Crofton) Dillon, c1873

Centre right: The "Photograph House" at Clonbrock built at a cost of £10 in 1869

Right: A strange image, apparently the intention being to photograph the frame of a mirror as this is the only part of the picture which is in sharp focus. The reflection of the two photographers, Luke and Augusta with their camera can be seen out of focus reflected in the mirror.

and flour merchant, was a keen stereoscopic photographer taking many views of the Castletownroche area as well as Cork city itself during the 1850s. He was probably transitional as far as processes were concerned, in so far as some of his images, although printed on albumen paper, give the appearance of having been printed from calotype negatives. However at least one of his images includes a portable wet plate darkroom in the background.

Humphrey Haines was a member of the Dublin Photographic Society and exhibited non-stereo views at the "Dublin International Exhibition" held at Earlsfort Terrace in 1865.[57]

Photography was practised at Clonbrock House near Ballinasloe, County Galway for most of the nineteenth century. Lady Augusta Crofton of Mote Park, Co. Roscommon probably introduced her new husband, the Hon. Luke Gerald Dillon, the future 4th Baron Clonbrock, to the mysteries of the wet plate process on their marriage in 1866.

There is a tradition in the Dillon and Crofton families that Augusta's interest in photography was kindled by the presentation of a camera from her father which was supposed to have been purchased at the Great Exhibition of 1851.

There are a number of problems in the acceptance of this as being true. Firstly Augusta was in her early teens at the time. 1851 was a transitional year in photography and the new wet plate process had just been introduced. Equipment to practice both this and the older calotype process were available at the exhibition. It is doubtful that any responsible father would allow a young girl to get involved with the complicated chemical procedures which were necessary to practice the wet plate process. On the other hand there are no records surviving of the calotype ever being practised at either Mote Park or Clonbrock.

It is much more likely that the exhibition at which Augusta's camera was purchased was the Great International Exhibition in London of 1862. Over the years confusion has probably arisen between the two exhibitions. There is, however, evidence to show that Augusta was familiar with photography before her marriage.

The Clonbrock Collection at the National Photographic Archive contains over 3000 negatives of all kinds – most of which are glass – which had accumulated at Clonbrock House during the latter half of the nineteenth century. It is significant that there are no paper negatives, the earliest are wet

Hon. Luke Gerald Dillon, photographed in his study by Lady Augusta (Crofton) Dillon, c1875

plate and appear to date from the 1860s. Wet plate negatives may be distinguished from other glass negatives by their light coloured emulsion coating carrying the image, the image on dry plates being black or otherwise dark in colour.

Most of the early material in the collection is almost certainly the work of Luke Gerald and his wife Augusta. There is no doubt that Augusta was the better photographer, there are charming child studies and well posed groups which are most likely hers. Augusta herself actually appears in many of the images, it is obviously safe to assume that her husband was responsible for these and for many others in the collection.

Much of the later material from the mid 1880s is probably the work of later generations of the Dillon family. Some historians have been inclined to attribute almost all of the important early images to Augusta alone. It may be attractive to think that all of this early material was produced by a young woman photographer, but there is, however, no basis for assuming this. Shortly after their marriage they had a "Photograph House" built on the estate. This included a glass roofed studio and a darkroom with a beautiful ruby red "safe" window, which amazingly has survived to this

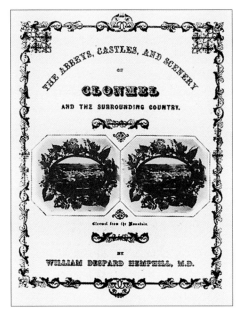

Above left: " Anner Castle",
a stereo card by William Despard
Hemphill, albumen prints on gold printed
card, c1860.

Above: Title page of Hemphill's book, 1860

Left: Pastoral scene, cutting the grass at
Newtown Anner. Co. Tipperary by William
Despard Hemphill, albumen print from
a collodion wet plate negative, c1865.

day. The cost of building it in 1869 was £10! [58]

The contents of Clonbrock were sold by
auction in 1976, including many albums of
photographs and items of photographic equipment. It was at this time that the collection of
negatives and other Clonbrock memorabillia
was acquired by the National Library from
where the photographic items have been
transferred to the new National Photographic
Archive.

This important collection, which is a
unique record of the life and times of a great
Irish house over a sixty year period, deserves
much more research.

Clonbrock House itself was mysteriously
destroyed by fire some years ago, the "Photograph House", however, survives and is being
restored.

Although many amateurs continued to
use the more simple and virtually obsolete
calotype well into the 1860s, the more
progressive, such as Francis Edmund Currey,
eagerly adopted the new process. All of
Currey's prints which turn up in the albums of
the Amateur Photographic Association appear
to be from collodion negatives.

It is interesting that Currey's membership
of this association has made him one of the
few Irish photographers of this period who is
known internationally. Because of this,
examples of his work are to be found in many
important foreign collections such as the Getty
and George Eastman House.

Many foreign historians, assuming him to
be English, are surprised to learn that he was
based in Ireland. This is not surprising as most
of the other A.P.A. members were English.

Another important Irish member of the
Association, whose work also appears in the
albums, was Dr. William Despard Hemphill.
He was probably the most ambitious of all of
these early Irish amateur photographers. A
surgeon who lived at Clonmel, he produced a
large number of stereoscopic photographs,
taken during the summers of 1857 and 1858,
of Clonmel and the surrounding countryside.

He had the idea of producing a book on
the area illustrated by mounted stereographs.
He had been encouraged to do this by friends
of his – many of whom came from the landed

Railway Station—Clonmel.

Clonmel Railway Station, c1858. One of the stereo views from William Despard Hemphill's book, *The Abbeys and Castles of Clonmel* 1860.

This is probably the earliest photograph of an Irish railway station.

gentry – who were interested in acquiring copies of his photographs. Prominent among these friends was a Mrs. Osborne of Newtown Anner, a large house near Clonmel. The completed book was dedicated to this lady "for her admiration of photography".

Books containing original mounted photographic illustrations were not new at this time, it was the only way of having photographs in printed books, as no satisfactory method had been devised up to this time of reproducing photographs. The most famous of such books was probably Fox Talbot's *"Pencil of Nature"* produced in parts in 1844. Hemphill was the first man, however, to consider the publication of a book with stereoscopic photographs. It did not work out that way in practice however. Less than a year before Hemphill was able to complete his book, another, on Tenerife by Professor Piazzi Smyth,[59] appeared. Piazzi Smyth was the Astronomer Royal for Scotland but was better known for his researches into the Great Pyramid in Egypt, claiming its construction had some astrological mystical significance, his rather disrespectful nick-name being "The Great Pyramidiot".

Hemphill insists that the photographs in his book were taken before Smyth's. The latter was able to get his book into print in faster time because it was much smaller, it contained approximately only twenty illustrations compared with over eighty in the book on Clonmel. It came complete with a special folding stereo viewer which allowed the stereographs to be viewed on the book pages.

Hemphill's book was published in 1860 by William Curry of Upper Sackville Street, the photographs being produced in London from Hemphill's negatives. As well as Clonmel it contained views of Lismore, Cahir, Cashel, Holycross, Mitchelstown and a series of nineteen country seats.

Originally it appears to have been brought out in parts, a label on one of his stereo cards states that the book was published in numbers, each containing four views and selling for five shillings each. He mentions in his introduction that shortly after his visits to Cashel and Holycross, in 1857, these places were visited by the London Stereoscopic Company and others, who later published. . .

> ". . . many beautiful and interesting views of those buildings, but as far as I am aware, the remaining subjects of the work have not as yet been visited by any *(other)* photographer for the purposes of publication".

The frontispiece of the book depicts him and his camera on the Rock of Cashel, posing beside the round tower.

Hemphill's book was a magnificent production for its time, and in the writer's opinion (admittedly biased!) is one of the most beautiful photographic books ever produced. It is not known how many copies were produced, but as it is extremely rare today,

Portrait of an unidentified young woman
by Sir Robert Shaw, c1865

great many non-stereo photographs. These, as has been mentioned, turn up in the A.P.A albums. His work was highly praised when it was shown in the great Irish International Exhibition at Earlsfort Terrace in 1865.

Hemphill was never a member of the Dublin Photographic Society. As most of the amateur photographers living either in or fairly near the city during the 1850s were members of the Society they will be dealt with in the chapter devoted to that organisation.

Hugh, fifth Earl Annesley of Castlewellan who was wounded during the Crimean War took up photography about 1855. Most of his surviving prints are in the PRONI in Belfast.

We are dealing here principally with those amateurs who lived at some distance from Dublin and for whom membership of the Society would probably have been impractical.

One amateur photographer who – although he lived in Dublin – was never, for whatever reason, a member of the Dublin Photographic Society was Sir Robert Shaw who lived at Bushy Park, Terenure. He was the older brother of Sir Frederick Shaw who was the Unionist M.P. representing Dublin at Westminster.

Sir Frederick was famous for being one of Daniel O'Connell's fiercest opponents in the House of Commons. His brother's interests were less political and were more in the military area, he being an officer in the local Militia. This is perhaps the reason why most of his surviving photographs are portraits of military officers and soldiers such as Field Marshall Gough (see plate 21).

These Shaws were of the same family as George Bernard Shaw. He came from a poorer branch of the family and is on record as saying that, even when he had become one of the most famous writers in the world, he was never fully accepted as an equal by the snooty Bushy Park Shaws.

one suspects it was only distributed to the photographer's landed gentry friends and was never available for sale to the general public. Very few copies turn up at auction or book sales, when they do they are extremely expensive. Unfortunately because of the nature of the book it often turns up incomplete with some or all of the views missing.[60]

Hemphill, as a successful surgeon, based in Clonmel – a fairly prosperous provincial town – was the quintessential amateur photographer who obviously had no financial need to sell his photographs. Copies of his stereo cards exist, however, carrying labels advertising them for sale, ". . . single slides 2s. each . . . to be had at Fitzhenry's and O'Neill's, Booksellers and Bradford, agent to the Stereoscopic Company, Clonmel." The fact that the London Stereoscopic Company should have an agent in a town like Clonmel is an indication of the popularity of stereoscopy at the time.

William Despard Hemphill also produced a

CHAPTER VI

Professional Photographers in Ireland 1850–1880

THE INVENTION of the collodion wet plate process by Frederick Scott-Archer in 1851 was one of the major developments in photographic technique of the nineteenth century. It was eagerly adopted by professional photographers, as it was totally free of copyright. Scott-Archer's decision not to copyright his invention was based on his criticism of Fox Talbot, which was shared by most photographic professionals, for retarding the development of photography by copyrighting his invention and thereby restricting its use by professionals. Ironically this decision had a rather unhappy outcome, he was to die prematurely a few years later leaving his wife and family virtually destitute. The photographic fraternity, amateur and professional, initiated a special fund and raised several thousand pounds to help alleviate the family's suffering. [61]

1851 was also the year of the Great Exhibition in London. For the first time large numbers of photographs were on display from around the civilised world. The large calotype prints by French photographers like Le Gray and Negrè were a revelation. Local photographers suddenly realised just how much the restrictions of the Talbot patent were retarding the development of photography in Britain. This realisation resulted in renewed attempts to persuade him to relax his patents which finally bore fruit. Pressure was being brought to bear on Talbot from many quarters; the commissioners of The Great Exhibition had planned a sizable project, the publication of a four volume *Report of the Juries* to be illustrated by photographs for presentation to dignitaries. The huge project entailed the making of 20,000 calotype prints for which Nicholaas Henneman, an associate of Fox Talbot, had quoted. Openly flaunting Talbot's patents the commissioners had the huge print order filled in France. [62]

As well as photographic images a great deal of equipment was on display at the Exhibition. Medals were awarded for daguerreotypes, many of which were won by Americans including one by Matthew Brady who was of Irish descent. He was later to become famous for his photographs of the American Civil War. A photographic curiosity which attracted the attention of Queen Victoria was the display of stereoscopic daguerreotypes. Stereoscopic photography was to become a great craze in the fifteen or so years after the Exhibition, an estimated half million stereoscopes being sold in less than five years.

The London 1851 Exhibition was the first great international exhibition. It was a peculiarly Victorian phenomenon and was intended as a celebration of the Industrial Revolution in Britain. It created the desire of other European and American cities to organise similar ventures.

A decision was made to organise a similar event in Dublin and in 1853 a large timber and glass 'crystal palace' was constructed on Leinster Lawn more or less on the site of the present National Gallery. A description of the planning and organisation of this exhibition would require a volume to itself, so here we will confine ourselves to the involvement of photography at the exhibition (*see Appendix VIII*).

Altogether there were twelve photographic exhibitors representing the daguerreotype, the calotype and the collodion processes. Claudet of London received the most praise for daguerreotypes some of which were as large as ten inches by twelve inches. Mayall also displayed daguerreotypes, some of the interior of the London exhibition of 1851. Local daguerreotypists were represented by Glukman and Pinkney whose view of Upper Sackville Street was highly praised.

The talbotype or calotype process was represented by Messrs. Moran and Quin and

41

Messrs. Henneman and Malone of London. Edward King-Tenison of Kilronan Castle exhibited large views of Spain. James Robinson of Grafton Street showed a large number of French photographs as well as cameras made in France. Robinson's firm was to become one of Dublin's most successful and longest lasting photographic establishments, the firm surviving well into the twentieth century. He had been operating his 'Gallery of Curiosities and Polytechnic Museum' for some years prior to 1853 when he appears to have expanded his operations to include the sale of photographs and equipment.

The new collodion process was represented by, among others, Philip Delamotte whose main claim to fame was the fascinating series of photographs taken during the re-erection of the London Crystal Palace at Sydenham after the Great Exhibition.

Leone Glukman exhibited, in the equipment section, a machine for polishing daguerreotype plates and an improved camera stand, which he had apparently invented. Glukman's range of interests, as we have seen, included electricity, in another section of the exhibition he is credited with the invention of an electric device for communicating between guards and drivers on railway trains and ships. In 1854 he applied for a patent for this invention,

Glukman's patent application, 1854

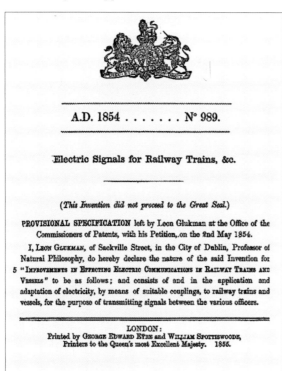

described on the patent document thus:

" I Leon (sic) Glukman, of Sackville Street, in the City of Dublin, Professor of Natural Philosophy, do hereby declare the nature of the said Invention for Improvements in Effecting Electric Communications in Railway Trains and Vessels to be as follows; and consists of and in the application and adaptation of electricity, by means of suitable couplings, to railway trains and vessels, for the purpose of transmitting signals between the various officers." [63]

As we shall see later this invention suitably altered for its use in coal mines was the means of making Glukman quite wealthy in his old age

Also on view in the equipment section were lenses and other accessories by Robert Beaufort of Sackville Street. Thomas Grubb of Rathmines, whose lenses for photographic use were later to become famous, was showing telescopes, and a double lantern for dissolving views. One of the principal exhibits at the exhibition, in a prominent position in the main building, was a great new telescope which he had just completed for the observatory at Melbourne, Australia.

The new collodion wet plate process although an improvement on the calotype as far as image quality was concerned, actually introduced complications into the chemical and manipulation part of the process. There were several who attempted to exploit this, as the following advertisements indicate:

Saunders News Letter 3/7/53
PHOTOGRAPHY,
THE COLLODION PROCESS
The chemicals necessary for the practice of the different modes of Sun-painting, manufactured under the superintendance of Dr. Aldridge *(later active in the Dublin Photographic Society)* can be obtained from Bewley & Evans, wholesale and retail chemists, 3–4 Lr. Sackville St., Dublin.

Saunders News Letter 19/8/1853
The Daguerreotype(?) simplified.
James Robinson begs to inform his scientific friends and the public generally, that he has lately devoted his attention to the new collodion process of photography by which every person can

be his own daguerreotypist(?). By this beautiful and highly interesting process, the most perfect picture can be obtained in a few minutes on a clean glass plate without the uncertainty and trouble of the daguerreotype and possessing moreover, the advantage of being seen in any light. James Robinson is prepared to teach the manipulation, which can be acquired in a single lesson by any person, and at a trifling expence. He has a large stock of cameras, lenses etc. and the chemicals necessary for its practice. Specimens can be seen daily at his establishment:
The Polytechnic Museum, 65 Grafton St.

At first sight this advertisement is confusing, the daguerreotype and collodion processes were quite different and it is difficult to understand the connection until one realises Robinson is promoting the ambrotype which was a different way of using the collodion process. Instead of producing prints on paper from the glass negative the negative itself went through a further processing stage after development, producing a positive image on glass. Used extensively for portraiture the ambrotype looked superficially like a daguerreotype but was much cheaper to produce.

Finally, intriguingly, the following advertisement issued from Horatio Nelson on October 11, 1853:

"POSITIVELY THE LAST WEEK
Daguerreotypes superceded, Nelson's Miniatures on ivory(?) taken in one sitting of one minute by the photographic process which guarantees a perfect likeness, most minutely finished in all the colours of nature. Guaranteed not to fade in any climate. The above extraordinary process is the invention of Mr. Nelson and practised only by him. Inspect specimens at: 9 Lower Sackville St".

Horatio Nelson, as an individual practitioner, disappeared from the Dublin scene shortly after this, a photographer bearing the same improbable name is seen to be operating in Edinburg later in the 1850s, it probably was he. Later still an Horatio Nelson is seen to be operating in London from 1863 to 1872. A photographic firm, Nelson & Marshall was operating in Dublin during the 1860s and 1870s but it has not been possible to establish

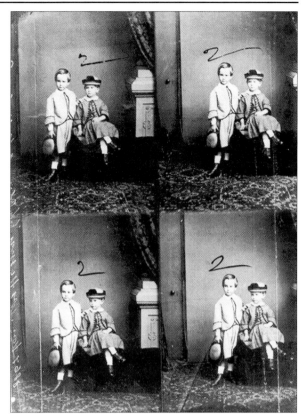

A print from a typical four image carte de visite negative. In "quality" establishments four would have been the norm. However, some photographers used six-image plates and even, occasionally, eight-image plates to produce even greater economies.

if Horatio had any connection with it.

The greatly improved image quality of the new process made it very suitable for large detailed views. The world was waiting to be recorded and many enterprising photographers were quick to exploit the possibilities. Some of the best known were Francis Frith's superb photographs of Egypt, Robertson and Beato's views of the Far East, Samuel Bourne's views of India and Roger Fenton's views of Russia, Britain and most notably of the Crimean War. This was the earliest coverage of any war, an achievement which was actually echoed by recently discovered Russian photographs of the same war from the opposing side. Over three hundred of Fenton's photographs of the war were exhibited in Dublin at the Royal Hibernian Academy gallery in Lower Abbey Street in February 1856.

Photography in the years up to 1860 was very much a rich man's preserve, the amateurs who practiced it were, on the whole, from the upper echelons of society and the high cost of having one's portrait taken ensured that it was most unlikely that anyone from the lower classes could ever afford it. During the 1850s to have an ambrotype portrait taken would have cost about five to ten shillings and to have an average sized portrait on paper would have cost about £2. If the photographer happened to be one of the more fashionable, such as Mayall or Silvy in London, the prices could be much higher. When these prices are compared with the average weekly wage of a working man, which at that time was less than £1, it is easy to see why photography would be exclusive to the moneyed classes.

Left: A typical carte de visite portrait by Lauder Brothers, c1862 with an untrimmed carte bearing the inscription "Mrs Lauder" which was obviously taken in the same studio – note the identical painted backdrop. Sometimes such items play an important part in helping to identify an otherwise anonymous photograph.

This situation was by no means confined to these islands, but was more or less universal as far as the civilised world was concerned. The solution to the problem, when it came, was quite simple. It was discovered that important savings could be made by taking several negatives on one glass plate and then developing and printing them as one. Andre Disderi, a Parisian photographer, is considered generally to be the first to use this idea and to be responsible for its popularisation.

The resultant photograph was of necessity small, measuring approximately 2.25" x 4" and, because of its size, became known as a carte de visite but which, however, was never actually used as a visiting card. By 1860 the demand for carte de visite portraits was so great that not even the leading and most fashionable studios could afford to ignore the business opportunities it provided.

With prices of 12/6 *(65p)* for a dozen and often less, there were few who could not afford to have their likenesses taken. Large numbers of new photographic studios were established; some by men whose photographic knowledge was considerably less than their desire to make money. On the whole they were successful as their clients were mostly quite uncritical.

In Dublin the number of studios is seen to increase from approximately twelve existing between the years 1850 to 1860 to over sixty which opened between 1860 to 1870.

The backs of the cartes were used by photographers to advertise their studios and sometimes provide valuable information to the photo historian regarding the photographers involved which also helps to date when the photographs were taken.

Until the coming of photography, the faces of the world's leaders, political or otherwise, were largely unknown to the general public. The carte de visite was mostly responsible for changing this. Practically everyone of note, from the Queen down, was persuaded to sit for their portrait, and cartes of well-known personages sometimes sold in tens of thousands. Fortunes could be made by photographers who were lucky enough to choose the right sitters. The London photographer, Mayall, is said to have received the sum of £35,000 alone for his portraits of the Royal Family.

Albums to take cartes soon made their appearance and these were used to collect, not only likenesses of members of the owner's family, but also cartes of the Queen and other royalty, well-known authors, actors, soldiers, criminals, clergymen and foreign heads of state, quite literally anyone who might, for the moment, be in the public eye.

George Mansfield was originally an apothecary or chemist, with a shop at 2 Lower Camden street in 1850, at the same time his brother had a fancy goods shop at 90 Grafton

Street. By 1857 he had joined George Yeates at number 2 Grafton Street where they were offering a photographic service as well as selling optical and photographic equipment. Because photographers of this period had to compound their own chemicals it was a distinct advantage for a photographer also to be a working chemist.

During the 1860s George joined his brother at 90 Grafton Street as Mansfield Brothers where they sold general fancy goods including pianos and other musical instruments, and had a photographic studio located on the first floor. Before long they had

George Mansfield's chemical knowledge served him well when in 1879 he made an important discovery which had the effect of greatly increasing the speed of the newly introduced dry plate process.[64] He appears to have exploited this discovery financially as he was soon to be seen living in a large house near Naas. Towards the end of the century he became a regular contributor to both the *British Journal of Photography* and *Photographic News*, the two leading British photographic periodicals at the time. He became a justice of the peace and, in 1898, his name figured on the Grand Jury at the Kildare Assizes rubbing

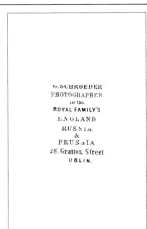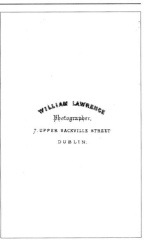

Four typical carte de visite photographs by Dublin photographers of the 1860s, backs and fronts

taken over the adjoining shop at number 89.

In 1865 the Prince of Wales visited Dublin to perform the opening ceremony of the Dublin International Exhibition which was being held at Earlsfort Terrace. While the Prince was in Dublin Mansfield received a command to photograph him and the sales of cartes from this commission must have been lucrative.

shoulders with such people as Lord Walter Fitzgerald, a son of the Duke of Leinster, and other gentry. He was president of the Photographic Society of Ireland in 1890–92.

The firm of Lauder Brothers in 1853 began trading at an address in Capel Street. They probably welcomed the invention of the carte de visite, as the increased business it brought enabled them to move to a more fashionable address in Westmoreland Street. Before long they had a second studio in Lower Sackville Street and a few years later they opened another branch in Kingstown (Dun Laoghaire).

John Chancellor, whose establishment in Lower Sackville Street had, since the early nineteenth century, specialised in the manufacture and sale of watches and clocks added photography to his range of activities during the 1860s,

The firms of Adolph Lesage and Thomas Cranfield had been long established in the field of print-selling and picture-framing. They both began taking carte de visite portraits in the early 1860s. John Fortune Lawrence, the older brother of the more famous William, went into business in 1857 at 39 Grafton Street. He along with the firm of Adolph, also of Grafton Street, held licences to produce "Diamond Cameo Portraits", which were four different small oval portraits of the same person on one carte.

Cranfield had, as his main operator during the mid 1860s, John Payne Jennings. Jennings, originally from London, after a brief period working for Robert Galbraith in Belfast set up a studio at Rathmines in 1870. His views of Ireland were much praised and later a series of views of the English lakes and the Norfolk Broads made him quite famous. He had moved to London in about 1878. [65]

Studios began vying with each other in the variety of the services being offered to customers, Jacolette of 40 Westmoreland Street was offering photographic Christmas gifts in the form of brooches, lockets, scarf pins, rings etc., and added that weather was no impediment to the taking of portraits. The Dublin Photographic and Philosophical Institution was one of the first Dublin studios to use artificial light in the form of magnesium powder.

Mark Allen of Westland Row advertised his studios as being at ground level, most other studios, for lighting purposes, were on the top floors of buildings and persons to be photographed had to climb many flights of stairs to reach them. Allen also mentioned that he was employing a French operator, the carte de visite being, after all, a French invention. His studio at ground level made it easy for him to offer "equestrian" portraits. These were popular, as almost every gentleman wished to be portrayed on his favourite steed.

Blunt and Wyse (The Grafton Gallery) also specialised in equestrian portraits while Pring and Webb offered the photography of horses and carriages at their branch at Beggars' Bush.

Nelson and Marshall of Sackville Street offered "solar" photographs in very large sizes, these were enlargements made by utilising sunlight as the illuminant, hence the name.

Godfried Schroeder advertised at 28 Grafton Street in 1865 the "two largest studios in the country" with ascent to them by machinery. Not to be outdone, Simonton and Millard of Grafton Street claimed to possess the largest and best equipped studio in the whole world!

Adolph of Grafton Street offered cartes at 6/- (30p) per dozen, Forster and Scott charged 10/- (50p) for ten, while Richard Burton of the Hibernian Gallery was offering the "Popular Medallion Portrait" at 2/6d (12.5p) per dozen.

Various Dublin studios also competed with each other in the luxury of their appointments, a typical example being the "Royal Panopticon of Science and Art". Named after a similar establishment in London it was opened at 70 Grafton Street by James Simonton in 1862 and was considered the last word in luxury, as the following, from the *Dublin Builder* of 15 July 1862, describes:

"... The interior, which is entered from a central doorway in Grafton Street, through a handsome porch with encaustic tile pavement and richly ornamented soffet, is very tastefully fitted with mahogany counters, glass cases, and other fixtures, the accessory appointments being all in keeping. Here will be shortly displayed an unrivalled – at least as far as this city is concerned – collection of articles of vertu, vases, groups, figures and other objects of art, in ormolu, crystal and bronze, together with philosophical, photographic and optical apparatus, cartes de visite, albums, stereoscopic objects &c, &c.

A spacious staircase, adorned with sculpture, and attractively painted, leads hence to the first floor, which is divided into apartments, a principal and a minor, both being devoted to the exhibition of oil and watercolour paintings (for sale) by foreign and native artists, to photographs, &c, &c, of which the proprietor has already acquired a choice and varied collection.

Because of the increase in the numbers of photographers with the advent of the carte de visite craze "sandwich" men were employed to entice potential customers into the rival studios. *(From a stereo card, c1865)*

By two distinct smaller staircases ascent is obtained to the photographic gallery – situated in the structure above referred to – and comprising one large apartment for taking photographs from the life, and another for copying drawings, busts &c., with the requisite dark chamber intermediately placed. The general construction of the gallery is note-worthy, and the ventilation – so seldom regarded – is very complete . . ."

Competition was fierce, many of the firms which opened in the early 1860s lasted less than one year in business. Partnerships were continually being formed and dissolved, Simonton and Millard at 39 Lower Sackville Street from 1856 separated in 1862. Simonton went into business in Grafton Street as described above, Millard continued to operate from the Sackville Street premises alone until 1865 when he went into partnership with J. V. Robinson.

Edwards and Company, at 28 Grafton Street, were joined in 1865 by the above mentioned James Simonton, the Panopticon presumably having disappeared by then. Edwards were described as successors to Wonfer and Co., formerly Schroeders, this

statement describes, better than anything, the situation existing at the time.

Thomas Millard was typical of the type of person who was involved with photography at this time, he had been originally a cabinet maker from Cheltenham who came to Dublin in 1838. In 1841 he married Caroline Clayton who was a wood engraver. He went into business as a builder in 1846, with a premises in Mary Street. He also worked for a time as an instructor at the Mechanic's Institute, Lower Abbey Street. In 1856 we find him in partnership with James Simonton in Sackville Street. He died in 1882. *(see also p.16)*

In 1989 at their great 150th anniversary sale of photography Christies sold a very important Irish photographic album. According to the inscription on a flyleaf, it would appear to have been assembled by someone named Murphy. It contains some references to the Guinness family. More importantly, the album also contains many items relating to the Dublin photographer James Robinson, including a superb salt print of "The Death of Chatterton". This image was the subject of an interesting legal action in 1857. (see p.57). Included are intimate

Edward, Prince of Wales photographed by George Mansfield in 1865 during the prince's visit to Dublin to open the *Dublin International Exhibition.* Opportunities to take such pictures represented a valuable source of income for photographers from the sale of cartes.

photographs of Robinson and his wife and family as well as some very early stereo views of Dublin streets. Robinson's main connection with the Guinness family was obviously his photographing, in 1865, the restoration of St. Patrick's Cathedral which was funded by Benjamin Lee Guinness, of whom a portrait by Robinson also exists. Included also in the album are several prints of photographs by Oscar Rejlander the famous Swedish photographer working in London; unfortunately the fact that these were in the album pushed its selling price well beyond the means of Irish interests represented at the sale. At £14,000, it was bought for the National Museum of Photography, Film and T.V. at Bradford.

The presence of the Rejlander prints in this album poses the intriguing question as to whether Robinson might have had contact with him. Both men were interested in posed genre type subject matter, Robinson's "Death of Chatterton" was produced in 1859, at the same time as Rejlander was turning out some of his most famous work. Rejlander will be remembered for his moralistic "Two Ways of Life" which, at the Manchester Art Treasures Exhibition in 1857, scandalised Victorian society by being the first exhibited photograph to portray female nudity. It was later purchased by Queen Victoria for her husband, Albert's bedroom!

Perhaps the most interesting item in the album, from the Irish historian's point of view, was a caricature drawing purporting to portray a group of Dublin professional photographers. It shows a studio situation and carries the heading " The Perfessor instructs as to Pisition". This is probably a sly dig at those photographers who adopted the title "Professor". The principal character is named as "Perfessor" Currie, who is shown taking a portrait of a cross-eyed seated lady with her head in a clamp. The "Perfessor" is shown standing beside a camera, with, incongrously, a crutch under his right arm, the lens cap in his left hand and saying "Now Mary the only way to obtain a true portrait is to keep steady and preserve the natural expression".

Looking on are three other figures identified as "Perfessor" Simonton, Monsieur Jackolett and Monsieur Adolph, all prominent Dublin photographers of the 1860s. Adolph is shown holding a top hat, probably referring to the fact that these were sometimes used by early photographers as lens capping devices.

Lying in disarray on the floor are five other portraits identified as: "Perfessor" Glukman, "Perfessor" Robinson, Monsieur Mares, Monsieur Lauder and Monsieur Cannon who is actually portrayed in the shape of a cannon.

"Perfessor" Currie is obviously meant to represent a Professor Currie who claimed to have been operating as a miniature painter

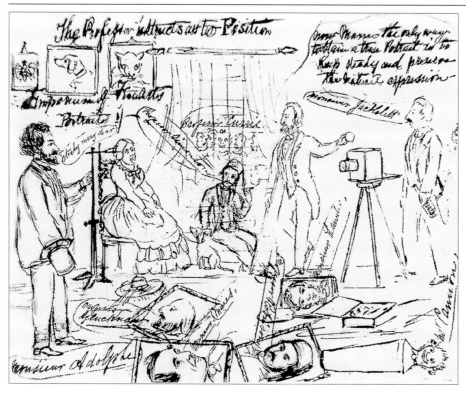

Anonymous cartoon depicting a group of Dublin professional photographers, c1865, included are:
Professor Leone Glukman,
James Robinson,
"Monsieur" Adolph,
(?) Jacolette,
Frederick H. Mares,
"Professor" Currie,
(?) Cannon,
James Simonton and
"Monsieur" Lauder

from a premises at 88 Grafton Street for about thirty years when he advertised in 1857 that he had recently taken up photography. In the advertisement he also stated that he had, not only a ladies toilet on his premises, but he also had the services of a female attendant.

The drawing which is obviously an amateur effort, is full of obscure references, like the series of animal portraits on the wall behind, labeled "Emporium of Famous Portraits" and the crowd of eager sight-seers peering gleefully through the window, and what is the significance of the crutch? These probably meant something to contemporary viewers. As to whether the portraits are accurate likenesses it is difficult to say, we know what both Glukman and Robinson looked like from contemporary photographs, and in the drawing they at least do bear superficial resemblances.

The identity of the artist who made the sketch remains to be discovered, he must have been a member of the Dublin photographic fraternity and the inclusion of Glukman indicates that it must have been produced some time before 1867. The version in the album is an albumen print copy.

The British Association for the Advancement of Science met in Dublin in 1857 and James Robinson ". . . respectfully invited those interested in photography to inspect his stock."

Robinson seems to have also specialised in medical photography. A large number of cabinet card photographs by Robinson of medical abnormalities and people with amputations has recently been found in New York. Dated approximately 1880, instead of having any prurient connotations, they would appear to have been taken as serious medical records. The close proximity of Robinson's studio to the Royal College of Surgeons on St. Stephen's Green might suggest for whom the work was carried out.

On April 1, 1857 Geary Brothers stated that they had just published a "First class likeness of the late Terry Driscoll". Driscoll appears to have been a Dublin character, perhaps a music hall comedian. The advert finishes with a quote from the man himself " I sat to Geary o' Grafton Street for a 'dagger-o-type" likeness and 'twas the real similitude. "

There were many firms, not actually taking photographs themselves, but who made a thriving business out of selling cartes and other photographs. Burke of Ormond Quay,

The small shop of John Gough where he sold cartes de visites and other photographs. Views of the International Exhibition of 1865 are clearly visible hanging in the window and are advertised on a poster in the window.

Yoakley of Grafton Street, and Gough of Eustace Street were three such Dublin firms. There appears to have been a ready market for such specialities as cartes of the Royal Family by Mayall of London and G. W. Wilson of Aberdeen. Views, stereo and otherwise, of many parts of the world could be bought, as well as cartes of practically everyone of note most of which could only have been obtained abroad, implying that these firms must have operated a fairly substantial import business.

The Dublin Stereoscopic Warerooms, Abbey Street specialised in selling stereo views and all the various accessories catering for the stereoscopic craze, which was at its height in the mid 1860s.

Leone Glukman began producing cartes about 1860, he was probably one of those photographers, and there were many, who resented the coming of the carte. This attitude tended to be common among established photographers who had been operating a lucrative business from the earliest days of photography when the number of studios were small and the prices high. Photography in its early days had an exclusive air about it, whereas after the introduction of the carte, competition had increased ten-fold and although business was better, prices were low and, inevitably, standards fell.

The established studios had, of course, no option but to start taking cartes themselves, if they wished to stay in business. Most of them, however, made no secret of the fact that they regarded the carte as a deplorable drop in standards, which of course it was in many respects.

There is a certain amount of evidence to show that by the early 1860s photography had ceased to be Leone Glukman's principal source of income, even though he had a life size portrait displayed at the R.D.S. exhibition of art in 1861. As already mentioned he appears to have been a painter originally, his Nelson Pillar illuminations show he was also interested in electricity. This interest probably led him to his invention of the railway telegraph on which he applied for a patent in 1854. He later adapted this for use in coal mines when it was rejected by most of the railway companies in Britain due, surprisingly, to the influence of Isambard Kingdom Brunel who called it "an invention of no consequence."[66]

At this time Britain was the most in-dustrialised nation on earth, and most of this industrialisation was powered by coal. Britain was by far the largest producer of coal, it was used not only to fuel transport and industry but also by millions of private homes. There were literally thousands of mines, some of them up to a thousand feet deep and extending for miles underground.

Any device which would allow those on the surface to communicate with the men at the coalface would be of immense importance to such a large industry. Actual details of Glukman's device are not clear from the patent documents which survive, but as telephones and microphones had yet to be invented, it is safe to assume it used morse code or some similar signaling system as a means of communication.

As early as 1857 Glukman appears to have been spending a great deal of his time travelling around Britain installing telegraphs in mines as the following letter to Clair Grece, William Constable's nephew, indicates:[67]

Gosforth, 15 Oct. 1857

My Dear Clair,
The letter I sent to the hotel, I fear never reached you, otherwise I would have heard from or seen you. I was waiting that Sunday until 4 o'clock. I shall be delighted to hear from you once more before I die, I hope to go to Heaven when I leave this mortal stage, I really deserve it.

I have been very good and pious, since you saw me I was twice in church, once I went with two old ladies and once to inspect a marriage registry. You will be surprised to hear that William Andrews (his former assistant) is married, I could not almost believe it till I saw the register. He married a pretty girl with plenty of hair on her head – I hope he will not "get entangled" when he gets of age.

I was in Dublin the first of this month, and since that have lived here amongst a people who have a taste for nothing else but eating, drinking and sleeping. I am quite disgusted, yet I cannot leave for a week or so. Last week I put up a telegraph in Leghill Colliery, one of the largest in England. The shaft is 85 fathoms and the workings extend 8 miles. To be wheeled down and up, is no trifling. Last Saturday I was wheeled up and down 33 times. In some parts the excavation is so low that even a little fellow like me must stoop. Right after the men ceased work I went down with a dozen men to lay down wires 3 miles distance. While the men were working, I went in a place to examine some wires which were broken. I was obliged to walk half a mile in the shape of a horseshoe. Tired and with almost a broken back due to the stooping, I decided to rest myself on a block of coal, but as there is "no rest for the wicked" I was soon punished for my laziness, I slipped, upset my lamp and ended up in the dark! You may guess my position – for two hours I could not leave the spot – every second seemed an hour. Every piece of coal I scraped my foot against I fancied the devil was coming to carry me some fathoms deeper!

At last I perceived a man with a lamp (a watch man?) I was delighted and called out, "Here, here, this way". The poor man not expecting to meet anyone this time of night, dropped his lamp and took to his heels – I could not stop laughing. I did not care what became of him, I was full of joy to have a light, my joy did not last long. The lamp had a broken door and I did not walk 5 minutes before I was again in darkness.

As I was close to some very deep places my terror increased. I imagined a heavy thunder descended into the pit and I felt paralysed by a much more painful and mysterious torture for I positively felt pieces of coal dropping on my head and one time I thought it is all over with my acting and that I am walking off the stage, and had it not been for my extraordinary presence of mind I don't think I would have survived all the torture! A colliery is nothing less than a Hell on Earth. The people here don't think much of Christ, yet they look very healthy and are good natured and were it not for the cursed sins of their forefathers they might have been bishops instead of coal diggers. I can tell you they are great cheats, and very sharp cutters *(card playing ?)*.

I am off to Glasgow tonight, pray let me know how you are and how your mother enjoys life. I saw uncle William *(Constable)* I was very pleased with his appearance. Extreme haste.

Leone Glukman
H. Morton & Co. Leeds
2 Bosinghall Building

William Andrews had been Glukman's apprentice and assistant from 1845 to 1857 when he left to set up his own studio at 32 Westmoreland Street.

It is not known if Glukman actually manufactured the telegraphic equipment himself or if this was done by others and he was merely working on a royalty basis.

Another of Glukman's projects was advertised in the *Irish Times* of January 26th 1863:

"Just arrived from Berlin, the Grand Continental Museum of Anatomy, Science and Art, now open at 24 Upper Sackville Street for gentlemen from 12 to 10 o'clock. Lectures every evening at half past four and half past eight. Admission one shilling".

An interesting aspect was that it was "for

gentlemen", it was probably felt that such a presentation might offend the sensibilities of the fair sex. It is not known whether it was exclusively for gentlemen, and that ladies might actually have been refused admittance.

Glukman's museum apparently consisted of wax or plaster models of the different races of mankind, as well as paintings and engravings of an anatomical nature. Special features were life sized wax figures of famous dwarfs, giants and other abnormalities. One figure could be "dissected" to show its internal parts. A carte de visite produced by Glukman for publicity and souvenir purposes show assistants posing with an assortment of exhibits. *The Irish Times* of the 27th of January carried the following report:

"Yesterday evening an anatomical museum intended chiefly for the aid of medical students was opened by Mr. Glukman at his establishment at Upper Sackville Street. The proprietor has been for some time engaged in bringing together the collection which he now possesses and to those gentlemen who desire to study the mechanism of the human system, whether professionally or as amateurs, the illustrations exhibited

From a carte de visite produced by Glukman to publicise his "Museum of Anatomy, Science and Art", 1863.

will provide aids to them in acquiring a knowledge of how the human frame is admirably and wonderfully constructed.

A lecture is delivered each evening on a model figure which is 'dissected' by being taken asunder like any piece of well-formed machinery, and the action of the heart, lungs and other organs of the body is explained from the model, so to be readily understood even by those of ordinary intellegence. Several phrenological busts are also exhibited besides sketches of man so as to show the framework stripped to sinews and muscles".

The museum seems to have been successful in attracting large numbers of curious visitors. By March, after three months, the claim was made in an advertisement that upwards of 8,000 people had seen it.

The actual place and date of Leone Glukman's birth remains unknown. He married Mary Ann Whitley in 1845 when she was 45 years old. We can calculate this from her death certificate in 1870 which gives her age as 70. Leone was probably at least the same age. The daguerreotype which is entitled "The Communion" *(see p.20)* portraying him with William Constable and dated c1844 shows a man in middle age.

This would probably put him in his early 60s in 1860. His advancing age coupled with the increasing competition in photography probably induced him to retire from the Dublin photographic scene. The fact that the telegraphic side of his business was doing well also was a probable further inducement.

The R.D.S. Exhibition of 1864 was the first in which he was not represented for nearly twenty years, and by 1868 his name had disappeared from the Dublin street directories. The lease on the premises in Upper Sackville Street was sold to a Mrs. Begg in 1867.

He and Mary Ann moved to Hove in the Brighton area of Southern England, which, would appear to have been where he had been working with William Constable, prior to his arrival in Dublin in the first place. His extensive correspondence with William Constable and his family during his sojourn in Dublin shows he had friends in the Brighton area and Mary Ann may actually have had family connections with the Constables. He may also have felt that the milder climate of Southern England would be kinder to him than Ireland during his retirement.

Mary Ann died at Hove in 1870 in her seventieth year and for most of the next ten years or so Leone seems to have spent a lot of his time travelling around the world, apparently seeking cures for the various minor ailments he appeared to be suffering and referred to in some of his letters written to William Constable's nephew, Clair Grece over the period, (Constable had died in1861).[68] This was obviously an indication that his financial situation must have been quite healthy at the time.

Unfortunately, he appears to have completely abandoned photography and does not mention it in any of his letters. In contrast to their general cheerfulness a rather disquieting theme runs through many of the letters about the various ailments he was suffering, perhaps not so surprising considering his age.

He was in Contantinople in 1873. In May 1877 he mentions he had fallen and broken some ribs. In April 1878 he was in New York and says he had just come from the hot springs of Arkansas, where he had gone to "take the waters". He explains that it was necessary to carry a loaded revolver at all times! He had apparently reached there by way of Mexico and Texas, having come from Cuba where he seems to have again fallen and injured a kneecap, necessitating the use of a crutch.

Later in 1878 we find him in Christiania (Oslo), Stockholm and Denmark. From Scandinavia he went to St. Petersburg from whence he travelled, by way of Berlin, to Paris where he visited the great exhibition then in progress. He was in Nice for Christmas 1878, moving on to Rome in February 1879.

For most of that year he seems to have

PHOTOGRAPHIC ESTABLISHMENT,
24, UPPER SACKVILLE-STREET,
PROFESSOR GLUKMAN
DAGUERREOTYPES DAILY
FROM 9 O'CLOCK, MORNING, TILL DUSK.
Portraits Engraved and Published;
ANIMALS, BUILDINGS, LANDSCAPES, CHALK DRAWINGS, OIL PAINTINGS, &c., &c.
COPIED BY THE DAGUERREOTYPE PROCESS.

An advertisement for Glukman's establishment which appeared in Shaw's Illustrated Directory of 1850, where he lists the various services which he had on offer including the engraving of portraits.

travelled around various European spas including Ems in Germany where he complains that drinking the waters has done him no good at all, claiming he would be better off if he had drunk a gallon of good Irish Whiskey! His final letter, dated October 1879, finds him in Vichy from where he writes complaining that the only guests left in his hotel are himself and "three deplumed ladies". He ends this letter by saying he had to make up his mind as to which "port to follow the swallows to their winter quarters".

Leone's letters cease at this point and the next information we have about him is of his letters and other papers being delivered to members of the Constable family by a Mr. Carderosa in September 1882. This is a Spanish name and as we have some details, but no date, of his death in Barcelona, we can only guess that this must have taken place sometime between 1880 and 1882.[69]

Undue emphasis may appear to be given here to Dublin portrait photographers, the main reason for this is that there were many more photographers in the city than in any other part of Ireland, also, because they advertised regularly in the daily papers, it is much easier to obtain information about them.

However, with the introduction of the carte de visite most large towns in the country would have acquired their own photographer by the early 1870s. Also larger cities like Belfast and Cork would have had, by then, about a dozen practitioners each. Some of the most prominent in Belfast were: James Magill, Plimmer & Son, John Gibson, and Marcus Ward. In Cork the best known were: Edward Harding, Francis Guy, Madam Bosenquet and A. D. Roche.

Some of the better known provincial photographers were: A. H. Poole of The Mall, Waterford, whose business extended as far as New Ross and the southern areas of Co. Kilkenny; Thomas J. Wynne of Castlebar, who had a thriving photographic and general merchant business; Henry O'Shea of Limerick; D. Welch of Enniskillen, James Bond of Derry; Henry D. Brown of Kingstown (Dun Laoghaire) who always styled himself in his advertising as "from London"; Galbraith of Dundalk; J. Galway of

Clones; W. Mack of Coleraine and Simmons of Galway.

As well as photographers based in the cities and towns of Ireland during the 1860s and 1870s, itinerant workers were operating from covered wagons. These included the redoubtable Professor Blume. The following is an excerpt from a newspaper report from 1864:[70]

"After an absence of nine years Monsieur Blume paid a return visit to Athlone, with some beautiful specimens of his art as photographer. With the aid of the latest chemical discoveries and improvements he was able to take likenesses in a most finished style. He set up his studio at Guthrie's in Mardyke Street, and announced that no sunshine was necessary to take the most perfect likeness.

He specialised in taking photographs of ladies and gentlemen on horseback and of houses of the gentry.

He gave certain directions for dress which he pointed out as being expressly required by the peculiarity of his art. Patrons were advised that dark silks were best for ladies' dresses, adding that checked, striped or figured materials were also good, provided they were not too light. He warned that black velvet was unsuitable whilst white was the bane of the photographer's art.

Monsieur Blume was one of the first to introduce into this country the process of taking likenesses on glass (?)"

While on the subject of instructions to sitters, it is appropriate to present here a further set of instructions from a later period, these, relating to facial expressions are from the *Irish Society Magazine* of 28 October 1893:

". . . ladies, as a rule, find a greater difficulty in composing themselves for a portrait than gentlemen. A correspondent suggests the following rules, which should be posted up in every photographer's waiting room.

When a lady wishes to have a bland countenance she should, on entering the room, say "bosom" and allow her mouth to remain in that position into which it subsides until the photograph is taken. If she wishes to appear noble or somewhat haughty she should say "brush". If her mouth is to appear small, let her say "flip", but if she wishes to enlarge it, "cabbage" is the word required. If a mournful expression is desired she must say "kerchunk", and if an appearance of resignation is wanted, she must somewhat forcibly ejaculate "s'cat". The drawback about these rules is, that you cannot combine any two of them, for instance, if you desire to have a distinguished appearance and a small mouth you must say "brush" and "flip". The former word opens your mouth and the latter closes it. So you must sacrifice one or the other. We don't think that "cabbage" would be extensively used in photography"

The earliest commercially produced views of Ireland date from the mid to late 1850s, Strangman Davis-Goff, an amateur, was responsible for taking some of the earliest views of Waterford. The presence of integral titles and numbers on some of his prints might suggest that he pursued photography commercially; Integral titles were a common feature on professional prints, and it was unusual for an amateur to use them. He was from a Quaker family and may have had some commercial connection with the old established firm of Poole's (who were also Quakers) in Waterford city. In the nineteenth and early twentieth centuries, they produced photographic views mostly of the south of Ireland. One of Davis-Goff's prints depicts Poole's shop situated next to Reginald's Tower (see plate 15).

Probably the most popular type of topographical photograph, as far as the general public was concerned was the stereo view. This was a small oblong card containing two almost identical images of the same scene, when viewed through a suitable viewer a three dimensional version of the scene was seen.

Stereoscopic photography was popular with amateurs because of the smaller and more compact equipment required to practice it. With the professionals, it was the profits to be derived from the sales of stereo cards which attracted them. Queen Victoria's interest in the stereoscopic photographs at the Great

Exhibition in 1851 has been mentioned, this resulted in a stereo craze which was to last for most of the 1860s and later.

The principle of binocular vision had been known for many years before photography. Sir Charles Wheatstone the famous English scientist had realised in 1832 that a sense of depth could be artificially achieved by the use of prisms or mirrors, however it remained for the invention of photography to fully exploit his idea.

Fox Talbot and Roger Fenton both experimented and produced prints which were put on sale to the public as early as 1846, these were designed to be viewed in a Wheatstone's mirror stereoscope (see pp.32-33).

Little interest was, however, shown in the subject by the general public until it was noticed by Her Majesty in 1851. It has been estimated that in the three months following the Exhibition over 250,000 stereoscopes were sold in Britain and France alone.

Stereoscopic photographs began to be produced in large numbers and the London Stereoscopic Company, formed in 1854, claimed a stock of 1,000,000 in 1858 and they were by no means the only company in the market.

Stereoscopic views of Ireland appear to have been produced and put on sale to the public from the early 1850s, but it is impossible to say who was responsible for the production of them.

Perusal of the newspaper columns of the time does give some information. James Robinson advertised in 1856 that he had just imported a large quantity of stereo material. The following year Mansfield and Yeates of Grafton Street advertised stereoscopes and slides and also the taking of stereo portraits.

Bewley & Evans, also in 1857, announced a new collection of Irish views, however it is unlikely that they were the actual photographers.

In the same year Simonton & Millard of Sackville Street advertised, *The Scenery and Antiquities of Ireland.* This would appear to have been a very extensive series, over 1200 different views being claimed in the advertisement. Available at only 3d (1.25p) each they were extremely cheap. As most stereo photographers would have commenced working with the introduction of the wet plate process, it seems unbelievable that any one

"Where Spollen hid the Money"
one of a series of stereo cards,
possibly produced by James
Robinson, showing the various
locations of a murder which
occurred at the Broadstone railway
station, Dublin, in 1858 which
resulted in a famous trial *(see text)*.

A stereo card, one of a series of
views of the Dublin International
Exhibition published by The London
Stereoscopic Company in 1865.
Shown here in a prominent position
is the Stereoscopic Company's stand
at the Exhibition.

Westmoreland Street, Dublin,
Anonymous, c1870, possibly by
Frederick Holland Mares.
Later printed and published by
William Lawrence on yellow
card mounts.

would have been able to accumulate over 1200 different negatives of Ireland in the few years to 1857. It is more likely that the 1200 figure refers to their complete stock, including duplicates. Robinson again advertised in 1857 a comprehensive collection of Irish views of which he was the photographer and publisher.

There was obviously a ready sale in Britain for stereo views of the Irish beauty spots like Killarney,and Wicklow. This is illustrated by the fact that the London Stereoscopic Company saw fit to send a photographic team, which included William England, over to Ireland in 1857.

The London Stereoscopic Company at this time was probably the largest producer of stereo views in the world. Cards from their first series of Ireland – curved top prints mounted on grey cards not to be confused with their later series on yellow and green cards – are eagerly sought after by collectors today. One of these early cards is interesting in so far as it shows a group of gentlemen in the Dargle valley, some of them are carrying what look like camera cases and several of the men bear resemblances to prominent members of the Dublin Photographic Society. It is the writer's opinion that when the Stereoscopic Company sent their English operators to Ireland they used some of the D.P.S. members as guides to the most suitable photogenic locations in the country *(see plate 30)*.

This was the first involvement by the London Stereoscopic Company in Ireland;

later, in 1865, they were appointed to provide photographic views and other souvenirs including stereoscopic views and lantern slides of the Irish International Exhibition at Earlsfort Terrace.

Also available in stereo was a series of Parisian "Recherché" Photos from Mons. Emile Sevine of London and advertised in the Dublin papers, sent by post in a plain secure packing!

Internationally the subjects covered by most stereo photographers at this time tended to be the picturesque and the beautiful. A few practitioners were, however, interested in using the medium to show documentary subjects. Some of the best known, being the series produced of the launch of the Great Eastern in 1858 and the opening of the Suez Canal in 1869. Great fires and earthquakes were very popular subjects – particularly in the U.S.A. These so-called documentary subjects particularly lent themselves to stereo photography because of the relative portability of the equipment.

An early Irish example of stereo documentary photography was the series produced, probably by James Robinson, of the Spollen murder case in 1856 *(see illustration p. 55).*

On the morning of Thursday, November 13th, the city was shocked by the brutal murder of Mr. George Little, the cashier of the Midland & Great Western Railway Company. The murder had occurred the night before while he had been working late in his office at the Broadstone Station. A large amount of money was missing.

James Spollen, a handy man working at the station, was accused of the crime. Spollen lived on the premises with his wife and four children.

He was subsequently brought to trial and a sensational aspect of the case was the fact that two of his children, Lucy aged 10 and Joseph aged 14 were witnesses for the prosecution, contributing evidence particularly damaging to their father's case. It was later established that their mother had prompted them to do this, and had even tutored them as to what to say, her own evidence, as wife of the accused, being inadmissable. This was all part of her plan to dispose of her unfortunate husband in favour of another man, and also to claim the reward of £350 offered by the railway company.

Inconsistencies in the children's testimony were soon noticed and the jury acquitted Spollen.

It can well be imagined the kind of sensation which this trial must have caused at the time; it was widely reported in the newspapers and it is easy to see that there would have been a ready sale for the stereoscopic photographs mentioned earlier.[71]

Several of the amateurs previously mentioned were interested in stereoscopy, Sir Joscelyn Coghill, Sir Robert Shaw and Thomas Brownrigg (who received the Dublin Photographic Society's medal for the best stereo negative in 1859) are each known to have taken stereo photographs

The barristor, Henry T. Vickers, Honorary Secretary of the Dublin Photographic Society in 1858 also appears to have specialised in stereo, having had views shown at the Great Exhibition in 1865.[72]

Photographers were beginning to realise the potential of their medium for recording such happenings and soon very little of any consequence ever occurred anywhere without it being recorded for posterity by the camera.

Until the invention of photography, if one had wished to be sure of getting an accurate impression of a famous painting, like the Mona Lisa, it would have been necessary to travel to Paris to see it; the only reproductive processes available i.e. engraving or lithography, were interpretive and could not be guaranteed to produce accurate representations of the actual works. During the 1850s the practice was established of photographing great works of art and then publishing photographic copies. This meant that, for the first time – albeit in monochrome – it became possible to purchase accurate reproductions of paintings and sculpture.

The sale of engraved and later photographic reproductions of famous and not so famous works of art seems to have been quite a thriving business in Dublin at this time, judging from the number of firms specialising in this form of business. Some of the more prominent were, Adolph Lesage 40 Lower Sackville Street, Thomas Cranfield 115 Grafton Street, Mark Allen 12 Westland Row, Thomas Webb 47 Lower Sackville Street and James Del Vecchio 200 Brunswick Street Great. Most of these firms had, by the early 1860s, begun to include photography among their activities but during the 1850s they were still operating solely as printsellers.

A feature of this type of business was the temporary exhibition of some topically famous work, then selling engraved copies of it to the people who came to see it. The columns of the Dublin papers of the time contain numerous advertisements for this type of promotion.

One typical example was the painting 'The Death of Chatterton' by Wallis, which had been much admired when exhibited in London, at the Royal Academy in 1856, and was subsequently shown at other exhibitions around the British Isles. The painting had been purchased with the exclusive rights to engrave, print or otherwise reproduce it, by a certain Mr. Augustus Egg.

In 1859 the painting went on display, in the usual way, at Cranfield's Gallery in Grafton Street and presumably reproductions were available for sale. James Robinson, the photographer, who had a studio at 65 Grafton Street, happened to see it. He went back to his studio and proceeded to construct a set, similar to the scene in the painting and to enlist the aid of his apprentice, whom he dressed in a similar fashion to the dying poet. He photographed the scene and subsequently put on sale stereoscopic and other views which were entitled "The Death of Chatterton" in the advertisements which he placed in various Dublin papers.

It is difficult to know just how long he expected to get away with this very obvious copyright infringement, presumably he felt, that as his versions of the work were purely photographic and were not actually copied from the original, he was safe from legal action. He discovered differently, however, when in June 1859 an injunction was taken out against him, and in the subsequent court action a petition was filed to restrain him from "exhibiting, publishing, selling or exposing for sale, or in any way parting with the photographic picture entitled 'The Death of Chatterton'."[73]

Dublin photographers appear to have been rather notorious as far as piracy was concerned – maybe they were more unlucky than others in being found out – as just two months later a similar case came before the court. On this occasion action was being taken against Messrs. Bewley and Evans, who were well known chemists and photographers (Thomas Bewley was Treasurer of the Dublin Photographic Society). Details of the case are not clear, but the injunction was granted to restain them from taking and selling copies of paintings owned by a certain Ernest Gambail of London and Paris.

Frederick Holland Mares showed views and stereograms of Irish scenery at the Dublin International Exhibition of 1865, he probably first went into business in the late 1850s when he was operating from a premises at Portabello Harbour. He moved to a more fashionable address at 79 Grafton Street about 1860 and began taking carte de visite portraits. He would appear to have started taking his series of views a year or so later. A copyright document exists in the P.R.O. at Kew for the first twelve cabinet views of Dublin, dated 1863. These, numbered integrally 1 to 12, would appear to be the earliest views put on sale by Mares. During the early 1870s all of Mares' view negatives were acquired by William Lawrence who continued to use some of them well into the twentieth century (see later). The negatives of numbers 3, 4, 6 and 10 from this series are still occupying the same numerical positions in the cabinet series in the National Photographic Archive. The numbers 1, 2, 5, 7, 8 and 9 are of scenes, such as Sackville Street (1), which changed over the years necessitating re-photographing. Mares' series were numbered approximately 1 to 500 and the negatives may be identified in the Lawrence Collection by the distinctive lettering style used for the integral titles. This was slightly different to that used later by Lawrence on his own negatives. Typical examples would be:

SACKVILLE STREET, DUBLIN 1.
(Mares, larger initial capitals)

SACKVILLE STREET, DUBLIN, 1. W.L.
(William Lawrence, uniform capitals with W.L. initials)

This series was the most comprehensive and best known collection of Irish views available, prior to William Lawrence entering the field in the early 1870s.

Mares published most of his views in the cabinet or half plate size – although larger views are known – and was one of the first Irish professional photographers to use integral titles and numbers. Many of his views were used as book illustrations, most notably in a series of volumes brought out in 1867 by Andrew Duthie of Glasgow, who had already published a similar series of books on Scotland using views by Annan and others. The most charming of the Irish series was probably *Photographs of Dublin with Descriptive Letterpress*; this included the twelve views of the city including Kingstown mentioned above, the original prints being pasted into the book. Other titles, also with descriptive letterpress, in the series, all including twelve images, were *Photographs of Killarney etc., Gems of Irish Scenery etc., Photographs of Co. Wicklow etc., Photographs of Connemara etc., Castles and Abbeys in Ireland* and *The Giants Causeway and the North etc.* The book on Killarney, however, did not have photographs by Mares, instead it contained twelve views by John Hudson who actually lived in Killarney and who also contributed several views to the Giant's Causeway book.[74]

The books were published in two sizes, the larger was quarto and containing 7" by 5" prints sold for 21 shillings (£1. 5p). The smaller format book was octavo and had 4.5" by 3.5" images. It sold for 10/6 (62.5p).

The fact that Mares' photographs were not used in the Killarney book may have been the reason why, also in 1867, Mares undertook the publication of *Sunny Memories of Ireland's Scenic Beauties, Killarney* containing twelve views by himself. The way that the title is worded might suggest that he was planning a series of books, but, as far as we can tell, no other titles were ever published.

There is also the possibility that Mares' *Sunny Memories* may have appeared first, and on seeing it, Andrew Duthie may have suggested that he would take over the publication of further titles, suitably rewarding Mares for the use of his photographs. Mares might, indeed, have welcomed Duthie's intervention, removing from him the onerous and expensive task of publication. This would also explain why the book on Killarney did not contain views by Mares.

Frederick H. Mares' compositions are easy to recognise when looking through the Lawrence Collection, they are distinguished by a particularly romantic view of the country. This was the fashionable way of looking at Ireland in the middle of the nineteenth century, and it contrasts markedly with the more factual or documentary, and perhaps less imaginative, approach evident in the later Lawrence views taken by Robert French, Mares' photographs show an apparently deserted city and country covered, on the whole, by mist laden ivy-covered ruins. The

lack of people was obviously caused by the long exposures necessary in the early 1860s (it is only in the later stereo views of Dublin, taken in the late 1860s that people are present). This, however, is probably only part of the reason; it is quite obvious from examining the photographs, that he was deliberately setting out to portray Ireland in a romantic pictorial style.

Mares also published an extensive series of stereoscopic views of Irish scenery. These were produced on the very common yellow card mount which were used by many stereo photographers of the 1860s. There is no indication on them as to who was responsible for them, however, in many cases he used the same distinctive compositions as in his cabinet views and it is relatively easy to identify them – they were probably taken at the same time. An attractive boxed set of these views of Dublin was published by Andrew Duthie of Glasgow, previously mentioned in connection with the publication of the books containing Mares' views. Further corroboration of Mares as a stereoscopic photographer – if that were necessary – is provided by the fact that the views contained in this set are the same as those in the Dublin book.

Identification of two stereo views by Mares can be made in a novel way, they are of Grafton Street in Dublin in the late 1860s looking down on the street from an upper storey window. When one works out just where the camera was located, it would appear to have been from the first floor front window of Mares' studio at number 79.

Mares also produced a number of genre type stereo cards in the early 1860s, the copyright documents of which are to be found in the P.R.O. at Kew, in London.

All of Frederick H. Mare's cabinet and stereo negatives were acquired by William Lawrence during the early 1870s and have subsequently ended up in the Lawrence Collection at the National Photographic Archive..

Although Mares abandoned the publishing of views about 1870, he did not go out of business at that time. Evidence of the Dublin streets directories shows him to have been still taking portraits at 79 Grafton Street up to 1880 when he sold out to James McFarland who had been his employee, and who went on using Mares'

Carlisle Bridge and Sackville Street,
and Sackville Street from Rutland
(Parnell) Square,

Both from stereo negatives by
Frederick Holland Mares, c1862, in
the National Photographic Archive.

carte and cabinet mounts
overprinted with his own name
for a time.

This was still not, however,
the end of Frederick H. Mares on
the Dublin scene; he seems to
have opened another, probably
smaller, studio further up the
street at 118 Grafton street where
he worked until 1895, when he
finally disappeared.

The name pre-eminent in
Irish commercial view photography is obviously William
Lawrence. Most people will be
familiar with the Lawrence
Collection now at the National
Photographic Archive. Strictly
speaking it is not a collection at all
more an accumulation.

The photographic firm from
which the Collection came had its
beginnings in the small toy and
fancy goods shop of Elizabeth
Lawrence in Sackville Street
during the 1840s. William Mervyn
Lawrence, Elizabeth's second son
was born in 1840. A tragic,
accident in childhood resulted in
the loss of his right arm, because
of this – although often quoted as being a
photogapher – it is most unlikely that he
would have been able to manipulate the large
cumbersome cameras of the nineteenth
century. His considerable talents as a business
man and entrepreneur were, however, responsible for building up the great organisation which bore his name. William's older
brother, John Fortune Lawrence, had opened
a carte de visite studio in Grafton Street in
1857. In 1865 the toy premises in Sackville
Street were extended and a photographic
studio under the direction of the younger son
was included in the renovation.

Initially, for the first few years, he seems
to have concentrated on carte de visite and

other portraits. It was about 1870 that he
entered the topographical view side of
photography by acquiring Frederick H. Mares'
negative stock

The conditions of the acquisition are now
difficult to establish, with Mares actually
continuing in business for many years after the
take-over. Presumably, he merely sold the
topographical view part of his business and
thereafter concentrated on the taking of
portraits.

A close scrutiny of the first five hundred
or so views in the cabinet series of the
Collection, undoubtedly the oldest non-stereo
negatives in the Lawrence Collection, reveals
most of them to have been taken by Mares in

When William Lawrence acquired Frederick H. Mares' negatives during the early 1870s he retained Mares' integral titles and numbering system but added his initials (W.L.) Their presence is an easy way to roughly date a print. Prints without the initials are by Mares himself and date from 1863 – when the images were copyrighted – to about 1870. A curious example of Lawrence's "up-dating" methods in the above illustration is the addition of the conical cap to the the round tower, missing in the original Mares version. The cap was probably replaced on the tower during the 1870s.

According to Kieran Hickey, he also took over the stereo negatives of his brother, John Fortune Lawrence, when he ceased to trade as a photographer. John Fortune, however, remained in business in Grafton Street selling cricket gear and other sporting goods.

By 1872 William Lawrence appears to have acquired sufficient confidence to take on the appointment as official photographer to the large International Exhibition held in Earlsfort Terrace. At the exhibition he was offering stereoscopic and other views.

The 1870s also saw the introduction of Lawrence's Eblana series of stereoscopic views on their distinctive orange coloured cards, *Gems of Irish Scenery* as they were styled were the most comprehensive stereo series ever produced in Ireland.

the early to mid 1860s. The negatives of nearly all of the views from the previously mentioned books by Mares are there. The titles and numbers allocated to them by Mares are still on the plates with the addition of the initials W. L. in a slightly different style of lettering *(see p.57 and above)*.

As mentioned earlier, where necessary, new views of the same subjects have been substituted to update the series when buildings or public transport vehicles changed over time. Plate No.1 shows Sackville Street complete with electric trams, obviously taken in the 1890s whereas Mares' No. 1 – from his book – shows exactly the same location but very obviously taken in the 1860s and therefore unsuitable for use later in the century. Plate No. 2, on the other hand is the original and beautifully atmospheric view of the Custom House, a careful examination of the costumes worn by the people in the photograph reveal them to be of the 1860s period, apparently not a sufficient reason to re-photograph the scene.

Lawrence seems to have always been interested in buying negatives from other photographers going out of business. In the 1870s he acquired the negatives (and thereby any repeat orders) of Lesage's, who had been photographers to the Catholic Hierarchy.

The old troublesome wet-plate process became obsolete in the late 1870s, and this in practice was the cause of much greater activity among professional view photographers. It is from around this time that the vast majority of the plates in the Lawrence Collection were taken. This period also saw the appearance on the scene of Robert French, the photographer who, more than anyone else, was responsible for the general overall quality of the photographs in the Collection.

There is a generally held view that Robert French was responsible for taking all of the Lawrence photographs. We have seen that most of the earliest negatives – those dating from the 1860s – were taken by Frederick H. Mares and possibly others. William Lawrence, or his employees only began taking view photographs in his own name around 1870. It is not clear if French was working as a photographer this early – his first jobs with Lawrence involved in-house dark room work.

If it is assumed that he began working about 1875 and retired about 1912, we see a working life of approximately thirty five years. The number of individual photographs in the Collection is greater than 50,000. A little

Robert French, the photographer of many of the photographs in the "Lawrence Collection" liked putting himself into some of his pictures. He is easily recognised with his fine full beard.

Left: Robert French in old age

simple arithmatic will show that if Robert French was the sole photographer, and allowing for unsuccessful exposures at a time when modern exposure meters did not exist, he would have had to take about six successful photographs every day of his working life not allowing for holidays. When we consider the amount of travelling involved, the primitive travelling conditions prevailing at the time and the uncertain weather which all Irish photographers, even to this day, have to cope with, little work would have been possible during winter months. When all this is considered we can see it would have been quite impossible for one man to have taken all of them.

Also, different visual styles are apparent in the Collection so it would appear obvious that Lawrence must have employed more than one photographer.

As the numbers of individual pictures multiplied up to the end of the century, so also did the number of different ways in which they were used. William Lawrence, to use a modern expression, "didn't miss a trick". Every conceivable way of exploiting photography was employed as a means of improving business.[75]

The Sackville Street premises were destroyed during the Easter Week rising in 1916 and everything therein was lost, including portrait and general commercial negatives taken over more than a fifty year period. Thankfully the view part of the business had been transferred to another premises, and this accounts for the survival of those negatives.[76]

The name Mason has long been associated with photography in Ireland. However, having been founded in 1780, the firm greatly predated the invention of photography. Initially Masons manufactured and sold scientific, mathematical and optical instruments. The term mathematical instruments included such things as levels, theodolites, drawing instruments and surveying quadrants.

Operating originally from a corner site at 11 Essex Bridge (now occupied by The Sunlight Chambers) Masons moved to its famous Dame Street location in 1894. In 1887 Thomas Mason had returned from London to take over the management of the family business which had fallen on hard times and was near bankruptcy. Having worked in

The Lawrence premises at 5, 6, and 7 Upper Sackville Street, Dublin, c1890

Right: Kingstown (Dun Laoghaire) Harbour probably photographed by Robert French for Lawrence c1880

London for the optical and photographic firm of Negretti & Zambra he successfully set about rebuilding the business and establishing a photographic department for the first time.

Masons were not a commercial photographic firm in so far as they did not take portraits. They offered a developing and printing service for amateurs as well as selling all types of photographic materials, cameras and other equipment, particularly magic lantern slide projectors. They were one of the few Dublin firms offering a slide making service. A religious or university lecturer could take a miscellaneous collection of photographs, prints, maps and other documents into Mason's and have them made into a set of slides for projection. Many people finding old slides with the Mason name on them assume that the original image was taken by one of the Mason family, whereas it is more likely that, in many cases, they were only responsible for the making of the actual glass lantern slide.

The North Dublin quays from the dome of the Custom House, photographed by Robert French for Lawrence c1890.

Photographically, the most important member of the family was Thomas Holmes Mason, Thomas's son. Born in 1877, he had a wide range of interests, before taking over the management of the business. At his father's death in 1913, he had been responsible only for the photographic department.

He journeyed around the country on a bicycle taking photographs, particularly of items of archaeological interest, eventually

amassing over 8,000 neg-
atives. In 1932 Masons began
publishing picture post-cards.

Thomas H. Mason was
elected a member of the
Royal Irish Academy and
wrote a classic book *The
Islands of Ireland* illustrated by
his own photographs. He was
a member and president of
the Photographic Society of
Ireland where his services as a
competition judge werc
highly valued. He died in
1958.[77]

The firm of Werner &
Son was established in Dublin
during the late 1850s. Louis
Werner, a French miniature
painter came to Ireland from Alsace with
Augustine, his wife, and set up a studio at 15
South Leinster Street, Dublin. Werner had
studied in Paris, the Academie des Beaux Arts,
with the famous painter, Paul Delaroche. He was
a fellow student with the son of Louis Jacques
Mandé Daguerre, a fascinating early Irish
connection with the beginnings of photography.[78] It would appear that Louis Werner
initially concentrated on painting society portraits
and that the photographic side of the business
was handled by Augustine. The earliest surviving
cartes by the Werner studio bear the name
Madame Werner.

By the mid 1860s, however, the firm was
known as 'L. Werner, 15 Leinster Street, Dublin'.
By the 1870s the Werners were exploiting their
Frenchness by calling their establishment
'Photographie Francaise'. It should be re-
membered that this was the period following the
Third Empire when everything French had
become the height of fashion.

Alfred, their son, eventually joined the firm
about 1880, the name then being changed to
'L. Werner & Son' and then later to simply
'Werner & Son'. Alfred's joining the firm
almost coincided with a move to the more
fashionable address of 39 Grafton Street, and
these two events marked an upswing in the
fortunes of the Werner studio, it eventually
became one of the most exclusive in the city
for society portraits.

Alfred Werner was also interested in
pictorial or art photography, as well as

The premises at 11 Essex Bridge which the Mason family occupied from 1780 to 1894 when they moved to their well known Dame Street location. The site is now occupied by the building known as " The Sunlight Chambers"

exhibiting at the various exhibitions organised in Dublin by the Photographic Society of
Ireland, his work during the 1890s became
increasingly well known at International
Salons abroad winning many awards and
medals. He built up an international rep-
utation and travelled widely as a judge of
photographic competitions and exhibitions.
He was one of the first to be awarded the
distinction, Fellow of the Royal Photographic
Society during the 1890s.

Alfred Werner's main claim to fame is the
large photograph of Maud Gonne which he took
in 1893. He had J. V. Robinson – a designer of
cameras and a fellow member of the P.S.I. – build
for him a large camera to take a plate nearly six
feet by four feet. His intention was to take life-size
portraits, but, the only surviving portrait taken
with it is the negative and the platinum contact
print from it preserved in the P.S.I. collection –
slightly less than life-size – of Maud Gonne, later
Maud Gonne McBride and mother of the
statesman Sean McBride *(see plate 40)*.

This portrait was among a group of
photographs by Werner that won for him the
premier gold medal for photographs at the
Chicago World's Fair in 1893. A contemporary
description is of interest: [79]

"The large portrait of Miss Maud Gonne
was taken by Alfred Werner in 1893 using a
specially designed camera. This camera was
built by Mr. J. V. Robinson of Malahide and
measures 8 feet high, 4 feet wide and 10

The Belfry of Cashel, from *Notes on Irish Architecture* by Lord Dunraven, 1875. Photography by William Mercer.

Notes on Irish Architecture written by Lord Dunraven in 1875 was a survey of ancient Irish eclesiastical architectural remains as they were at the time. It was produced in two monumental volumes which contained over one hundred photographs taken by William Mercer of Rathmines.

The illustrations are not original photographic prints, as is usually assumed, but are carbon transfer prints. This process was one of a number of extremely expensive – even in late Victorian times – pigment processes which were used when the exact reproduction of photographs was required and of necessity was only used for expensive works published in fairly small editions. One of the advantages of using carbon prints or other pigment prints over original photographs was the fact that they did not fade with exposure to daylight. With the Woodburytype, a similar pigment process, the carbon print process has never really been bettered – even today – for the reproduction of photographs for quality book illustrations. They are commonly mistaken for original silver based prints. The introduction of half-tone blocks in the late 1880s – although greatly inferior to the pigment processes – was responsible for their decline because of the much lower costs involved. The fact they could be printed with letterpress type allowed for the use of photographic illustrations in newspapers and periodicals for the first time.

It is most unlikely that the expertise to produce carbon prints in quantity would have existed in Ireland at the time. Mr. Mercer's negatives were probably sent to England where the necessary reproduction prints would have been made from them. Not a lot is known about William Mercer, it is assumed he was the same Mercer who is listed in the directories of the time as a photographer living in Rathmines. A lady named Blanche Mercer who was active in the P.S.I. during the 1920s and 1930s may have been his daughter or grand-daughter.

feet long. It could take a plate of over 6 feet high but the present exhibit measuring 5 feet 4 inches by 3 feet 2 inches was the largest actually used. Focusing is accomplished by two men inside the camera directly onto the sensitive plate itself, a ruby filter being placed over the lens during the operation.

The lens is a specially made 50 inch Ross doublet and the plates were also specially made from plate glass. Development was carried out in five gallons of pyro-gallic developer in a special tank with a glass bottom illuminated by a ruby light.

The print is a platinotype. It is a full length portrait, the treatment is clever and bold and the drapery has been managed with rare skill. Great credit is due to the young subject for the easy and motionless way in which she held the pose for what must have seemed to her the interminable exposure of 10 seconds at F.16."

CHAPTER VII

The Dublin Photographic Society 1854

ONE OF THE RESULTS of the relaxation of Fox Talbot's patent, coupled with the invention of the collodion process was the great increase in the number of people practising photography, particularly in an amateur capacity. Soon the desire to form clubs or societies was felt as a means of sharing technical knowledge. The first photographic societies to be set up were the Calotype Club in London in 1847, and the Societé Héliographique which came into existence in Paris in 1851.[80]

The Calotype Club in 1853 became the Photographic Society of London with Roger Fenton as secretary. Fenton, it will be remembered, was soon to gain fame for his photographic coverage of the Crimean War.

In Dublin a small group of photographic enthusiasts had been accustomed to meet informally at the apothecary shop of William Allen in Henry Street and discuss their technical problems. It was decided that a proper society would be desirable, so a public meeting was called. The Dublin Photographic Society came into existence at this meeting, held in Leinster House (then headquarters of the Royal Dublin Society) on the 8th of November 1854, with Lord Otho Fitzgerald in the chair. Fitzgerald was also Lord Mayor of Dublin at the time. The draft rules and regulations were approved, a number of members were enroled and the following officers were appointed to act for the ensuing year:

Chairman: Lord Otho Fitzgerald;
Vice Chairmen: Captain Henry of the 4th Dragoon Guards and J. A.Fenton;
Secretary: Sir John Joscelyn Coghill Bart;
Treasurer: Samuel Bewley.
Committee: William Allen, John Barker, F. Brady, Thomas Grubb, Vere Hunt, Joseph Kirk RHA, William Cotter Kyle, James Robinson, Frederick Saunders and M. Stapleton.[81]

The Dublin Photographic Society, Council for 1856

Left to right, standing:
Henry T. Vickers (Secretary)
Thomas Bewley (Treasurer)
Lord Otho Fitzgerald
William Allen
Michaelangelo Hayes RHA
James Robinson
Captain Hartley

Seated:
Gilbert Saunders
William Cotter Kyle
Thomas Grubb
Sir John J. Coghill (President)
Frederick Saunders
Captain Henry (V. President)
Joseph Kirk RHA

Meetings were held monthly at the Royal Dublin Society's Kildare Street premises, and consisted of two or more short talks by members on experiences with different processes, demonstrations of technique or displays of new apparatus. Occasionally there was a visiting lecturer, a travel talk or a discussion on the artistic side of photography.

On January 1st 1855 the Society published the first number of *The Dublin Photographic Journal,* which consisted of sixteen pages of closely printed matter and was published at three pence. It reported all meetings, but unfortunately no copy of this or any subsequent issue is known to exist.[82]

The following advertisement appeared in the Dublin papers in January, 1855:

Dublin Photographic Journal
First issue this month, edited and published in connection with the Dublin Photographic Society. Copies sent on application to Edward J. Milliken, Publisher,
15 College Green.
Subscription 3 shillings per annum.
Single copies 3d.

Some of the people associated with the Society at this early time are worthy of note. The first chairman, Lord Otho Fitzgerald, born 1827, was the third son of the Duke of Leinster and along with Sir John Joscelyn Coghill, the first secretary, was active in the "Amateur Photographic Association". This had its headquarters in London, with Prince Albert as its patron and was probably the most exclusive photographic society ever founded. Expensively bound albums of members' work were published annually in limited editions.

Coghill had been an amateur painter and originally took up photography as an aid to drawing before becoming one of the best

An illustration from *The Delineation of Animals in Rapid Motion,* Dublin 1877 by Michael Angelo Hayes RHA

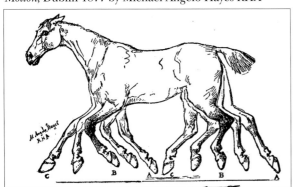

Captain Henry with his wet plate camera, c1855

photographers and most energetic promoters of the medium in Ireland.

Another interesting founder member of the Photographic Society was Michaelangelo Hayes RHA, the well-known painter of equestrian subjects, who later became president of the Royal Hibernian Academy from which position he resigned over some disagreement with other Academy members. No photographic work by him appears to have survived. Many painters had an interest in photographs which they used merely as reference material for paintings. He was however, the author of an interesting little pamphlet *The Delineation of Animals in Rapid Motion* published in 1877 describing, with drawings, the true action of the legs of a horse galloping. His researches into the subject almost parallel those of Eadweard Muybridge in America at about the same time. Apparently neither man appears to have been aware of the other.

Another Academician, Joseph Kirk, the well-known sculptor, was also a founder member. He was responsible for, among other statues, the memorial plaques on the Wellington Testimonial in Phoenix Park, he was a committee member during the first years. Other founder and committee members were the previously mentioned Thomas Grubb, the telescope maker and James Robinson, previously mentioned in connection with the Dublin International Exhibition. Leone Glukman and John Shaw Smith were also active as committee members in later years.

The Lion Arch, Avoca, Co. Wicklow, by Thomas M. Brownrigg, albumen print from a collodion negative, c1855.

The Castle of Chillon, by Sir John Joscelyn Coghill, albumen print from a collodion negative, 1855

doubt, was tolerated because of the technical knowledge and skill which he brought to the Society. Glukman, in particular, appears to have been under no illusions as to his presence as a member. Reports of various verbal exchanges during discussions, show that he considered himself a cut above the other members as far as photographic knowledge was concerned.

This is obvious from the following. Sir John Joscelyn Coghill was delivering a talk on travelling and taking pictures in Switzerland, and was indignantly declaring in no uncertain terms that Continental shop keepers were robbers. He cited an example of his being charged eight shillings per ounce for some chemical which he needed to buy, when, he declared, that the same could be obtained in Dublin for four shillings. Glukman remarked that if he, Coghill, had asked for his purchase in the language of the country, he in all probability would have got it for four shillings, he had been charged an extra four shillings for not speaking the local language!

Another report from the journal is concerned with a yachting trip which Coghill and the then President of the Society, Captain Henry, made in 1859. They sailed, in Henry's yacht, down the coasts of France and Spain landing at various points on the coast and taking views. This gives an indication of the type of lifestyle which these men enjoyed.

They proceeded as far as Gibraltar, where Coghill was obliged, for some reason, to leave the party and return home, taking the stereoscopic plates which he had exposed on the Spanish coast with him. These were later the subject of a lecture which he presented to the

Reports of the monthly meetings were published in the *Photographic Journal*, the organ of the Photographic Society of London —[83] presumably publication of the Dublin journal had been discontinued — and these provide a valuable source of information regarding the early days of the D.P.S. It is quite clear from these reports what kind of society the D.P.S. was in those early years. Practically all of the members seem to have been drawn from the upper or upper middle classes, very occasionally one comes across the name of a professional photographer, whose presence, no

The giant 72 inch telescope at Birr, photographed by Mary, Countess of Rosse during the 1860s. Built by her husband, the third Earl of Rosse during the 1840s this was the largest telescope in the world and remained so for many years. The third Earl was a distinguished astronomer and Birr was to become a Mecca for astronomers during the 19th century. Hence the presence of the Rev. Dr. Thomas Romney Robinson *(above right)* who was photographed by the Countess, c1856. Dr. Romney Robinson was a noted mathematician and was director of the Armagh observatory for sixty years.

Society. Captain Henry continued alone, through the Straits of Gibraltar, spending the entire summer months sailing in the Mediterranean and returning home in the Autumn.

On reaching home, and having moored his yacht at Kingstown Harbour with all his photographic materials on board, he learned that "The Great Eastern", then recently launched and the largest ship in the world, was visiting Holyhead. Undaunted, he again set sail to see the ship. While at Holyhead the weather abruptly changed and in a squall Henry's yacht was fouled by another and she sank taking all his precious photographic equipment and several hundred collodion plates, exposed on his travels, to the bottom. The report concluded with the members expressing their commiserations to their president on his loss.[84]

Thomas Grubb's name crops up in quite a number of reports as well as in letters to the editor, usually complaining about infringement of his lens patents. It appears that there was a great deal of competition between lens makers, and as the number of possible designs was limited, it was fairly easy to accidently or otherwise, use another manufacturer's design.

The Society held competitions for its members and organised an annual exhibition, as the following notice, taken from *Saunder's Newsletter* of May 25, 1856, indicates:

"The Annual Exhibition of the Dublin Photographic Society, under the patronage of the Lord Lieutenant, at the Royal Irish Institution, College Street.
Admission 1/-
By order of Thomas Grubb, Hon. Sec."

The Society was also responsible for the arrangement of the photographic sections in the annual R.D.S. Arts and Manufactures exhibitions. The Society had a special silver medal, bearing the head of Minerva, designed by the well known Dublin medal designer Woodhouse in 1859, for use in competitions. One of the first of which was won by Lady Rosse of Birr Castle.

Mary, Countess of Rosse had joined the Society on November 28, 1856; the Countess of Caledon from Co. Fermanagh, who was probably a friend of hers, also joined on the same day.[85] (Contrary to popular belief Lady Rosse was not the Society's first lady member, that distinction belongs to a Miss M. Grubb who was probably a daughter of Thomas Grubb. She became a member at the inaugural meeting on November 1, 1854). Lady

Above: Member's invitation card signed by Thomas Brownrigg, 1859

Left: Lough Long, Scotland by Captain Henry, c1857

Rosse's medal is still preserved at Birr Castle and is probably the only surviving example of the Society's Woodhouse medal.

Many of the Countess of Rosse's photographs were of her husband's great telescope and of other parts of the demesne as well as the town of Birr and its environs. Many of her photographs are in the form of wet plate negatives, which she adopted when the calotype became obsolete. She also included stereoscopic photography among her activities.[86]

The name of the Society was changed to the Photographic Society of Ireland in 1858 and continued to hold its meetings in the boardroom of the Royal Dublin Society at Leinster House. This apparently was a privilege reserved for certain societies of a scientific nature and which were approved of by the R.D.S. The societies were independent from the R.D.S. and were merely holding their meetings on that society's premises for convenience. However, in 1858, the decision was taken by the senior society that all of the smaller societies should affiliate with the Fine Arts Section of the R.D.S.; and all meetings would be held, henceforth on the same night, presumably for logistical reasons.

This decision was not very well received by the Photographic Society. The conditions relating to the P.S.I. affiliation to the R.D.S. are not very clear from contemporary documents which survive, it

is, however, clear from reports of meetings that there was a certain amount of disquiet being felt by members that the P.S.I. might be losing its separate identity under the wing of the older larger society.

In 1860 the Council of the P.S.I. decided that meetings should be held elsewhere than on R.D.S. property. Subsequent meetings were held at the Royal College of Science. After this date, and in fact until 1879, no records of meetings of the Society appear to exist. Oscar Merne who wrote a history of the Photographic Society in 1954 on the occasion of its centenary states that it continued to hold meetings at the Royal College of Science, however he was unable to give names of presidents for the years 1860–1885. Lack of information for these years and the fact that former prominent members of the P.S.I. are seen to be active in other photographic organisations during this period, draws one inevitably to the conclusion that the Society was not operating at the time.

In the first flush of enthusiasm after 1851 many photographic societies were set up all over Britain, however there is clear evidence that by 1860 a great many of these had not lasted the pace. Societies in Liverpool and other large British cities had disappeared, so it is entirely conceivable that the Dublin society should have gone the same way. A short lived Belfast Photographic Society, founded in 1857 was also gone by 1860.

Another reason for the loss of interest

among amateurs at this time was probably the introduction of the carte de visite photograph; this popularised the medium to the extent of its being no longer the exclusive pastime which they would have liked it to remain.

This is in fact the reason, which is on record, as to why the famous Lewis Carroll abandoned the practice of photography.

The introduction of the wet plate process was universally recognised by photographic professionals – because if its lack of patent – as a giant step forward; but to the gentlemen amateurs on the other hand, it appeared to complicate photography on location by the necessity of needing a portable darkroom. This is illustrated by the fact that for many years after the introduction of the wet plate process, many amateurs were still seen to be practising the simpler technique of the paper negative calotype process, even though its image quality was much inferior.

Another possible reason why some amateur photographers preferred the older process has been suggested by some historians. When the first photographs on paper appeared they were inevitably compared to the existing modes of artistic pictorial presentations on paper as opposed to oil paintings. The three most favoured processes were the mezzotint, the aquatint and the lithograph, all of which were ink-based and in which the image appeared to be in the paper rather than on the surface of the paper, which was the case with the newly introduced albumen print.

These three processes, together with the watercolour, all presented matt surfaces which to cultured tastes were associated with so-called artistic ideals. To such tastes, the calotype, with its similar matt surface was to be preferred to the shiny surface of the albumen print with its deep blacks and the daguerreotype with its metallic silver surface.[87]

A contemporary critic, Thomas Sutton writing on the subject in *The Liverpool and Manchester Photographic Journal* in 1859 stated:

From a stereo card taken on board Captain Henry's ill-fated yacht, probably taken by Henry, before 1857

"As a matter of taste, he *(Sutton)* extremely dislikes prints on albumenised paper, and no doubt there are many who entertain the same feelings, and its for them that the present article is intended. Those who prefer that peculiar kind of vigour and brilliancy which is exhibited by a piece of black sticking plaster, or a well polished Wellington boot, to the depth and vigour of the blacks of a fine engraving on plate paper need not concern themselves with this process; for the best results which it appears capable of yielding do not surpass, in point of vigour, the best proofs from the press of the copper plate."

No details of the activities of the Photographic Society of Ireland appear to exist for the years between 1860 and 1879 when it was re-founded. *(see chapter X)*

CHAPTER VIII

The Dublin International Exhibition 1865

ONE OF THE GREAT events of the 1860s in Dublin was the International Exhibition of 1865. This was held at the Exhibition Palace, specially built for it at Earlsfort Terrace. Elements of this building still stand, greatly altered, as part of the old U.C.D. buildings and the National Concert Hall. It is not generally realised that the present Concert Hall was originally built as a concert hall as part of this exhibition in 1865.

Unfortunately the impressive "Winter Garden" part of the complex, built of glass like a smaller version of the Crystal Palace in London, has disappeared. It seems to have been demolished around 1900, probably because it had become derelict or dangerous. As in 1853, when the inspiration for the Dublin Exhibition was the London exhibition of 1851, inspiration came, on this occasion, from the London Exhibition of 1862.

The London Stereoscopic Company was appointed to handle all the photographic publicity. The appointment of a non-Irish firm must have caused some raised eyebrows in Ireland, however, the reason for the appointment was probably the fact that the Stereoscopic Company had also acted in the same capacity for the London Exhibition. It is doubtful whether any Irish photographic firm at this time could have provided the same facilities for the mass production of the many items made available by the Stereoscopic Com-

pany. These included cartes, cabinets, stereocards, lantern slides and views in many sizes.

By the time the next great Dublin exhibition was being held, in 1872, William Lawrence had arrived on the scene and was more than capable of providing all that was required on that occasion.

The photographic section of the exhibition was the most extensive yet seen in Ireland, it was organised by Sir John Joscelyn Coghill, former President and Secretary of the Photographic Society of Ireland. Containing over 4000 actual photographs, it must surely have been the largest photographic exhibition ever held in Ireland. Many world famous names were represented among the exhibitors, Camille Silvy, Francis Bedford, Henry Peach Robinson, Oscar Rejlander, John Jabez Mayall, William

The sculpture gallery of the Dublin International Exhibition, 1865 It is now part of the National Concert Hall complex at Earlsfort Terrace. The actual National Concert Hall itself was originally built as a concert hall for use at the exhibition. Photographed by the London Stereoscopic Company in 1865

England, James Annan, Lady Hawarden and Julia Margaret Cameron. Mrs Cameron's work at the exhibition received surprisingly bad reviews in the photographic press of the time.

As far as local amateur photographers were concerned, Coghill's own work was highly praised; the Countess of Rosse and other members of the Amateur Photographic Association also had work on display. Irish professional photographers on view included Beauford and Bruce, Schroeder, Millard and Robinson and Frederick Holland Mares.

A contemporary description of a journey from London to Dublin to specifically see the photographic section of the exhibition makes fascinating reading.

From *The Evolution of Photography* by John Werge, published 1890:

TO DUBLIN AND BACK WITH A GLANCE AT THE EXHIBITION, 1865
(Excerpt)

As we approach the Bay, the Carlingford Hills can be seen on the right, and a little more southwards Lambay and Ireland's Eye. The latter island is rugged and precipitous, seaward, in the extreme – a barren and desolate-looking spot, possessing an unenviable notoriety on account of the murder of a lady by her husband having been committed there a few years ago: Howth, the light-house, and the Bailey Rock, where the *Queen Victoria* Steamer was wrecked, now attract our attention. And, as nearly as we can remember, these are the most striking features on the north side of the Bay. On the South the Harbour of Kingstown is distinctly visible, and we saw the mail steamer which crosses from Holyhead to Kingstown, a distance of sixty miles, in three and a half hours, blowing off her steam. By paying a little extra you can cross in the mail steamers, if you wish, but it is not worth while paying the difference, as the ordinary steamers cross from Holyhead to Dublin in about five and a half hours. All round the south side of the Bay we could trace the Kingstown and Dublin Railway, which is the oldest line but one in the United Queendoms of Great Britain and Ireland. An obelisk commemorates the visit of the last of the four Georges to Ireland in 1821.

Right over Kingstown the Killinny *(sic.)* Hills are to be seen, and all along the water line the Bay is studded with pretty little villas, and the scene is truly beautiful. If possible, arrange your entrance into the Bay of Dublin in the early morning, for then the sun, rising in the east, lights up the subjects to the very best advantage, and throws a charm about them which they do not exhibit at any other time of the day. By waiting at Holyhead for the early morning boat you can easily manage this.

But now we are at the North Wall, and on landing are besieged by carmen to have a "rowl" and jumping on to one of those light, odd-looking, jaunting cars which are one of the institutions of the country, we are "rowled" up the North Wall for nearly a mile, past the Docks, over the drawbridges, and past the Custom House – a large stone building, too large for the business of the port – along Carlisle Bridge, down Westmoreland Street, past the Bank of Ireland – once the Houses of Parliament – and up Dame Street, leaving the College on our left, and passing King William III statue, representing a mounted Roman with gilded laurels and ornamental toga, we arrive at Jury's Hotel, a commercial and family house of superior arrangements; which was well recommended to us before we left London; and here we rest.

After breakfast, and having made ourselves internally and externally comfortable, we start for the Exhibition, which is within easy walking distance of the hotel; but the car fares are so very moderate that we prefer a "rowl". The fare is sixpence a "set down" that is, you may ride from one end of the city to the other for sixpence, but if you get off to post a letter, or buy an umbrella to keep the rain off – for the cars have no covering – that is a "set down", and so every time you get down and get up again you have sixpence to pay, no matter how short the distance you are taken each time. So we hailed a car at the door of the hotel, determined to be "rowled" to the Exhibition for sixpence each. We go down Dame Street, across College Green, up Grafton Street, along the west and south sides of St. Stephen's Green or Square to Earlsfort Terrace and the principal entrance to the Dublin Exhibition, which occupies the site of what was formerly Coburg Gardens.

Arriving at the entrance hall, we pay our admission fee, and on passing the registering turnstiles we are at once in the sculpture Hall on the ground floor, the contents of which we shall notice more particularly by-and-by. Passing through the Sculpture Hall we are within the western transept, or Winter Garden portion of the Exhibition. This transept is 500 feet long and of lofty proportions, with galleries on each side, and tastefully hung with the banners and flags of the nations exhibiting. The northern court is about 300 feet long, also of iron and glass, with galleries running round both sides similar to the western transept. The ground floor and part of the galleries of the northern court are devoted to the productions of the United Kingdom. The Exhibition building is small, but well arranged and compact, and partakes of the character of an art and industrial exhibition and place of amusement and recreation, like our Crystal Palace at Sydenham, with ornamental gardens and archery grounds attached. The gardens are small – a little larger than the area of the building itself – but most tastefully laid out. And there are fountains and grottoes, and rookeries and cascades, with flowers growing about them, which give the whole place a pleasant, healthy, and delightful appearance.

On the first day of our visit there was a grand archery meeting, and the turn-out of Dublin belles was double in numbers. There was a large attendance of bowmen, too, and belles and beaux were banging away at the targets most unmercifully in keen contest for the prize; whether it was a medal, a ring, or an heiress, we could not learn; but if nothing more than the privilege of entering the lists against such lovely competitors, the bowmen ought to have been satisfied; but we don't suppose they were, for men are both ambitious and avaricious, and probably some of them hoped to win a prize medal, kill a beauty, and catch an heiress all at once, with one swift arrow sent whizzing and quivering into the very heart and gilded centre of the gaily-painted target. Perched up on the top of the cascades we noticed a double sliding-front stereoscopic camera, and doubtless Mr. York was busy photographing the scene we have been describing, impressions of which the London Stereoscopic Company will probably issue ere long. We must, however, leave this gay scene and turn our attention to other things, certainly not more attractive; but duty calls us away from beauty, and we must submit.

Re-entering the Exhibition building, we seek the photographic department, which we readily find on the ground-floor, between the music hall and the first class refreshment-room. Entering from the Belgian department in the western transept, we find three rooms in the main building devoted to the exhibition of photographs, and a lobby between the rooms pretty well filled with apparatus. To Sir J. Joscelyn Coghill are photographers indebted for obtaining so much space for their works, and in such a get-at-able situation; but it is a pity the rooms are not better lighted. Many of the pictures on the screens are very indistinctly seen, and some are in dark corners scarcely to be seen at all.

The foreign department, which is the first room we enter, is mainly made up of reproductions of old and modern engravings and copies of drawings and paintings. One very remarkable photograph on the wall of this room is an immense magnification of a flea, by A. Duvette. What a subject for the camera ! – one that suggests in sporting phraseology something more than the "find", the "chase", and the "death".

A panoramic view of Rome, by M,

Petagna, is a great achievement in panoramic photography. There are seven impressions from 15" by 12" plates, all carefully joined, and of equal tone. The point of view is "Tasso's Oak", and the panorama gives us an excellent idea of Rome at the present day.

The British part of the Photographic Exhibition in Dublin might be very properly denominated by an enlargement of the *(Photographic)* Society's exhibition now open in Conduit Street, London. Nearly all the principal exhibitors there have sent duplicates of their chief works to the Dublin Exhibition. There is Robinson's beautiful picture of "Brenda", his "May Gatherers", "Sunshine", "Autumn", "Somebody Coming", "Bringing home the May", &c., all old and familiar pictures, every one of which we have seen before, Robinson himself in his study – a beautiful piece of photography, even to his black velvet coat. Blanchard also repeats his "Zealot", and other subjects, and sends a frame full of his exquisite stereographs. William England also sends some of his charming stereoscopic pictures of Switzerland and Savoy.

Francis Bedford's contribution is much the same as his pictures in the London exhibition. Among them are his lovely Warwickshire pictures. Wet-plate photography is well represented, both in landscape, portraiture, and composition. Among the latter, Rejlander is most prominent. One frame containing some pictures showing the "expression" of the hands, illustrates Rejlander's artistic knowledge and ability more than many of his other pictures. None but a thoughtful and accomplished artist could have disposed of those members in such a skilful manner. His pictures of "Grief", "The Mote", "The Wayfarer", "'Tis Light within–Dark without" and his "Home, Sweet Home", reveal exquisite feeling in his treatment of such subjects. Thurston Thompson also exhibits some of his fine reproductions of Turner. There is "Crossing the Brook", and "Childe Harold's Pilgrimage"; but a much larger collection of these beautiful copies of Turner's pictures are now on

view at Marion's, in Soho Square. Dry-plate photography is exemplified in all its phases, from the oldest form of albumen alone, to the latest modifications with collodion, collodio-albumen, Fothergill, tannin, malt, &c. The most prominent and largest contributor to this department is Mr. Mudd. In addition to the duplicates in the London Exhibition, he sends a few others, the most remarkable of which is a large view of "Borrowdale", a noble picture, exquisitely treated, showing masses of light and shade and pleasing composition which stamp it at once as a work of art.

Mr. G. S. Penny exhibits some very fine examples of the tannin and malt process. They are soft and delicate, and possess sufficient force to give powerful contrasts when necessary. Mr. Bull's tannin and malt pictures are also very good; his "Menai Bridge" particularly so.

The amateur photographers, both wet and dry, make a good show and among the Irish followers of our delightful art are Sir John Joscelyn Coghill, who exhibits twelve very pretty views of the neighbourhood of Castletownsend. Dr. Hemphill, of Clonmel, also exhibits a variety of subjects, many of them pretty compositions and excellent photography.

Dr. Bailey, of Monaghan, contributes both landscapes and portraits of very good quality. Mr. T. M. Brownrigg shows seventeen photographs all excellent examples of the wet collodion process. Many of them are exquisite bits of photography, and evince an amount of thought and care in selecting the best point of view, arranging the lines of the subject, and catching the best effect of light so as to make them pictures, which is seldom attended to by professional photographers.

Amongst the Irish professional photographers in landscape work, Mr. F. Mares, of Dublin stands pre-eminent. His pictures of Killarney, and views in the county of Wicklow, are very beautiful, and give evidence of a cultivated eye and artistic taste in the selection of his subjects and points of view. There are other excellent views and architectural subjects by Irish photographers; but we are sorry to observe some that really ought not to have been admitted. They are not even average photography, being utterly destitute of manipulative skill, and as deficient in art-excellence as they can well be.

One branch of landscape, or, we should say, marine photography, is without competition. We refer to those exquisite and charming transparencies by Mr. C. S. Breese. His moonlight effect is wonderfully managed; the water looks "alive", and the moonlight Is dancing on the waves juat as we have seen it far away upon the sea. His "Breaking Wave" is marvellous coming to shore with it's cavernous curl; we almost fancy we hear its angry howl as it dashes itself into foam on the beach. We have seen such a wave sweep the deck of a ship before now, and know well with what a ponderous weight and velocity it comes, and we wonder the more at Mr. Breese's success in catching the wave in such a position. We cannot, however, speak so highly of the "Sunlight" effects by the same artist. The transparencies as photographs are inimitable; but there is colour introduced into the skies which ought to have been taken up by the rocks, and so carried into the foregrounds of the pictures, to be natural. Such warm skies and cold middle distances and foregrounds are too antagonistic for the harmony of nature.

In portraiture, our Irish brethren of the camera contribute somewhat liberally. In that branch we noticed the works of Messrs. Robertson and Co., S. (*John Fortune*) Lawrence, and G. Schroeder, of Grafton Street; Millard and Robinson, Nelson and Marshall, and S. (*John*) Chancellor, of Sackville Street, Dublin. T. Cranfield, Grafton Street, also exhibits some photographs beautifully coloured in oils.

The most eminent English photographers also show up well. We saw the well-known works of Mayall, Silvy, Claudet, Maull and Co., and others, eminent in plain photography. Messrs. Lock and Whitfield exhibit a Royal case of exquisitely coloured photographs of the Prince and Princess of Wales, and Prince Albert Victor. Mr. G. Wharton Simpson also exhibits a few specimens of his beautiful colodio-chloride of silver printing process. There are some lovely specimens of that process with such a frightfully ugly name, but which, in plain parlance, are pictures on opal glass, though Mr. Helsby has christened them "Helioaristotypia miniatures." As a set-off to this, surely the next dry process that is discovered should be called "Hydrophobiatypia".

In amateur portraiture, Mr. H. Cooper, Jun., exhibits a large number of his clever life studies, as well as those quiet and charming representations of his friends in their habits as they live.

Solar camera enlargements are very numerously contributed. Mr. Claudet sends some good pictures enlarged by solar camera, and developed with gallic acid. Mr. Solomon also has some very good examples of enlarging. Dr. D. Van Monckhoven is an exhibitor of the capabilities of his direct printing camera. Mr. Mayall exhibits two series of very interesting enlargements by the Monckhoven camera, printed direct on albumenized paper; one is Tennyson, in eight different sizes, from a one ninth to a life-size head on a whole sheet of paper; of the other, Captain Grant, there are seven similar pictures. These photographs are all bold and vigorous and uniform in colour, and come nearer to our idea of what an enlargement should be than anything we have yet seen. Of the two, that of the Poet Laureate is the best; the other is harsher, which is in all probability due to the difference in the subjects themselves. We can easily imagine that the face of Captain Grant, bronzed and weather-beaten as it must be, will present more obstacles to the obtaining of a soft negative than that of Tennyson. Specimens of plioto-sculpture are also to be seen at the Dublin Exhibition, many of which are very pretty and life-like statuettes; but some of the figures seem much too large in the busts, and the plinths on which the figures of ladies stand are in very bad taste; being diminishing beads of a circular form, they suggest the idea of a huge crinoline just dropped.

Nearly all the denominations of photography have their representative forms and impressions in this Exhibition; and the history of the art, from the early days of the Daguerreotype to the latest vagary of the present day, may be traced in the collection of photographs spread before you on the walls and screens of the Dublin International Exhibition. There is the Daguerreotype, the Ambrotype, and the collodiotype, which ought to have been known as the Archertype; for the wet collodion process, although it is the most important of all the discoveries in photography that have been made since the first pictures were obtained by Wedgwood, is without a name conferring honour on the man who first applied collodion to photography. Archer's name is generally associated with it, but without taking that definite and appellative form it ought to. We know that another claimant has been "cutting in" for the honour, but unless that claim can be "backed up" by data, we are not disposed to believe that it was anterior to 1851 – the year of the first exhibition – at that date we know that Mr. Archer took photographs on collodionized glass plates. Then why should we not honour Archer as the French honoured Daguerre, and call the wet collodion-process the Archertype ?

In printing and toning, there are samples of nearly all the formulæ that have been discovered since the days of printing on plain salted paper and fixing in "hypo" only. There are prints on plain paper and on albumenized paper, toned and fixed in every conceivable way. There are prints on glass, porcelain, and ivory; prints in carbon, from the negative direct; and impressions in printer's ink from plates, blocks, and lithographic-stones, which have had the subjects transferred to them by the aid of photography. There are Wothlytypes, and Simpsontypes, and Tooveytypes, and all the other types that have sprung from a desire to introduce novelties into the art.

In graphs and the various forms and fanciful applications of photography to portraiture, &c., there are stereographs and micrographs, and the old-fashioned "sit-on-a-chair" graphs, the "stand-not-at-ease" graphs, the "small carte" graph, the "large carte" graph, the "casket gem" graph, the "magnesium" graph, the "cameo" graph, the "double-stupid " graph, and the latest of all novelties, the "turn-me-round" graph. The latter is a great curiosity, and must have been suggested by a recollection of that "scientific toy" of ancient manufacture with which we used to awaken the wonder of our little brothers and sisters at Christmas parties when we were boys, by twirling before their astonished eyes a piece of card-board with, a bird painted on one side and a cage on the other, both pictures being seen at the same time during the rapid revolution of the card.

In apparatus there is not much to talk about, the Pantascopic camera being the chief novelty. There are several of the manufacturers exhibiting in the photographic department, but we could not reconcile ourselves to the circum-stance of Mr. Dallmeyer not exhibiting in the right place. His name is honoured by photographers, and he should have honoured Photography by going in under her colours. If he must go to the "scientific department," he ought to have gone there with his scientific instruments alone, and shown his photographic apparatus in the place assigned for that purpose. True, he makes a handsome show, but that does not atone for his mistake. Photographers are queer animals – jealous of their rights, and as sensitive to slight as their plates are to light; and we fear we are ourselves not much better. A large majority of photog-raphers stand by Mr. Dallmeyer, and very justly believe in his 1 and 2 B's as shippers do in A1's at Lloyd's; and his stand should have been in the photo-graphic department".

A group of gentlemen photographed by the London Stereoscopic Company in connection with the Dublin International Exhibition. They were probably chairmen of various selection committees.

Included are: Michaelangelo Hayes RHA, Sir John Joscelyn Goghill and Joseph Kirk RHA founder members of the Dublin Photographic Society.

Also included is Henry Moore, *(second right, standing)* first director of the National Gallery of Ireland, the Hon. Lewis Wingfield, a painter and photographer and several others who were active in the visual arts in Ireland at the time.

One of the series of stereo cards published by the London Stereoscopic Company in 1865 as a souvenir of the Dublin International Exhibition.

Notes on the Photographic Department

By Sir John Joscelyn Coghill, Bart.

Having been requested by the compilers of this work *(Catalogue of the Exhibition)* to furnish them with such details of the working of the Photographic Department as may likely to prove of general interest, I need hardly premise that such observations as I shall offer are to be considered as supplimental to, and in some points explanatory of, the Report of the Jury in that section, and in no sense either opposed to, or in favour of the views taken by those gentlemen.

From the commencment of the undertaking it was the earnest wish of the Executive Committee that this attractive section should be fully represented, and that every inducement should be held out to photographers to secure their co-operation. For the first time in the annals of International Exhibitions their remonstrances were listened to, and their works relieved from the degradation of being officially branded as the mere products of machinery. The small jealousies of a few narrow-minded art-pedants which proved so injurious, and indeed nearly fatal, to the formation of a collection of photographs in the London Exhibition of 1862, found no favour in the councils of those who watched over the interests of the Dublin Exhibition of 1865, and Photography was publicly assigned her rightful place among the sisterhood of "the Fine Arts."

That the liberal views of the committee were not confined to the bare recognition of the position of the art will appear from the following circumstance. In all previous Exhibitions, both generally and exclusively, it had been customary to award medals or prizes and certificates of merit to the most successful photographic exhibitors, and the competition thus produced was found to act most beneficially on the art; but in the present Exhibition a difficulty arose from the fact of Photography having been admitted into the Fine Arts Class, in which it was ruled that no such distinctions should be given. Under these circumstances it was to be feared that while every true lover of the art must hail with pleasure its elevation to its proper place, many of the best of its artists, deprived of their accustomed stimulus, might consider it not worth their while to contribute. To meet this difficulty it was promptly decided that the Photographic Department should be made an exception to the above general rule, and that, as formerly, medals and certificates should be awarded to the most deserving among the exhibitors.

In considering the fitness of the rooms for the purposes of a Photographic Exhibition, the jurors have expressed their regret that they were not lighted from above instead of from the side. This was a regret fully shared by the hanging committee, and in no point was their duty more difficult than in the endeavour to diminish, as far as was in their power, the unpleasant glare and reflection that is almost impossible to be got rid of under such circumstances. The case, however, was one of which there was no help. It must be remembered that the total space available for exhibition purposes was altogether inadequate to the demand, and that the directors of each department were all equally desirous of obtaining the best and greatest amount of room. Photographers, therefor, cannot complain that the few top-lighted rooms at the disposal of the

Executive fell to the lot of the senior branches of the Fine Arts, viz., Painting and Sculpture. The rooms accorded were, with this one objection, admirably suited, being light, airy, spacious, of easy access, and, what was of great importance, en suite.

On entering upon their work it became evident to those entrusted with the management of the Department that a general principle must be laid down to guide their labours. This general principle they found in the international character of the Exhibition. No doubt had the covering of their walls with the most perfect photographs obtainable been their object, it would have been possible to have presented the public with an intrinsically more beautiful collection than was exhibited, but to have done so it would have been necessary to have accepted only the works of a few, and to have sacrificed the peculiar advantages derivable from the universal competition. It was felt that such Exhibitions should be the tide-marks of the progress of nations, and should exhibit fairly the ebb and flow, the progress or decline in each department of knowledge and its results among the various families of the world. The contributions of each country should be kept as distinct as possible, so as to allow their various peculiarities to stand forth in relief whether they are faulty or meritorious, and the competition should be regarded less as one of individuals than as one of nations.

That this programme was not carried out as successfully as could have been desired is much to be regretted, but the blame for it must rest with the photographers of those countries who have supinely allowed the opportunity to pass. There was no civilised nation but received a pressing invitation to cooperate, and it can only be a matter of regret, but not of reproach, to those in charge of the Department that the Foreign contributions, though some of them of a high class merit, are so few and so little representative. With regard to the British portion of the collection this supineness is less observable; and although, as remarked by the jurors, the names of a few – a very few – are "conspicuous by their absence," it may be safely asserted that rarely (in Ireland never) has there been collected together under one roof, so complete and beautiful collection of the kind.

In attempting some slight analysis of the photographs exhibited it may be convenient to classify them as follows:

1193	Portraits
1189	Landscapes and Architectural &c.
159	Composition subjects
330	Copies of Paintings, Sculpture &c.
136	Microscopic photography
525	Stereoscopic photography
640	Ethnological photography
1	Enamel processes
27	Enlargements
6	Photo zincography &c.
19	Photo sculpture
4225	Total

It would be ill of me to express an opinion upon the comparative merits of individual items – that is a task which the Executive Committee has confided to the jurors in the several departments without restriction or interference, and to their report the reader is referred without comment on my part; but I cannot allow the present opportunity to pass without acknowledging a peculiar debt of gratitude due to one foreign exhibitor – Monsieur Fierlants, of Brussels – whose photographic reproductions of the Old Masters, in the Musée at Antwerp and elsewhere, have astonished and delighted all true lovers of art, no less by the great difficulties attending this branch of photography than by the admirable success which has rewarded his skill. This gentleman, in the truest spirit of art-brotherhood, has presented the whole valuable series exhibited by him, to the directors of the Winter Garden Palace Company as a nucleus for a permanent Photographic collection in Ireland. It is only to be hoped that many will follow so liberal an example.

Lastly, I may perhaps be allowed to acknowledge the signal service done to the department by the Photographic press, both British and foreign, not only in giving publicity to all official notifications, but in keeping the subject constantly before their readers in the spirit of the warmest co-operation; to the exertions of the gentlemen conducting these journals may be attributed much of that success which rendered the Photographic Department one of the most popular and attractive in the building.

J. J. COGHILL
Director Photographic Department

CHAPTER IX

Art Photography and
Irish Amateur Photographers

ALFRED WERNER, with his contribution to the artistic side of photography, was something of a rarity in Ireland. The vast majority of professionals were only interested in the commercial aspect of photography, and the interests of most of the amateur members of the reformed P.S.I. operating during the 1880s were involved in the technical or scientific areas of photography.

Werner appears to have been influenced by the ideas of Dr. Peter Emerson, who founded the movement of naturalistic photogaphy which was a reaction against, and in opposition to, the contrived so-called high art photography then practised by Henry Peach Robinson and others, and which was then very fashionable in Britain. He demonstrated his theory in his beautiful photographs of the Norfolk Broads.

Alfred Werner's surviving prints are very similar to Emerson's in style, including rural studies of peasants working in fields, mostly taken in Alsace and Belgium.

It is worth explaining here the situation which existed in the photographic world at this time and the way it had evolved ever since photographers first began showing their work and submitting it for appraisal by the artistic establishment and the public at large. It has been earlier mentioned that the first amateur photographers in Ireland, as elsewhere, were mostly from the upper classes of society. It was usual for such people to have had a classical education and when they came to taking photographs they tended to naturally choose and arrange their subject matter according to the various rules of drawing and conventions of composition which they would have acquired as part of that education.

The natural progression of this attitude, particularly in England, was for photographers to copy the popular painting styles of the period. This had the enthusiastic support of the art journals and was to lead to terrible abberations of taste. Photographers were encouraged to strive for loftier themes than the mere reproduction of reality, subjects that would "fire the imagination." As one art critic remarked "For photography there are new secrets to conquer, new difficulties to overcome, new madonnas to invent and new ideals to imagine. There will be perhaps, photograph Raphaels, photograph Titians, founders of new empires and not subverters of the old". [88]

Even some of the most distinguished

Centre: "At Newtown Anner" by William Despard Hemphill, 1862

80

Victorian photographers, including Julia Margaret Cameron, succumbed to the "art photography" craze.

The two photographers whose names were most associated with this type of photography were Henry Peach Robinson and Oscar Rejlander. Both of these men specialised in constructing complicated compositions from many different negatives with such titles as "Fading Away", "Dawn and Sunset" by Robinson, and "Head of John the Baptist in a Charger" and "A Penny Please" by Rejlander. The ultimate was, perhaps, "Two Ways of Life" by Rejlander which was purchased by Queen Victoria in 1857, bestowing a certain respectability and Society's acceptability of this type of photography. The technique of photographing individual figures and later combining them on one print had to be resorted to because of the problem of getting large groups of people to stay still for the overlong exposure times then necessary. This technique, – although totally manual – is quite similar to the current trend of manipulating and assembling photographic compositions on a computer. The methods used are vastly more sophistocated, but the general theory is very similar.

Picture Making by Photography, Henry Peach Robinson's most influential book, ran to many editions and was still in print during World War I. It promoted the idea of picture "making" as opposed to picture "taking" and had a profound effect on the type of photography being produced in camera clubs and societies in Britain and in Europe, right up to the 1920s. Most of those practising "Art Photography" did not resort to the multiple negative technique, being simply content to somehow manipulate the image, by using Bromoil or another of the numerous techniques then available to make their prints less photographic and more "artistic".

"Artistic Photography" was the style to which the majority of serious amateur photographers in Britain and Europe aspired during

Alfred Werner's large camera with which he took the large, almost life-size portrait of Maud Gonne in 1893 (*see plate 40*). Its largest negative size was approximately 6 feet high by 3.5 feet (180cm. by 10.5cm.) Focussing was accomplished by men inside the camera moving the huge plate with a red filter over the lens!

the years between 1880 to as late as 1930. The only dissenting voices were Emerson with his "Naturalistic Photography" and later in the early years of the new century Steiglitz, in America, with the "Photo Secession Movement".

In 1900, Britain – that is the so-called "British Isles" which included Ireland – had 256 photographic clubs as against only 99 in the United States and a mere 23 throughout the whole of Europe. It is difficult to know how many Irish clubs were included in the British figure (they could probably have been counted in single figures). The *Amateur Photographer's Annual* for 1892 lists Irish clubs as follows: Dublin, "Photographic Society of Ireland" and the "Y.M.C.A. Camera Club"; Cork, "The Munster Camera Club" and Belfast, the "Y.M.C.A. Camera Club," a total of only four.

The idea of forming clubs and societies to cater for interests or hobbies has always been more popular in Britain – or more correctly, England – than in most other places. Photography was no exception. The first organisation to cater for the interests of early photographers was the Calotype Club, founded in London in 1847.

This was to pass through several metamorphoses by the end of the century, eventually becoming the Royal Photographic Society. By the mid 1850s many large towns and cities in Britain had photographic societies, including Dublin *(see elsewhere)* and

Belfast. It was not, however, until the invention of the dry plate process in the late 1870s, that the vast majority of clubs were founded, eventually leading, by 1900, to the figures mentioned earlier.

Very few Irish photographers practised "art photography"; James Robinson's "Death of Chatterton" and some of the genre stereo photographs by Frederick H. Mares and Robinson, although made for commercial purposes, could be said to qualify.

Probably William Despard Hemphill was the Irish photographer whose work most closely resembled the "art photography" produced in England, although, apparently, he never resorted to building up pictures from multiple negatives or technically manipulating the image.

During the 1880s the newly revived Photographic Society of Ireland initiated an ambitious series of triennial international photographic exhibitions in conjunction with the Royal Hibernian Academy at the Academy's rooms in Lower Abbey Street.

Two lofty top-lit rooms were allocated by the Academy to the first exhibition in1884, which consisted of over 600 prints in most of the various processes then in use by many of the leading photographers of the day. This was an extraordinary instance of enlightenment for this time, the artistic establishment in Ireland actually recognising photography as an art form, no less, and thinking it worthy of hanging on the walls of their gallery which, alas, was destroyed during the "Rising" in 1916.

Unfortunately only two such exhibitions were held, in 1884 and 1887. However, these were not the first photographs to be shown on those hallowed walls, Roger Fenton's Crimean War pictures had been presented there in 1856.

One of a series of double (trick) portraits by Victor Smyth, c1893

International Photographic Exhibition at the Royal Hibernian Academy's gallery, Lower Abbey Street, Dublin, 1884. One of two which were organised by the Photographic Society of Ireland. The second was in 1887

By the 1880s, most amateur photographers were coming fromthe increasingly affluent middle classes. This was due to the invention of the new dry plate processes which simplified technique and the reduction in costs due to the introduction of more compact cameras by Kodak and others.

Kodak was also the first manufacturer to be entirely responsible for the processing and printing of the film, "you press the button and we do the rest" was their famous slogan and it soon caught on.

CHAPTER X

The Introduction of Dry Plates
1880–1900

THE COMPLEXITIES of the old wet-plate process up to the late 1870s were responsible for curtailing the activities and output of photographers. Many experiments had been made, endeavouring to produce a less troublesome dry plate process, but to no avail. In 1878, after the discoveries of Dr. Richard Leach Maddox, the first successful dry plates were put on the market by Wratten and Wainwright of Croydon. No longer was it necessary for photographers to transport darkrooms and chemicals with them, on their travels, a camera, tripod and a few plates were now all that were required.

The "Original" Kodak camera introduced in 1888 had the effect of revolutionising photography in a few short years

The 1880s were to be years of technical innovation and change in photography, as the introduction of the dry plate process paved the way for other, equally revolutionary changes.

In America George Eastman had begun to market dry plates in 1881. In 1885 he developed a roll holder for attachment to any standard plate camera, that took a roll of paper negatives which could be wound on after each exposure. This type of product could not really be successful until after the introduction of some kind of transparent flexible base material, this took place in 1888 with the invention of celluloid, and from this year Eastman began to dominate the popular photographic market with his new roll films.

Also in 1888 he marketed the first "Kodak" box camera, which sold for five guineas in Britain, and was capable of taking 100 circular pictures which were returned to the makers for processing – the first time this concept was used by a photographic manufacturer. The familiar slogan "you press the button, we do the rest" was coined. The word "Kodak" is interesting in that it has no meaningful significance, apparently its value lies in its pronunciation being the same in all languages.

The Kodak was only one of many new portable "hand" cameras to be introduced during the 1880s. Up to this time most photographs had to be taken with the camera on a tripod. There was the craze for so-called "detective" cameras one of the most interesting of which was the "Stirn" this was circular and flat, and could be worn under a waistcoat with the lens peeping through a buttonhole. Interestingly the selling agent in the British Isles for this camera was James Robinson of Grafton Street, who, by the end of the century, had a branch in Regent Street, London. Another of Robinson's imports from America was the "Luzo", another type of portable "detective" camera. Cameras came in a bewildering range of shapes and sizes, but their general trend was for them to be inconspicuous, portable and small, or small by the standards of the time.

There were cameras disguised as hats, cravats, brown paper parcels, watches, binoculars and, most unlikely of all, guns. Actually this was not the first instance of a camera being made in the form of a gun, in

1857 Thomas Skaife, an eccentric designer of cameras made a camera in the shape of a revolver. He attempted to photograph Queen Victoria as she was driven down the Mall and was instantly jumped on by several hefty guardsmen. He was lucky to escape with his life!

It is difficult for modern readers to understand the change which this, even partial, abandonment of the tripod meant to the amateur photographers of the 1880s, suddenly a whole new range of candid and documentary subject matter became possible.

The simplification of technique brought about by the introduction of dry plates attracted many more amateurs to photography. This had the effect of rejuvenating the dormant photographic societies. The first meeting of the reformed Photographic Society of Ireland was held at the Queen's Institute, Molesworth Street, on Wednesday July 9th 1879, with Professor J. Emerson Reynolds in the chair.

James Emerson Reynolds F.R.S., who became president of the P.S.I. in 1882, had been editor of the *British Journal of Photography Almanac* in 1864 before his arrival in Dublin to take up the post of Chemistry Lecturer at the R.D.S. Having been a prominent member of the London Photographic Society and editor of the *British Journal*, he obviously brought welcome knowledge and expertise to the Irish Society. He later became Professor of Chemistry at Trinity College Dublin. He was only one of a distinguished group of men which the P.S.I. was able to attract to its ranks at this time, mostly from the University. [89]

In 1885, another Trinity professor, J. Alfred Scott, compiled tables of the actinic values of light in different parts of the world and these were widely published in photographic handbooks and manuals. It should be realised that before the invention of exposure meters photographers had to rely on their experience in being able to calculate the correct exposure required for a particular situation. Scott's tables were the first of their kind and although they were complicated to use, they were enthusiastically received by photographers. Ilford Limited used the information contained in the tables as the basis for the design of what is considered to be the first exposure meter. It was basically a type of slide rule which could be easily carried in

Professor J. Alfred Scott, president of the Photographic Society of Ireland in 1893, and compiler of the tables of light values which were the basis of the first exposure calculator, marketed by Ilford Ltd. in 1885.

the pocket. Scott later was president of the P.S.I. in 1893. [90]

Sir Howard Grubb, son of Thomas Grubb, a founder member in 1854, was the President in 1888 and like his father, was an optician who designed photographic lenses. He was also, like his father, responsible for the design and manufacture of large refractor telescopes at his factory at the appropriately named Observatory Lane in Rathmines. He also appears to have worked extensively for the British Admiralty for whom he designed new gun sights and is credited with the invention of the submarine periscope. He received his knighthood for services to the Royal Navy.

The Grubb manufactory in Rathmines was working for the Admiralty right up to the end of the British regime in Ireland, the firm seems to have disappeared during the early 1920s. This was not surprising for such a firm, given its sensitive history; there is a rumour that during the "Troubles" an armed guard was kept on the premises night and day.

Another distinguished member at this time was Professor John Joly, also of Trinity College. A complete "renaissance man", he concerned himself with many subjects. A number of his researches concerned sea water and much of his research took place in the sea in and near Dun Laoghaire Harbour. Joly was Professor of Biology at Trinity until his death in 1933. He invented the thalometer and meltometer to determine the melting point of minerals. He realised the importance of radio activity in determining the earth's history and introduced radioactive methods to date geological formations. He was famous for inventing new apparatus to further various researches and, from the strictly maritime viewpoint, is above all celebrated in introducing the estimation of the earth's age by the length of time taken by salt to accumulate in the sea. He was also for a time the Kingstown Harbour Commission's Special Scientific Adviser and was considered to be one of the greatest scientists of his time.

His photographic activities appear to have begun in the late 1880s and he was a member of the Photographic Society from about 1890. His experiments into colour photography would appear to have started about the same time.[91]

John Joly is internationally credited with producing what was probably the world's first practical colour process. He took the researches and theories of Clerk Maxwell and Ducos du Hauron which had been undertaken and formulated during the 1860s and applied to them the improved technology of the 1890s. What had been impossible in the 1860s was capable of being achieved in the 1890s. He used ordinary monochrome plates sandwiched with specially made screens inscribed with red, green and blue lines, about thirty to the inch. When a plate was exposed through such a screen, developed and printed, reversed and then bound up with a similar screen a crude colour transparency resulted.

Joly applied for a patent in 1894 and wrote extensively about his invention in learned journals during 1894 and 1895 (see Appendix IX). He subsequently discovered that a certain James McDonough of Chicago claimed to have used exactly the same idea to produce colour photographs two years earlier and had in fact patented it in America in 1892. Details of the argument at this time are unclear, suffice to say that Joly was challenged in the American Courts and was defeated.[92]

The whole affair was shortly to be made of academic interest, however, by the introduction by the Lumiere Brothers, in Paris, of the greatly superior Autochrome process. Although it is generally believed that John Joly did not exploit his invention commercially, there is some evidence to show that he

did put on sale a small number of special kits for amateurs to try out the process.

While Reynolds, Scott, Grubb and Joly were all of a scientific turn of mind, and although distinguished in their fields, they did not contribute much to the creative side of photography in Ireland. However, they were more than compensated for by the activities of Alfred Werner F.R.P.S. who exhibited internationally and whose most famous picture was the large portrait of Maud Gonne mentioned earlier.

Alfred Werner remained a member of the P.S.I. for many years, delivering many lectures and becoming president on two occasions, and when the Dublin Camera Club was set up by the Society in 1920 he was also president of that for some time.

A curious fact about Werner was that when he died in 1944 at the advanced age of 85 after many years of retirement, he had become very wealthy and living in a large house in Dundrum, Co. Dublin. This was most unusual as, unfortunately, many photographers tended to die poor, if not actually in poverty. This was the lot of some quite famous photographers, including Frederick Scott Archer, inventor of the collodion wet plate process, O. G. Rejlander and the first Irish photographer, Francis Stewart Beatty. It is not easy to amass great fortunes practising this profession; a few Irish exceptions were William Lawrence and the Lauders who established Lafayettes, these, however, were not merely practising photographers but photographic entrepreneurs, who exploited the medium for most gain.

Werner's secret was that he was shrewd enough to invest in George Eastman's Kodak Company when it was formed in 1888. It is said that by the year 1900 his original investment had appreciated by a factor of over one thousand.[93]

The years after 1880 showed a marked decline in the number of photographic studios at work in the country. This was due more than anything else, to the fact that many more people were now capable of taking their own photographs. Apart from those amateurs who were prepared to join the photographic societies and camera clubs which existed, there were many who were using the new Kodaks, or other "simple" cameras and who relied on books and magazines – of which during the 1880s there were several – for the necessary knowledge. In 1889 the *Freeman's Journal* saw fit to publish a small handbook *Photography for Fun* stating it had been reprinted from a series of articles in the *Weekly Freeman*.

The studios which survived tended to be the larger quality establishments like Lafayette's, Chancellor's, Lawrence, Glover's, and Lauder Brothers in Dublin; The Vienna Co., Abernathy's and Church's in Belfast and Guy's in Cork.

Messrs. A. & G. Taylor, in Dublin, were the first studio in Ireland to introduce portraits by subscription, where clients paid by instalments.

Without doubt the firm of Lafayette's were the most outstanding of these studios. It was founded in 1880 as an offshoot of the long established Lauder Brothers and presented the last word in luxury.

The Countess of Warwick,(Daisy), as Marie-Antoinette, the costume she wore to the famous "Devonshire House" Ball. Photographed in London by Lafayette, 1897

Its name reflected the feeling that everything French represented the height of fashion and sophistication at that time.

Lauder Brothers had been founded as a daguerreotype studio in 1853 by Edmund Stanley Lauder a son of George Marsh Lauder of County Offaly, the Lauders originally came from Scotland, and had settled in Offaly during the eighteenth century. Although the firm always traded as "Lauder Brothers" exhaustive research has failed to produce a trace of any other "brothers" being involved. Perhaps another brother did originally exist and may have died young.

Over the following thirty five years Lauder Brothers became one of the most successful portrait studios operating in Dublin,

eventually having, by 1880, three branches – the original premises at 30 Westmoreland Street, another one at 45 Lower Sackville Street and a third in Kingstown (Dun Laoghaire).

A separate firm, E. & J. Lauder was opened, during the 1870s, at 22 Westmoreland Street. Edmund Stanley Lauder had four sons and this new firm appears to have been a partnership venture by him and his eldest son James Stack Lauder.

This was to be the first small photographic step by James Lauder who was responsible for setting up the first premises of Lafayette at 30 Westmoreland Street in 1880.

The Lauders, now with three premises on Westmoreland Street, dominated the photographic scene on that important principal city

The Growth of a Photographic Empire: No other Irish photographic firm attained the size or international importance of the Lauder/Lafayette organisation *(see text)*. The growth of the parent firm, Lauder Brothers, may be indicated by the changes in the design of the backs of their cartes over a 30 year period, c1860–1990

c1860

c1865

c1868

c1870

c1872

c1875

c1880-90 (Westmoreland St.)

c1880-90 (Sackville St.)

Lafayette's, founded in 1880 by James Stack Lauder, won many international medals.
Pictures of these were proudly displayed on the backs of their cartes and cabinets.
Photographs may be dated by the dates of the latest medals shown (see below)

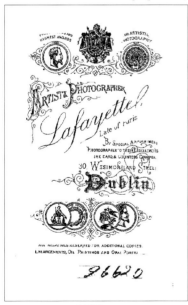

c1880

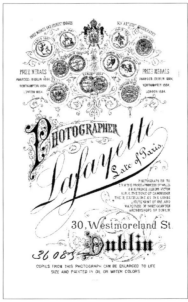

c1885

c1900 (London)

thoroughfare. They were eventually to almost dominate the photographic scene in the city as a whole, today Lauder or Lafayette photographs represent almost a third of all old carte and cabinet portraits which may be found.

In time they would become the leading society photographers in the country. James Stack Lauder or Jacques Lafayette, as he sometimes liked to call himself for trading purposes, had almost immediate success. He exhibited widely, winning many prize medals internationally. He reproduced pictures of these on the backs of his print mounts and Lafayette photographs may be dated by the number of medals displayed.

The Lafayette premises were rebuilt during the 1890s and were furnished in the latest art-nouveau style, it was probably the only photographic studio and gallery in Dublin to be purpose built. It represented the last word in luxury with special drawing rooms for ladies and gentlemen and with galleries to display the firm's products. The actual studio was on the top floor and a Parisien open style lift – one of the first in Dublin – was installed to carry the wealthy society patrons upwards to have their portraits taken.

Lafayette's took their first royal portraits, of Alexandra, Princess of Wales on the occasion of her visit to Ireland in 1885. Being lucky enough to be granted such sittings could be extremely profitable for photographers. One portrait alone, showing the princess in the robes of an honourary Doctor of Music, is said to have earned for Lafayettes at least £100,000 in print sales, a vast sum in those days. From this it is easy to see how they were able to afford to rebuild their premises. In 1887 they were commanded to photograph Queen Victoria at Windsor Castle and were granted a Royal Warrant as "Her Majesty's Photographer in Dublin" the only Irish photographer to be so honoured.[94]

Originally Lafayette's headquarters was in Dublin. By 1900 they had branches in many of the large cities of Britain; Glasgow 1890, Manchester 1892, London 1897 and Belfast 1900.

In 1897 with the opening of the London studio the firm's headquarters was transferred there to their plush new studio at 179 New Bond Street. The year was significant as the Diamond Jubilee (60 years) of the Queen's reign, and Lafayette's move to London is a

Edward, Prince of Wales, a cabinet card, photographed by Chancellors, c1890

measure of their business acumen. There was obviously going to be a lot of work for society photographers.

One of the most important social events which was staged to celebrate the Queen's Jubilee was the Devonshire House Ball. This was a glittering affair, a fancy-dress ball, organised by the Duchess of Devonshire at her home in Piccadilly. Over 700 high society guests were invited to attend in "allegorical or historical costume."

Many of the most important guests were photographed on the night of the ball in a special photographic studio tent, erected in the grounds, by Lafayette. To have obtained this commission was an incredible plum for the newly opened studio and it is possible that the move to London was probably instigated by this fantastic event alone, it certainly was responsible for establishing Lafayette's as one of the leading society photographers in London. The Lafayette business was floated on the stock exchange in 1898 and it continued trading as a single company until 1922. [95]

During the early years of the twentieth century yet another offshoot of the Lauder empire, called J. Stanley, was operating in Dublin. In 1916 the Sackville Street branch of Lauder Brothers was totally destroyed and in

Mr. Wynne of Castlebar, 1872.
The Wynne family published views of
the west of Ireland over many years.
The Wynne collection is now at the
National Photographic Archive,
Temple Bar, Dublin.

Marey. Of Irish interest was his assistant Lucien Bull. Lucien Bull was born in Dublin in 1876, the son of an Irish father and a French mother.

Lucien had a French education and at an early age developed an interest in photography. He became an assistant to Dr. Marey and later had a distinguished career himself in researching high-speed photography and as an inventor in his own right.

He became director of the Marey Institute in Paris in 1914 after Dr. Marey's death. His ultimate achievement was perhaps his taking one million images in a second in 1952.

He is greatly honoured in France where among other distinctions he was appointed an Officer of the Legion of Honour. He is, alas, virtually unknown and unsung in Ireland, the place of his birth. It may also be noted that his brother, René, invented a method of firing machine guns through the blades of aeroplane propellors during the first World War, a major contribution to aerial warfare at the time.[97]

As mentioned earlier, the half-tone block gradually came into use during the 1890s as a means of reproducing photographs. For the first time photographs could now be printed directly along with type on a printing machine. Before this, if photographs were required to be in close proximity on a page with type or other printed matter, it was necessary to physically mount them laboriously by hand.

The half-tone block made profound changes in the appearance of such things as newspapers and popular magazines. In Dublin a new weekly publication, *The Illustrograph* made its appearance profusely illustrated with photographs. It provided the Irish photographers of the day with a marvellous vehicle for their work and, for a time, it organised a

1922, shortly after James Stack Lauder's death, Lafayette's was split up, each of the branches becoming separate entities. The Dublin branch still survives, albeit under a different ownership.

Lafayettes were not the only Irish photographers to open branches in London, it has already been mentioned that James Robinson did so during the 1880s where he was British selling agent for a number of European and American miniature spy cameras such as the "Luzo" and the "Stirn".

On the 17th of February 1890 the P.S.I. was responsible for bringing to Dublin the famous lecture on "Animal Locomotion" by Eadweard Muybridge. It was held at the Antient Concert Rooms.[95] It was Muybridge, who in 1872, by using a series of cameras, first demonstrated the true action of the legs of a galloping horse. It is considered that the Muybridge experiments led indirectly to the invention of cinematography.[96]

Another inventor who carried on experiments into the analysis of movement by photography was the Frenchman Etienne Jules

George Mansfield's photographic studio as part of the department store in Grafton Street, Dublin, c1890

Left: Messrs Guy's photographic establishment at Patrick's Street, Cork, c1880. From a Lawrence stereo negative.

weekly competition for amateur photographers for a time.

An outstanding photographic event of 1894 was the holding of the annual meeting of the Photographic Convention of Great Britain in Dublin in July. It was organised locally by a formidable committee consisting of 116 members, drawn from every branch of society; the nobility, the Corporation, the professions, the arts, the press, the Church and the photographic community. The programme included an address by Sir Howard Grubb, past President of the P. S. I., an exhibition and the General Meeting, held at the R. D. S. The rest of the programme included excursions, garden parties, dinners, the reading of six papers on photographic subjects and even a smoking concert *(see Appendix XI).*

The introduction of new portable cameras was mainly responsible for encouraging photographers to take a more candid type of picture. For the first time the minute details of everyday living were capable of being recorded. The collections which have survived from this period constitute valuable social documents, showing life as it was in Ireland at the end of the nineteenth century in much greater detail than was possible earlier.

Into this category would fall the large collections built up by Pooles of Waterford and the Wynne family of Mayo, now in the National Photographic Archive. Many similar collections exist in Northern Ireland notably by Robert Welsh, D. J. Hogg and H. T. Hutton. Individual

amateur photographers were also responsible for leaving important collections, Captain Langford of Kingstown, and John Joseph Clarke of Castleblayney being examples.

Clarke, who took exciting candid photographs of Dublin at the turn of the century while studying medicine at the old Catholic University from which he qualified as a doctor in 1904. His photographs display a modern, almost documentary, approach which was remarkable for its time and it is to be regretted that after he qualified as a doctor he seems to have abandoned photography altogether. Clarke's negatives have recently been acquired by the National Photographic Archive. His style has been compared to the French photographer Lartique who was working at the same time in Paris.

The playwright John Millington Synge was also a keen amateur photographer who was responsible for taking a fine series of photographs of the Aran Islands.

George Bernard Shaw was also interested in photography and, for a time, actually wrote critical reviews of photographic exhibitions for various art journals in London.

Also active at this time was Victor Smyth, he was a member of the prominent Dublin family who owned "Smyths of the Green" a famous provision shop on St. Stephen's Green, catering to the landed gentry. Rather than entering the safe family business, he took up instead the uncertain occupation of professional photographer. A member of the Photographic Society

Above:
The first floor studio of Robert Forbes on the corner of Grafton Street and South King Street, photographed by John Joseph Clarke about 1900

Left:
A small booklet on photography published by the *Weekly Freeman's Journal* in 1889 reflecting the new popularity of photography as a hobby which was generated by the introduction of the new simple portable cameras.

91

Part of the annual exhibition of the Photographic Society of Ireland, held at the Dawson Hall, Dublin, 1893

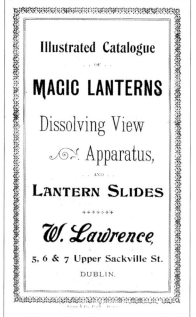

An outing by members of the Photographic Society of Ireland to Dalkey Quarry, c1895

of Ireland, his most interesting surviving photographs are a series using a split screen trick technique, one shows him taking a picture of himself *(see plate 39, and p.82).*

Photography was being used to document the architecture and topography of the country, most notably by the Royal Society of Antiquaries of Ireland where the results of their photographic surveys of the 1890s may be inspected today. Ephraim MacDowel Cosgrave was responsible for a great deal of the photography undertaken by this Society. He produced an *Illustrated Dictionary of Dublin,* with photographs by himself, as well as contributing many articles and papers to the Journal of the R.S.A.I. His large collection of photographs and slides were presented to the Society when he died in 1925. He was also a member of the Royal Irish Academy and the Photographic Society of Ireland.

Photographers with a more socially oriented conscience were now able to use the medium to record and publicise the terrible conditions under which many people were forced to live in the slums of Dublin and other Irish cities. One example of this is the collection of lantern slides depicting slum conditions, "Darkest Dublin" preserved by the R.S.A.I. Photography was also being used to highlight conditions in the so-called congested districts in the West of Ireland.

The culmination of the nineteenth century development of photography was obviously the introduction of movement. The Lumière Brothers in Paris invented the "Cinématographe" in 1895. This was later to develop into the cinema. The first Irish demonstration of the new invention took place at the Star of Erin music hall, now the Olympia Theatre, in 1896, and by the end of the century the earliest Irish films had been made.[98]

APPENDIX I

Some Historical Recollections of Photography

by Francis Stewart Beatty

Francis Stewart Beatty of Belfast is generally considered by most photographic historians to have been Ireland's first photographer, and very possibly the first native person of these islands to successfully produce daguerreotype images independently of the inventor in Paris.
This is an article by him which appeared in the *Photographic News* of the 8th August, 1879.

"We are aware of Mr. Beatty's long connection with photography, and of his labours in connection with permanent printing, which we have the pleasure at all times recognising,
Photographic News, September 16th, 1864"

MY LONG CONNECTION with photography, a connection now entering upon its fortieth year, induces me to give a brief statement showing now how far I have been instrumental in the infancy of photography of fostering and promoting its interest, which may be interesting, and useful to those who admire and follow the art as a profession.

About this time, 1839, the scientific journals of all countries made the announcement that M. Daguerre, of Paris, had discovered a means by which the fleeting images of external objects depicted on the ground glass of the camera-obscura could be retained on a tablet of polished plated silver plate, and be permanently fixed thereon. Splendid specimens were exhibited in Paris of its architectural buildings, bridges, &c. The most distinguished and scientific men of that day were taken by surprise by the publication of so wonderful an invention, and intense anxiety was experienced by all awaiting the publication of the details. Although communicated to the Academy of Sciences the 7th January, 1839, the process was not published until the 15th June by M. Arago to the French Chamber of Deputies on the occasion of the French Government awarding to M. Daguerre, in conjunction with M. Isidore Niépce, each a pension for the discovery and publication of all details.

Ever watchful then, as well as now, to investigate into any new discovery that may be useful and beneficial to the advance of science or art, I resolved at once to exercise what ability I possessed to accomplish what M. Daguerre had discovered, and proceeded to work at the problem, being at the time an amateur optician, chemist, and careful manipulator (my profession being an engraver).

After many failures and up-hill work, I was surprised when I succeeded in my object to my entire satisfaction, as a letter of mine dated 20th September, 1839, published in the *Belfast News Letter* of that date will more fully show, which is annexed :

From *Belfast News Letter,* of September 20th,

THE DAGUERREOTYPE — On this curious subject, the following interesting letter has been addressed to us by Mr. Beatty, the well-known engraver of this town. We have also received the specimen to which he refers, and the effect noticed by him is extremely singular.

To the Editor of the *News Letter.*

Sir, Being occasionally engaged since the announcement of M. Daguerre's extraordinary invention of fixing on silver, plated on copper, the minute images of external objects, produced by means of the camera-obscura, after a number of experiments, I was somewhat surprised to find, that in using silver paper, the effect was different from silver plated on copper, although treated in a similar manner. Silver plated on copper gives the the true effect of light and shade — while silver on paper gives the opposite namely, the light parts of the subject are dull, and the dark shades are, in a proportionate degree, light *(negative image).* In order to convince you of the fact I send you a specimen; but our days of late having been cloudy, you cannot expect it to be as perfect as I would wish. I hope before your next publication to be able to submit to you a specimen upon silver plated on copper, and silver on paper, in order that you may more completely understand the difference. Hoping that this communication may have the effect of promoting inquiry on the subject, I remain, your obedient servant,

FRANCIS S. BEATTY.

It is only now after the lapse of nearly forty years, in which I have had experience of many vicisitudes of fortune intermingled with pleasure for the love of our beautiful art, and which entailed upon me endless expense of time and money in endeavouring to promote its interests and at a time when there could be no reasonable prospect of a return for the outlay. However, I can never divest myself of the pride I possess in having taken an active part in the infancy of this invention, and by my humble abilities aiding to bring it forward to its present state of perfection. I question whether there is any record of a successful accomplishment of a Daguerreotype picture in Great Britain at so early a date, September 20th, 1839, nearly three months after its first publication of June 15th, 1839.

In the *Photographic News* of November 29, 1878, there appears a critical notice of a work (*Scientific Memoirs, by John William Draper, M.D., L.L.D.*), which, to me, is very interesting. I therefore take the liberty of quoting a paragraph. "In the early days of photography a galaxy of the most distinguished philosophers of the day, were fascinated with the field for investigation and discovery which it opened out to them, and they devoted themselves to aiding in establishing the new art. Treasures of time, thought, learning, and experiment, were lavished on it by the most capable chemists and physicists of the period. Probably the only survivor of those who have prosecuted their researches with unabated ardour is Dr. Draper".

All I assume to be is that of an humble individual of a practical turn of mind not trained to scientific investigation. My authorship extending only to such matters as can be conveyed in a letter on a scientific subject in a periodical, and without wishing in the least to detract from others their merits of discovery, or their practical application of it into practical results, I think from the facts I have already stated in this communication, that photographers will concede to me as proved that I had the good fortune of recording myself in the field earlier than any other person.

It was in March, 1840, that the first photographic portrait from life was effected by Dr. Draper as recorded in the *Philosophical Magazine*, and consequently nine months from the date of the publication of M. Daguerre.

In the latter part of 1839, and continued in 1840, Belfast, my native place, its architectural buildings, old long bridge, spanning the river Lagan, was delineated by the Daguerreotype executed by me, and were much admired by the nobility and gentry of the town and neighbourhood, and noted in the most flattering terms by the local newspapers of that day.

In June, 1840, Mr. Richard Beard patented in Great Britain the concave silvered mirror for the production of Daguerreotype portraits, being a communication from Mr. Woolcot (*sic.*) an American photographer; and being desirous of giving this method a trial, I immediately set to work to grind and polish a concave mirror of short focus in speculum metal, having previously ground and polished them for reflecting telescopes.

After considerable delay I accomplished my object, and in 1841 was enabled to produce portraits. Having communicated my success to Mr. Beard, he invited me over to London, and in the October of that year found me in the Polytechnic Institution, when I was introduced to Messrs Cooper and Goddard. At this time Mr. Beard was establishing a similar institution in Southampton; he, therefor, desired me to take my part as an operator until he would come home. In the meantime he would examine my specimens, which he took with him.

So great was the excitement created in London amongst the nobility, gentry, and moneyed classes at this new species of portraiture which was then being produced at the Polytechnic, that during my stay the average amount of money taken each day amounted to, I was told, £150. However this included expensive cases, frames and jewellery. In the waiting rooms of this establishment you would see waiting their turn to enter the blue-glass roofed operating rooms, the noble dames and daughters of England's aristocracy accomodating each other as. well as their limited space would allow, awaiting for hours together before desires were accomplished. I venture to say that if our present race of photographers were to present to the domestics of any of our aristocracy, portraits such as were supplied at the Polytechnic of that day, they would not accept them, so beautiful and cheap as they are now produced, showing the onward march of improvement.

On the arrival of Mr. Beard from Southampton, he mentioned to me his intention of establishing a Daguerreotype gallery in Dublin, and that if I would accept the operative management he would pay me a percentage of work done. Having been in pretty good circumstances at the time, his terms did not meet my approval, and I therefore declined the offer.

The Parabolic glass mirror soon gave place to the original camera in consequence of the use of more sensitive chemicals being employed to sensitize the Daguerreotype plate in addition to simple vapour of iodine, bromine and clorine were used.

Opticians of note applied their abilities to make lenses for the camera of Daguerre. The most successful were the late Mr.

Alexander Ross, of London and also Voightlander *(sic.)*, of Vienna. Photography now got a start in the right direction, and exquisite portraits were the result, the patented mirror was abandoned, and the art became free to all. The glare of the silver plate was got rid of by subjecting the finished picture to the action of the galvanic battery by depositing upon it a film of gold, which not only preserved it, from atmospheric injury, but gave to the picture a warm flesh-coloured tint which had a pleasing effect, while the splendid detail made portraiture of that day unequalled at the present.

Their multiplication by printing being unpracticable, their value was considerably enhanced by their cost, therefore limiting their productions as a profitable commercial transaction.

In 1842, in connection with another, we built a gallery for Daguerreotype portraiture in a central situation in Belfast, which was carried on for a considerable time. However, the expense of a Daguerreotype portrait being above the means of the general public, we had to abandon the undertaking.

"It is not so generally known among our citizens as native merit demands that it should be, that the first person who introduced this new and beautiful art of imitating nature into Great Britain was Mr. Francis S. Beatty, of Castle Street, a gentleman whose talent in several branches of the arts are as varied as they are creditable. We have seen both portraits and architectural views produced by Mr. Beatty, which, in our opinion, could not be surpassed, either for accuracy of copy (which, however, is inseperable from the art), or for the *(sk)*ill with which the most minute details had been fixed. His skim *(?)* to public patronage is supported by abilities of which his fellow classmen ought to be proud, independently of the credit due to him for his succesful prosecution of the photographic art."

Banner of Ulster, **1842.**

Mr. Fox Talbot's Calotype pictures were executed by me, positives from paper negatives; some of them are now before me of that date; a Daguerreotypist would not admire them. Time went on, and progress was slow until Mr. Archer's collodion process was made public; this gave a new impetus to the subject, to portraiture as well as landscape, cheapening the process, and placing before the public a beautiful glass positive *(ambrotype)* for a trifle.

Photography became at once an established and fashionable business, and, of course, I once more joined the Profession. Then came the carte-de-visite or Albion portrait, followed by the cabinet, and enlargements of all dimensions, &c.

APPENDIX II

Presidents of the
Dublin Photographic Society 1854–1857
and the
Photographic Society of Ireland 1858–1954

The Dublin Photographic Society was founded in 1854,
the name of the society was changed to The Photographic Society of Ireland in 1858
The names of all known presidents are listed up to the Society's centenary in 1954
List extracted from *The History of the Photographic Society of Ireland* (1954) by Oscar Merne

Lord Otho Fitzgerald	1854
Sir John Joscelyn Coghill, Bart.	1855–1856
Captain Henry	1857
Gilbert Saunders, M.R.I.A.	1858
John Bayly, J.P.	1859–1860
Society presumed dormant	**1861–1878**
Society re-founded	**1879**
?	1879–1884
Dr. J. Emerson Reynolds, F.R.S.	1885–1887
Sir Howard Grubb, F.R.S.	1888–1889
George Mansfield, J.P.	1890–1892
Prof. J. Alfred Scott, M.A., M.D., F.R.C.S.I.	1893–1895/1923–1926
Alfred Werner, F.R.P.S.	1896–1901
Prof. John Joly, F.R.S.A.	1902–1903
Hugh Pollock, B.A., B.L.	1906–1908
Robert Benson	1909–1910
Thomas H. Mason, M.R.I.A.	1911–1912
W. N. Allen	1913–1915
Serjeant Henry Hanna, K.C.	1916–1919/1929
John Rowland	1920–1922
Major R. H. Plews	1927–1928
T. V. Cleary	1930–1931
G. Prescott	1932–1933
H.M. Dockrell, T.D.	1934–1935
J. V. Aiken	1936–1937
J. L. Campion	1938–1939
A.V. Henry, B. Sc.	1940–1942·
J. H. Roch	1943–1944
C. A. Bowles, B.E.	1945
Oscar. S. Merne	1946
Major P. J. McDonagh	1947–1948
P. Kelly	1949–1950
W. F. Aylward	1951–1952
Denis Crowley, M.Sc.	1953–1954

Sir John Joscelyn Coghill, Bart.
President 1855–1856

Professor John Joly, FRSA
President 1902–1903

Alfred Werner, FRPS
President 1896–1901

APPENDIX III

"The Photographers' Mile"

Lower Sackville Street from *"Shaw's Illustrated Directory of Dublin, 1850"*
showing Glukman's first Dublin studio at number 13 (arrowed).

During the nineteenth century the majority of the portrait studios operating in Dublin had premises located on the main centre city streets from the Rotunda at the top of Sackville Street through Upr. Sackville Street, Lwr. Sackville Street, Westmoreland Street, College Green, Grafton Street with a few on St. Stephen's Green. This continuation of streets became known in photographic circles as **The Photographers' Mile**
The list below is based on information gleaned from Dublin street directories
from 1841 to 1900 and is most probably not complete.
The dates shown are when the individuals or firms advertised as photographers although they
may have occupied the same premises either before or after these dates.

Rotunda	Richard Beard (?)	1841–1842	34	W. Kirkpatrick	1865–1869
	Alexander Doussin Dubreuil	1842–1844		M. Morganti	1870
				Henry Finning	1870–1880
Upper Sackville Street			39	Simonton & Millard	1859–1862
5	William Lawrence	1875–1900		Thomas Millard	1862–1864
6	William Lawrence	1890–1900		Millard & Robinson	1864–1890
7	William Lawrence	1865–c1875	40	Adolph Lesage	1870–1885
11	Nelson & Marshall	1860–1884		Francis Grieffield	1885–1890
	W. G. Moore	1885–1900	45	Edmund Lauder	1853–1885
15	Pring & Webb	1862–1863		Lauder Brothers	1885–1900
18	Photo Transfer Co.	c1869	46	Francis Martin	c1853–1860
22	Mrs. O'Neill	c1865	48	W. C. McKee	c1885
23	Scott Brothers	c1864	55	John Chancellor	c1855–1875
24	Prof. Leone Glukman	1848–1867		Chancellor's	1875–1900
Lower Sackville Street					
5	W. C. McKee	c1885–1895	**Westmoreland Street**		
6	T. F. Geoghegan	1895–1900	9	The Grosvenor Gallery	c1865
7	Stark Brothers	1868–1884	22	Fleury Mooney	c1865
12	Mr.(?) Treffry	1841–1842		W. H. Monney	1864–1870
13	Prof. Leone Glukman	c1844–1848		London Metropolitan	1870–1880
	Joseph H. Pinkney	1848–1859		J. & E. Lauder	1880–1890
	Professor Blume	1850– ?	30	Forster & Scott	1862–1863
15	Hutchinson & Keegan	1866–1870		W. C. Forster	1864
	James Hutchinson	1870–1875		Forster & Haskoll	1865–1875
19	J. Lewis	1875		W. B. Samuel	1875–1888
32	M. Morganti	1864–1870	31	J. Lafayette	1885–1900

Westmoreland Street (continued)

32	William Andrews	1859–1860
32	Lauder Brothers	c1855–1900

College Green

16	Francis Stewart Beatty	c1854-70

Grafton Street

3	John Robertson	1863–1894
	The Photo-Transfer Co.	c1863
20	Horatio Nelson	1843–c1849
24	P. O'Reilly	c1870
28	Auguste Schroeder	1865–1880
	Godfried Schroeder	1869–1880
	Edwards & Co.	1880–1885
	Edwards & Simonton	1875–1880
39	John Fortune Lawrence	1860–1875
	Alfred Werner	1885–1900
41	W. R. Kiernan	1895–1899
43	Henry Neale	c1862–1869
	Adam Sauvy	1870–1875
	Wilson & Talbot	c1875
	London Photographic Co.	c1875
49	M & S Eaton	1870
54	Godfried Schroeder	1880–1884
	Adam Sauvy	1884–1992
	Robert Forbes	1892–1900

65	James Robinson	1850–1900
70	James Simonton	1862–1874
71	Thomas North	1863–1900
72	(?)Coakley	c1865
75	E. Adolph	1860s
78	Julius Ahlborn	1860–1865
	Julyan & Ahlfred	1865
	G. H. Wonfer	1875–1879
79	Frederick H. Mares	1860–1880
	James McFarland	1880–1890
88	London Metropolitan	c1880
	The Photographic Studio	c1875
90	Barrett & Stanley	1848–c1859
	George Mansfield	1860–1900
	F. P. Darcy	1900
93	Horatio Nelson	c1850–c1853
95	M. & S. Eaton	1870
112	C. E. Bagot	1864
118	Theodor Haskoll	1862–1864
	J. Walsh	1869–c1874
	W. B. Samuel	1868–1869
	Frederick H. Mares	1880–1895

St. Stephen's Green

3	Geary Brothers	c1848–1855
6	Oliver F.X. Sarony	c1859–1864
124	M. Glover	1885–1900

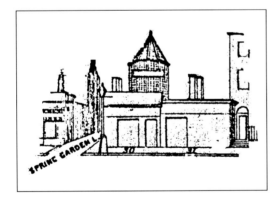 

Left: Doussin Dubreuil's glasshouse and premises on the corner of Spring Garden Lane, in Great Brunswick Street (now Pearse Street) which he opened in 1845 after his bankruptcy at the Rotunda. *Right:* Leone Glukman's second studio at 24 Upper Sackville Street to which he moved in 1848; he was to spend the rest of his stay in Dublin – until 1867 – at this address. He occupied the entire house, living as well as working there, whereas with his previous address he was merely occupying the top floor. Both illustrations have been taken from *Shaw's Illustrated Directory of Dublin*, 1850.

APPENDIX IV

Members of the Dublin Photographic Society 1854–1859

Founder members' names are shown in bold type

Date joining	Name	Address	Proposer	Seconder	Occupation
1/11/1854 FIRST MEETING	**Lord Otho Fitzgerald**	**Carton, Maynooth, Co. Kildare**			**Gentleman**
	Sir John Joscelyn Coghill, Bart	**Belvedere House, Drumcondra, Dublin.**			**Baronet**
	Captain Henry, Dragoon Gds.	**8 Waterloo Place, Dublin**			**Soldier**
	William Cotter Kyle	**8 Clare Street, Dublin**			**Barrister**
	T. A. Fenton Esq.	**1 Mountjoy Square E, Dublin**			**Barrister**
	John Garret Rathborne Esq.	**Dunsinea, Castleknock, Co. Dublin**			**Candle Manufacturer**
	Samuel Bewley Junior Esq.	**6 Dame Street,**			**Tea/Coffee Merchant**
	James Robinson Esq.	**65 Grafton Street, Dublin**			**Photographer**
	William Allen Esq.	**Henry Street, Dublin**			**Chemist**
	Michael H. Stapleton, M.D.	**1 Mountjoy Place, Dublin**			**Surgeon**
	Michaelangelo Hayes. R.H.A.	**4 Salem Place, Dublin**			**Painter**
	Edmund W. Davy Esq. M.D.	**Royal Dublin Society, Dublin**			**Prof. of Chemistry**
	Thomas Grubb Esq.	**14 Leinster Square, Rathmines, Dublin**			**Optician, Lens maker**
	Henry Yeates Esq.	**1 Grafton Street, Dublin**			**Optician**
	John Barker Esq. M.D.	**48 Waterloo Road, Dublin**			**Physician**
	William C. Plunkett Esq.	**30 Upper Fitzwilliam Street, Dublin**			**Gentleman**
	Francis Brady Esq.	**Lower Leeson Street, Dublin**			**Barrister**
	Vere Hunt Esq.	**13 Harrington Street, Dublin**			**Money Broker**
	Joseph Kirk Esq. R.H.A.	**94 Harcourt Street, Dublin**			**Sculptor**
	Frederick Saunders Esq.	**30 Lombard Street, Dublin**			**Engraver**
	W. E. Steele Esq. M.D.	Royal Dublin Society	W. C. Kyle	W. Allen	
	Davenport Crosthwaite Esq.	21 Mount Pleasant Avenue, Dublin	J. Rathbone	V. Hunt	
	Miss M. Grubb	14 Leinster Square, Rathmines, Dublin	T. Grubb	M. Stapleton	
	William Dalgleish Esq.	Ordnance Survey, Phoenix Park, Dublin	J. Robinson	S. Bewley	
	William Aldridge Esq. M.D.	3 Lower Sackville Street, Dublin	T. Fenton	M. Stapleton	
	George Sharpe Esq.	Wentworth Place, Dublin	J.J. Coghill	T. A. Fenton	Artist
	James P. Sheridan Esq.	Buenos Aires, Argentina	J. Robinson	M. Stapleton	
	Rev. W. Hartigan	Delgany, Co. Wicklow	J. Kirk	F. Saunders	
	William Lover Esq. M.D.	46 Talbot Street, Dublin	T. Grubb	M.Stapleton	Surgeon/Author
	Thomas Millard	43 Mary Street, Dublin	J. Robinson	W. Allen	Photographer
	Thomas Mayne	Wellington Street, Dublin	W. Allen	J. Robinson	Optician
29/11/1854	Miss Greaves	Bird's Grove, Ashbourne, Derbyshire	J. J. Coghill	Capt. Henry	
	William LeFanu Esq.	7 Fitzwilliam Square, Dublin	J.J. Coghill	Capt. Henry	
	George Porte Esq.	43 Great Brunswick Street, Dublin	J. Robinson	F. Saunders	Engineer
	J. McMahon Royal Engineers,	Islandbridge Barracks, Dublin	J. Robinson	Capt. Henry	
	James Vance Esq.	Sussex Place, Kingstown, Co. Dublin	J. Robinson	T. Grubb	
	T. Elrington Esq.	24 Upper Fitzwilliam Street, Dublin	J.J. Coghill	J. Robinson	
	James S. Mulvany Esq.	Lakelands, Dundrum, Co. Dublin	J. Robinson	J.J. Coghill	Painter
	George Mulvany Esq. R.H.A.	Lower Mount Street, Dublin	M.Stapleton	T. Fenton	Painter
	James McCurdy Esq. C.E.	Westland Row, Dublin	D. Crosthwaite	V. Hunt	
	Harry Draper Esq.	Mary Street, Dublin	M. Stapleton	T. Fenton	
	Charles H. James Esq.	19 Cavendish Row, Dublin			
	Samuel V. Pratt Esq.	17 Summer Hill, Dublin	S. Bewley	J.J. Coghill	
	Charles Cameron Esq.	5 Dame Street, Dublin	J. Robinson	Capt. Henry	
	Alfred Wilson Esq.	Dame Street, Dublin	S. Bewley	J.J. Coghill	
	Holland Atkinson Esq.	Ely Place, Dublin	C. James (?)	J.J. Coghill	
	Thomas H. Young Esq.	Marlborough Street, Dublin	W. Allen	S. Bewley	
	Gilbert Saunders Esq.	The Hill, Monkstown, Co. Dublin	J. Barker	J. J. Coghill	Engineer
	H. Spiers Esq.	28 College Green, Dublin	J. Robinson	J. J. Coghill	
	Rev. Charles Graves D.D.	Trinity College Dublin	J. Robinson	J.J. Coghill	
	Nicholas Balfe Esq.	3 Proby Square, Blackrock, Co. Dublin	H. Stapleton	J. J. Coghill	
	Edward Dyer Esq.	St. Stephen's Green, Dublin	J. Robinson	Capt. Henry	
	James F. Donevan Esq. M.D.	19 Gardiner Place, Dublin	J. Robinson	Capt. Henry	
	James Claridge Esq.	28 Marlborough Street, Dublin	J. Robinson	Capt. Henry	
	R. Ball Esq. L.L.D.	Trinity College, Dublin	Capt. Henry	S. Bewley	Astronomer
	Jasper Kelly Esq.	Herald's Office, Tuam, Co. Galway	J. J. Coghill	Capt. Henry	
	William Hodges Esq.	Bank of Ireland, College Green, Dublin	T. Grubb	J.J. Coghill	
	William Wilkinson Esq.	4 Barlow Terrace, Dublin	S. Bewley	J. J. Coghill	
	John Shaw Smith Esq.	Fairy Hill, Blackrock, Co. Dublin	J. Robinson	M. Stapleton	Gentleman

Date joining	Name	Address	Proposer	Seconder	Occupation
29/11/1854	Captain Lyon	Military Provost, Arbour Hill, Dublin	J. J. Coghill	J. Robinson	
	James Kelly Esq.	45 Upper Gloucester Street, Dublin	J. Robinson	M. Stapleton	
	Stewart Black Esq	20 Gardiner Place, Dublin	T. Fenton	J. J. Coghill	
	Bernard Mulrennen Esq	Great Brunswick Street, Dublin	T. Fenton	J.J. Coghill	Painter
	A. McGwire-Gyles Esq.	Coolnagoor, Dungarvan, Co. Waterford	W. Allen	S. Bewley	Gentleman
	J. B. Barnett Esq.	40 Gardiner Street Lower, Dublin	W. Allen	S. Bewley	
	Frederick Robert Smith. L.L.D.	7 Grantham Street, Dublin	J. Robinson	F. Saunders	
	Richard Pring Esq.	Medical Hall, Cornmarket, Belfast	O. Fitzgerald	Capt. Henry	Apothecary
	? Fraser Esq.	Hyde Park, Borristown	J. J. Coghill	S. Bewley	Gentleman
	James Clarke Esq.	Birch Lodge, (illegible)	J. Robinson	J. Rathbone	
	S. Y(e)ates Esq	1 Grafton Street, Dublin			Optician
	Thomas Shaw Esq.	Kingsbridge Station, G.S.W.R.	J. Robinson	J. J. Coghill	
	Rev. Ogle Moore	Blessington, Co. Wicklow	J. Robinson	J. J. Coghill	
	William Brocas Esq.	120 Baggot Street, Dublin	J. Robinson	J. J. Coghill	Painter
	Henry T. Vickers Esq.	8A Lower Leeson Street, Dublin	J. Robinson	J. J. Coghill	Barrister
	Edward Barton Esq.	Kildare Street Club, Dublin	J. J. Coghill	J. Robinson	Gentleman
	R. Bruce Armstrong Esq.	31 Eccles Street, Dublin	J. J. Coghill	J. Robinson	
	William Telford Esq.	109 St. Stephen's Green, Dublin	J. Robinson	W. Allen	
	James Mallery Esq.	40 Upper Sackville Street, Dublin	J. Robinson	S. Bewley	
	Samuel Nugent Esq.	29 Rutland Street Upper, Dublin	H. Stapleton	J. Robinson	
	Captain Edward King Tenison	Kilronan Castle, Roscommon	J. J. Coghill	O. Fitzgerald	Gentleman
	James H. Aylmer Esq.	Walworth Castle Darlington	J. J. Coghill	O. Fitzgerald	Gentleman
	J. C. F. Kenny Esq.	Kilclogher, Athenry, Co. Galway	H. Spier	S. Bewley	Gentleman
	John Scouler Esq. M.D.	Kimmage Hse, Roundtown, Co. Dublin	R.D.S.	R.D.S.	Prof. Mineralogy
	Robert D. Lyons Esq. M.B.	Upper Merrion street, Dublin	R.D.S.	R.D.S.	
	Edward Lees Esq.	2 Sussex Place, Kingstown, Co. Dublin	W. Allen	S. Bewley	
	Edward Pring Esq.	Bank of Ireland, Westmoreland St.	W. Allen	S. BewlS. Bewley	
	Joseph Goff Esq.	Kildare Street Club, Dublin	J. J. Coghill	E. Barton	
	William Allen Esq (junior ?)	5 Little Ship Street, Dublin	W. Allen	S. Bewley	
	John W. Grief Esq.	Upper Sackville street, Dublin	J. Robinson	J.J. Coghill	
	Capt. Inglis 11th Hussars	United Services Club, Dublin	J. Robinson	Capt. Henry	
	Edward Roper Esq.	8 Upper Gloucester Street, Dublin	J. Robinson	M. Stapleton	
	Prof. Rev. J. W. McGanley	66 Leinster Road, Rathmines, Dublin	M.Stapleton	T. Fenton	
	Hon. Yelverton	Army and Navy Club, Dublin	J. J. Coghill	J. Robinson	
	James Pim Esq.	13 Upper Merrion Street, Dublin	J. Robinson	Dr. Lover	
	James Shackleton Esq.	Dundalk	Capt. Henry		Declined
	James Whitty Esq. L. L. D.	15 Henrietta Street, Dublin	Dr. Lover	J. J. Coghill	
1856 here	Dennis Packenham Beresford	Avisford, Arundel	J. Robinson	T. Grubb	Gentleman
	Captain Hartley	United Services Club, Dublin	J. Robinson	J. J. Coghill	Soldier
	Charles William Hamilton Esq.	40 Lower Dominick Street, Dublin	J. Robinson	T. Grubb	
	George Mansfield Esq.	90 Grafton street, Dublin	W. Allen	J. J. Coghill	Photographer
	Rev. James Dopping	Stone Hall, Multifarnham	J. Robinson	J. J. Coghill	
	John Bayley Esq.	30 Molesworth Street, Dublin	J. Robinson	J. J. Coghill	
	T. R. Fetherston Haugh Esq.	18 North Great George's Street, Dublin	J. Robinson	W. C. Kyle	
	Frederick Holland Mares Esq.	81 Grafton street, Dublin	J. Robinson	H. T. Vickers	Photographer
	T. M. Brownrigg Esq.	9 Besborough Terr., Phoenix Pk., Dublin	J. J. Coghill	W. C. Kyle	R. I. C.
	John Barrington Esq.	202 Great Britain Street, Dublin	Transferred in. .respect of . . former..sub. (?)		
	William LeFanu Esq.	7 Fitzwilliam Square, Dublin		,,	,,
	Luke McDonnell Esq.	4 Merrion Square East, Dublin	H. T. Vickers	T. Grubb	
	Professor Leone Glukman	28 Upper Sackville Street, Dublin	T. Grubb	Dr. Aldridge	Photographer
	Captain Barlow A.D.C.	United Services Club, Dublin			Soldier
	C. J. Thomas Esq.	Ballybrack, Co. Dublin	T. Grubb (HS)	Dr. Aldridge	
	Rev. W. H. Kennedy	St. Doulough's, Nth. Co. Dublin			
	Thomas Hutton Esq.	115 Summerhill, Dublin	T. Grubb (HS)	Dr. Aldridge	
28/11/1856	Arthur Barlow Junior Esq.	4 North Great George's Street, Dublin			
	William Corrigan Esq	4 Merrion square, Dublin			Solicitor
	Rev. William A. Willock	Clunish(?) Rectory, Enniskillen.			
	Countess of Caledon	Caledon House, Caledon, Co. Fermanagh			Noblewoman
	Countess of Rosse	Castle, Parsonstown (Birr), Co. Offaly			Noblewoman
	Miss O'Shaughnessy	20 Corn Market, Dublin			
11/2/1857	Strangman Davis-Goff Esq.	Horetown Hse, New Ross, Co. Wexford	J. Robinson	A. Barlow.	Gentleman
13/7/1858	William Barker Esq.	115 Grafton Street, Dublin	W. Allen	J.J. Coghill	
	Humphrey Haines Esq.	Cork City	T. Brownrigg	S. Bewley	Apothecary
	?Jackson Esq.		T. Brownrigg	S. Bewley	
	? Edmunds Esq.		T. Brownrigg	S. Bewley	
24/1/1859	Hugh Early Esq.	Croncrue(?), Wicklow	J. J. Coghill	W. Allen	
28/1/1859	James Wilson Esq.	Lark Hill, Rathmines, Dublin	H. T. Vickers	J.J. Coghill	
	John Nobber Esq.	38 Upper Mount Street, Dublin	J. J. Coghill	H. T. Vickers	
23/2/1859	Robert Staples Esq.	Dunmore, Durrow	W. Allen	T. Grubb	
	William Andrews Esq.	The Hill, Monkstown, Co. Dublin	G. Saunders	W. Allen	Photographer

Information extracted from the manuscript list of members of the Dublin Photographic Society in the National Archives, Dublin (M.1115)

An Index of Irish Photographers of the Nineteenth Century

ABBREVIATIONS

The figures 50, 60, 70 etc. after each name indicates decade of the nineteenth century when that particular photographer was active, i.e. 40 = 1840–49, 50 = 1850–59 etc. Note 00 = 1900–10.

The following letters indicate the main source of reference:
DPS: Dublin Photographic Society; PSI: Photographic Society of Ireland; C: Commercial (cdv., cabinets, etc.); APA: Amateur Photographic Association; A: Independent Amateur.

A.M. LLD., Ex STCD (?); Dublin, 60
ABERNATHY; Belfast, 70,80,/C
ABERDEEN Lady, 80,90,00,/A
ACADEMY STUDIO; Belfast, 70, 80, /C
ADOLPHE E; Dublin, 60, 70, 80, /C
AHLBORN Julius; 60,/C
ALBERT STUDIO; Fermoy, 80/C
ALBON L; Dublin,70, /C
ALCORN J J; Kingstown,80, 90,/A
ALDRIDGE (?) MD, 50, /DPS
ALLEN C E; Dublin, 80, 90, /C
ALLEN Mark & Co.; Dublin, 70,80,/C
ALLEN William ; Dublin, 50, /DPS
ALLEN W N; Dublin, 00, 10,/PSI
ALLISON & VIENNA STUDIOS; Belfast,90
AMERICAN PHOTO GALLERY; Dublin, 70/C
ANDERSON Samuel ; Dublin, 80./A?
ANDREW J J; Belfast, 90, 00./A
ANDREWS William; Dublin, 50, 60, 70, /C
ANNESLEY, Hugh Earl of ; 50, 60, /A
ARMAGH PORTRAIT CO.; Armagh, 70,/C
ARMSTRONG (?); Dublin, 90, /A
ARMSTRONG R; Dublin, 80, /C
ARMSTRONG R B ; Dublin, 50, /DPS
ARMSTRONG Thomas; Dublin, 90, /A
ATKINS Ringrose ; Cork. 1890-00./A
ATKINS William R; Cork. 1890-00./A
ATKINSON T ; Dublin, 90, /C
ATTHILL Miss A ; Monkstown, 00, /PSI
AYLMER J H ; Dublin, 50, 60, /DPS, C
AYTON Alex.; Derry, 60, 70, /C

BAGOT C E ; Dublin, 60, /C
BAILEY Rev. W R ; Monaghan, 60, /A
BAKER L ; Dublin, 90, /A
BAKER Ronald ; Dublin, 90, /A
BAKER Samuel ; Dublin, 90, /A
BALFE N ; Dublin, 50, /DPS

BALL R ; 50, /DPS
BARKER John ; Dublin, 50, / DPS
BAPTY Walter ; Dublin, 90,/A
BARKER Thomas; Cork, 00,/C (press)
BARKER W C ; Dublin, 50, /DPS
BARLOW Capt. Arthur ; Dublin, 50, /DPS
BARNETT J B ; Dublin, 50, /DPS
BALDWIN C ; Belfast, 50, 60, /C
BANTRY Earl of ; Bantry, 60/APA
BARRETT B ; Kingstown, 80, 90, /A
BARRET & STANLEY; 40, 50,/C
BARRINGTON J ; Dublin, 50, /DPS
BARRINGTON A ; Bray, 80, /A,C
BARTON Edward ; Dublin, 50, /DPS
BASSETT George Henry; Louth, 80./A
BAYLEY Prof. John ; Dublin, 50, /DPS
BEATTY Francis Stewart ;
   Belfast/Dublin, 40 to 80, /C
BEAUFORT & BRUCE ; Dublin, 60, /C
BEAUFORT R ; Dublin, 50, /C
BELCHER J; Limerick, 70?/A,C
BELL H ; Waterford, 90, /C
BELL T F; Belfast, 90, 00./A
BENNETT J ; Cork, 90, 00 /A
BENSON Robert ; Dublin, 00, /PSI
BERLIN STUDIO ; Cork, 70, 80, /C
BERNARD Thomas ; Limerick, 80, / C
BEWLEY Samuel ; Dublin, 50, / DPS
BEWLEY Thomas ; Dublin, 80, / PSI
BEWLEY W; Dublin, 90,00/A
BINKA (?); Dublin, 90, 00/A
BIRNEY Edward ; Belfast, 50, 60, /C
BIRRELL Bros. ; Belfast, 50, 60, /C
BLAKENEY R H ; Dalkey, 90,/PSI
BLAKE-FORSTER; Galway, 60, 80/A
BLUME Professor; Dublin/Itinerant, 50,60,/C
BLACK S ; Dublin, 50, /DPS
BLAIN Hugh ; Belfast, 50, 60, /C

BLIGH F A , RA ; Co. Meath, 90, /A
BLUNT & WYSE ; Dublin, 50, 60, /C
BOBS ; Dublin, 90, /C
BOND James ; Derry, 70, /C
BOSANQUET Madam ; Cork, 60, 70, /C
BRADDELL E ; Belfast, 90, 00 /A
BRADSHAW J ; Cork, 90, 00 /A
BRADY F ; Dublin, 50, /DPS
BRADY Miss P. J. ; Dublin, 00, /PSI
BRANFIELD J A C ; (?), 80, /A
BRINDLEY Louis ; Dublin, 00, /PSI
BROWN BROS. ; Belfast, 70, /C
BROWN John; Belfast, 90, 00/A
BROWNE Charles R; Mayo, 90/A?
BROWNE Henry D ;
   Kingstown, 60, 70, 80, /C
BROWNE Capt. L M ; 00, /PSI
BROWNE Robert ; Dublin, 00, /PSI
BROWNING Francis ; Dublin, 00, /PSI
BROWNRIGG T M ; Dublin, 50, /DPS
BURKE J H ; Dublin, 60, 70, 80, 90,/C
BURTON Richard ; Dublin, 60, 70, /C
BUTLER Miss Julian; Dublin, 80, /A
BYRNE John & Son ; Dublin, 50, 60, /C
BYRNE Thomas ; Dublin, 50, /A

CADDELL Col.; Dublin, 90, /PSI
CAIRNS H ; Bray, 70, /A
CALEDON Countess; Armagh, 50, /DPS
CALLAGHAN ; Cork, 70, /C
CANNON J ; Dublin, 60, 70, /C
 Alfred ; Roscrea, 50, /A
CAREW Lord and Lady;
   Enniscorthy, 60, /APA
CAROLIN Miss ; Dublin, 90, /PSI
CARSON James ; Kingstown, 90, /PSI
CARROLL H F ; Dublin, 00, /PSI
CHANCELLOR John ;
   Dublin, 60 to 00,/C

CHAPMAN Miss R ; Dublin, 00, /PSI
CHARLTON P;Dublin-Newbridge,70,80,/C
CHURCH E T ; Belfast, 60, 70, 80, /C
CHURCH J F ; Kildare, 70, /C
CINNANONT Miss ; Belfast, 50, /C
CITY OF PARIS Photo.Co.; Dublin, 60, /C
CLARIDGE J ; Dublin, 50, DPS
CLARENDON J ; Kingstown, 60 to 90, /C
CLARKE John J ; Castleblayney, 00, / A
CLARKE Lt. Col. J ; Dublin, 50, /DPS
CLARKE T T : Dublin, 90, /PSI
CLEARY Lester ; Dublin, 50, /DPS
COATES S B ; Belfast, 90, 00/A
COCHRANE (?); Dublin, 90, 00/A
COGHILL Sir J J ;
        Dublin/Cork, 50, 60, /DPS, APA
COGHILL A J ; Dublin, 90, /PSI
COLLET M ; Dublin, 70, /C
COLGAN N ; Dublin, 90, /PSI
COLLINS P ;
        Clonmel/Kilkee/Tralee, 60,70,/C
COOK (?) ; Cork, 60, /C
COOKE E A ; Dublin, 00, /PSI
COOKE & COOKE; Roscrea-Thurles, 70/C
COOPER W F ; Dublin, 00, /PSI
CONAN Alex.; Dalkey, 90, /PSI
CONSIDINE P ; Dublin, 00, /PSI
CONNOLY W P ; Kingstown, 90, /PSI
CONYERS Miss A ; Dublin, 00, /PSI
CONYNGHAM W (Baron Plunkett)
        Bray, 80,/A
COPELAND William ; Belfast, 50, /C
CORNWALL E M ;
        Dublin, 60,70,80, /C
CORRIGAN William; Dublin, 50, /DPS
COSGRAVE E McD; Dublin, 90, 00/A
COTTER-KYLE William;
        Dublin, 50, /DPS
COWLEY F ; Dublin, 00, /PSI
CRACE John Gregory; (?), 50, / A
CRANE & CO.; Enniscorthy, 70, /C
CRANFIELD Thomas; Dublin, 50–90, /C
CROFTON-DILLON Augusta;
        Galway,60-00/A
CROFTON W E C ; Dublin, 00, /PSI
CROKER G D ; Waterford, 80, /C
CROWDER G F ; Enniskillen, 70, /C
CURRAN Miss A ; Dublin, 00, /PSI
CURRAN C P; Dublin, 00,/A
CURREY F E.; Waterford, 50–90,/APA PSI
CURTIS BROS.; Dublin, 90, /C

DALGLEISH William ;
        Dublin, 50, /DPS
DALY J ; Tralee, 70, /C
D'ARCY F P ; Dublin, 90, /C
DAVENPORT C ; Dublin, 50, /DPS
DAVIDSON L; Dublin, 90,00/A
DAVIS Edward ; Dublin, 90, /PSI
DAVIS & CO.; Clonmel, 60, 70, 80, /C

DAVIS-GOFF Strangman; New Ross 50,/DPS
DAVY E W ; Dublin, 50, /DPS
DAY J ; Cork, 90, /PSI
DePINNA Prof. F; Dublin, 90, /C
DEWER Norman ; Dublin, 10, /C
DILLON Augusta; Co. Galway, 60,70,/A
DILLON Hon. Luke; Co. Galway, 60, 70,/A
DOME L ; Dublin, 90, /C
DOOLIN W G ; Dublin, 90, /PSI
DOPPING Rev. J ; Multifarnham, 50, /DPS
DOUGLAS-LYSAGHT Maj J; Cork, 90, /A
DOWLING J J ; Co. Dublin, 90, /PSI
DOWLING W P ; Dublin, 70, /C
DOYLE & CO.; Dublin, 80, /C
DRAPER Harry; Dublin, 50, /DPS
DRAPER H C ; Dublin, 90, /PSI
DRIMMIE A H ; Dublin, 90, /PSI
DROGHEDA Marq. of (H. Moore);
        Co. Louth, 60,/APA
DUBLIN PHOTO COPYING CO.;
        Dublin, 60,/C
DRURY George ; Dublin, 90, /PSI
DUBLIN PHOTO & PHILOSOPH. INST;
        Dublin,60,/C
DUBREUIL Doussin ; Dublin, 40, / C
DUNBAR C R ; Dublin, 00, /PSI
DUNCAN J F ; Dublin, 50, /DPS
DUNCAN R ; Armagh, 60, /C
DUNLO Visc. (Rich. Somerset);
        Ballinasloe, 60, /APA
DUNNING H ; Wicklow, 70, /C
DURHAM (?) ; Dublin, 60, /C
DUTHIE Andrew ; Glasgow, 60, /Publisher
DYER Edward ; Dublin, 50, /DPS

EASON F T ; Dublin, 90, /PSI
EATON M & S ; Dublin, 80, /C
EDGEWORTH Lt.Col; Longford,80,90/A
EDGEWORTH Michael Packenham;
        Edgeworthstown, 40, 50, /A
EDWARDS Capt.; Dublin, 80, /A
EDWARDS & CO.; Dublin, 80, /C
EDWARDS & SIMONTON;
        Dublin,70, 80, /C
EDWARDS & CO.; Dublin, 80, /C
EGAN C H ; Dublin, 00, /PSI
EGLISTON T ; Limerick, 80, /C
ELRINGTON T ; Dublin, 50, /C
EMERY H ; Dublin, 90, /PSI
ENGLAND W; G.B.,(L.P.S.Co.) 50, 60,/C
EVANS R J ; Belfast, 90, 00/A
ERWINE T ; Ballymena, 70, /C
EVANS T ; Cork, 60, /C

FARLEY C T ; Drogheda, 60, 70, /C
FENTON T A ; Dublin, 50, /DPS
FENTON Capt.; Curragh, 50, 60, /A
FERRIES W R ; Belfast, 50, /C
FETHERSTON-HAUGH S R;
        Dublin, 50, /DPS
FINNING Henry ; Dublin, 70, 80, /C

FITZGERALD Ld. Otho; Dublin, 50, /DPS
FITZHERBERT R B; Co. Meath, 50, 60,/A
FLYMING Miss R B ; Dublin, 60, /A
FLUERY-MOONEY W ; Dublin, 60, /C
FORBES Robert; Dublin, 90, 00, /C
FOLEY R; 90, 00/A
FORSTER W C; Dublin, 60, /C
FORSTER & HASKOLL; Dublin, 60,70/C
FORSTER & SCOTT ; Dublin, 60, /C
FRASER (?); Borristown, 50, /DPS
FRANKLIN Denham; Cork, 90-00./A
FRENCH Robert (Lawrence) ; 80, /C
FRITH Francis & Co.; G.B., 90,/C

GALBRAITH J & CO.
        Dundalk/Belfast, 70, /C
GARRETT Dr. ; Kingstown, 90, 00, /A
GALWAY J ; Clones, 70, /C
GANLEY Edward G ; Dublin, 70, /C
GEARY H. St, George; Dublin, 50, /C
GEARY BROS.; Dublin/
        Kilkenny, 50, 60, 70, /C
GEDDIS A M ; Kingstown, 90, /A
GEOGHEGAN T F ; Dublin, 90,00, /C
GEOWN M ; Lisburn, 80, /C
GERRARD J ; Dublin, 90, /PSI
GIBBON E P ; Dublin, 50, /DPS
GIBBON J G ; Dublin, 90, /PSI
GIBSON John ; Belfast, 50, 60, /C
GILLIES J M ; Dublin, 90, /PSI
GLASS I ; Derry, 70, /C
GLEN Henry G ;
        Belfast/Lurgan, 70, 80, /C
GLEN John ; Belfast, 80, /C
GLINDON T ; Dublin, 60, 70, /C
GLOVER M ; Dublin, 80, 90, 00, /C
GLUKMAN Prof. Leone ;
        Dublin, 40, 50, 60, /C
GLYDE Samuel ; Belfast, 50, /C
GODDARD (?); Dublin, 60, /C
GOFF James ; Dublin, 50, /DPS
GOODWILLIE Henry; Dublin,90,00,/PSI
GOUGH John ; Dublin, 60, 70, /C
GORDON A E ; Dublin, 90, /PSI
GRAFTON PHOTO STUDIO;
        Dublin, 80, /C
GRAHAM G H ; Cookstown, 60, /C
GRAINGER (?); Dublin, 90, 00/A
GRAY William; Belfast, 90,00/A
GREAVES Miss ; Dublin, 50, /DPS
GRIEFF J ; Dublin, 50, /DPS
GRIEFFELD F ; Dublin, 80, 90, /C
GROMANN E ; Dublin, 90, /C
GROSVENOR GALLERY;
        Dublin,60,70,/C
GRUBB Sir Howard; Dublin,80,90/PSI
GRUBB Miss M ; Dublin, 50, /DPS
GRUBB Thomas ; Dublin, 40, 50, /DPS
GUBBINS Miss A R ; Cork, 00, /PSI
GUERIN M ; Dublin, 90, /PSI

GUY Francis & Co;
    Cork/Limerick, 70, 80, 90, 00, /C
HAFFIELD Thomas; Kingstown, 60-00/A
HAINES Humphrey; Cork, 50, 60/DPS
HALLINAN P; Cork, 90, 00/A
HAMILL & HUGHES ; Belfast, 50, 60, /C
HAMILTON C W ; Dublin, 50, /DPS
HAMILTON Ian Trant; Dublin, 90, /PSI
HAMILTON James L; Belfast, 90,00/A
HANNA Mr. Justice ; Dublin, 10, /PSI
HARDING Edward J; Cork, 40, 50, 60,/C
HARGRAVE B A; Kingstown, 90, /PSI
HARGRAVE J H; Dublin, 90, 00./A
HARRINGTON W; Cork, 90, 00/A
HARRISON S J ; Dublin, 00, /PSI
HARTLEY Captain ; Dublin, 50, /DPS
HASKOLL Theodore F ; Dublin, 60,/ C
HASTING BROS; Dublin,70, 80, 90,/C
HASTINGS John ; Dublin, 70, 80, / C
HAUGHTON C C ; Dublin, 90, / PSI
HAUGHTON W S ; Dublin, 00, /PSI
HAWARDEN Lady Clementina ;
    Cashel, 50, /APA
HAWKINS C ; Dublin, 50, /DPS
HAYDEN Rev. J A ; Limerick, 90, /A
HAYES J ; Ennis, 70, /C
HAYES Michaelangelo; Dublin, 50,/DPS
HEDLEY M ; Kingstown, 90, /A
HELY Mrs C W ; Dublin, 00, /PSI
HEMBRY ; Belfast, 90, /C
HEMPHILL William Despard;
    Clonmel, 50 to 90, /APA
HENRY G ; Connemara, 90, /PSI
HENRY Capt. R J ; Dublin, 50, /DPS
HEWETT A W ; Dublin, 00, /PSI
HEWITT James ; Dublin, 00, /PSI
HIGGINS James ; Dublin, 70, /C
HOBAN J T ; Athlone, 80, /C
HODGES W ; Dublin, 50, /DPS
HOGAN A M ; Dublin, 90, / A
HOLBORN H ; Clonmel, 80, /C
HOLDEN J D ; Dublin, 90, /PSI
HOLLAND Atkinson; Dublin, 50,/ DPS
HOLLWEY P C ; Dublin, 90, /PSI
HONEY W G ; Cork, 70, 80, 90, /C
HUDSON John ; Killarney, 70, /C
HOPKINS W ; Bray, 90, /PSI
HUGHES R J ; Dublin, 90, /C
HUMPHREY Alex.; Dublin, 00, /PSI
HUTTON T ; Dublin, 50, /DPS
HUTTON W M ; Dublin, 90 /PSI
HUNTER H ; Cork, 60, /C
HUNTER John S ; Bandon, 60, /C
HUNTER Rev.; Delgany, 50, /DPS
HUNTER & CO ;
    Armagh/Monaghan, 90, /C
HURLEY Sean ; Dublin, 70, /C
HUTCHINSON James ; Dublin, 70, /C
HUTCHINSON & KEEGAN ;
    Dublin, 60, /C

HUTCHINSON W ; Roscrea, 70, /C

INGLIS Capt.; Dublin, 50, /DPS
INGLIS R M ; Dublin, 90, /PSI
INGOLDSBY J F ; Dublin, 00, /PSI
IVATTS E B ; Dublin, 90, /PSI

JACOBS Harold ; Greystones, 00, / PSI
JACOLETTE M ; Dublin, 50, /C
JAMES C H ; Dublin, 50, /DPS
JAMESON Col. J R;
    Blackrock, 90, /PSI
JENNINGS Payne John;
    Dublin/Belfast, 60,70,/C
JESSOP S ; Dublin, 60, 70, /C
JOLY Prof. John ; Dublin, 90, 00, /PSI
JOSCELYN Vicess; Dundalk, 60, /APA
JOSEPH A ; Dublin, 50, /C
JULYAN & AHLFRED ; Dublin, 60, /C
KANE Dr. ; Dublin, 40, /?
KEANE & SONS ; Kells/Navan, 70, /C
KEATINGE Reginald ; Dublin, 00, /PSI
KELLY Jasper ; Tuam, 50, /DPS
KELLY (?) ; Dublin, 50, /DPS
KELSALL Joseph ; Dublin, 90, /C
KENNAN W R ; Dublin, 90, /C
KENNEDY John ; Belfast, 50, 60, /C
KENNEDY W H ; Dublin, 50, /C
KENNY J C F ; Athenry, 50, /DPS
KEOGH J M ; Dublin, 90, /PSI
KEOGH M F ; Dublin, 00, /PSI
KEOGH BROS.; Dublin, 90, 00, /C
KERR Hugh ; Derry, 60, /C
KIERNAN W R ; Dublin, 90, /C
KILGANNON T ; Sligo, 70, /C
KILPATRICK ; Belfast, 70, 80, /C
KILPATRICK W ; Dublin, 60, /C
KINGSTOWN STUDIO; Kingstown,70,/C
KIRK Joseph ; Dublin, 50, /DPS
KNOX Rev. Thomas; Toomevara, 40,/ A
KNOWLES James ; Kingstown, 90, /C
KWIATKOWSKI Harry;
    Dundalk, 00?/C
LAFAYETTE Jacques ;
    Dublin etc. 80, 90, 00, /C
LAIDLAW G ; Strabane, 70, 80, /C
LANE Denny; Cork, 90, 00/A
LANGFORD Capt.; Kingstown, 90, /A
LAROCHE & WILLIAMS; Dublin, 80, /C
LATIMER F A; Dublin, 90, 00,/A
LAUDER E&J ; Dublin, 80, 90, /C
LAUDER J ; Dublin, 80, /C
LAUDER BROTHERS;
    Dublin, 50, 60, 70, 80, 90, 00, /C
LAWLESS Rev. C ; Blackrock, 00, /PSI
LAWLESS Hon.Frederick;
    Blackrock, 80, 90,00,/PSI
LAWRENCE Arthur ; Dublin, 90, /PSI
LAWRENCE John Fortune ;
    Dublin, 60, 70, /C

LAWRENCE M ; Cavan, 60, /C
LAWRENCE William Mervyn;
    Dublin, 60 to 00, /C
LEE R ; Portrush, 80, /C
LEES Edward ; Kingstown, 50, /DPS
LeFANU William ; Dublin, 50, /DPS
LENNON L W ; Roscommon, 70, /C
LENNON M ; Dublin, 70, /C
LEONARD D H ; Dublin, 00, /PSI
LESAGE Adolph; Dublin, 50, 60, 70, /C
LESLIE James; Belfast, 90, 00/A
LEVINGSTONE R R ; Dublin, 90, /PSI
LEWES J ; Dublin, 70, /C
LEWIS J ; Dublin, 60, 70, /C
LEWIS Milford ; Dublin, 80, /C
LEWIS-DAVIS D ; Itinerant, 40, 50, /C
LITTLE Harold ; Dublin, 00, /PSI
LONDON METRO.PHOTO. CO.;
    Dublin, 70, /C
LONDON PHOTO. GALLERY;
    Dublin, 70,/C
LONDON STEREOSCOPIC CO;
    G.B.; 50, 60,/C
LONGFIELD C M ; Dublin, 90, /PSI
LOVER W ; Dublin, 50, /DPS
LOXTON A S G ; Dublin, 00, /PSI
LUND H; Cork, 90, 00/A
LYON Capt.; Dublin, 50, /DPS
LYONS R D ; Dublin, 50, /DPS
LYNCH F ; Dublin, 90, /PSI
LYSAGHT J ; Douglas ; Cork, 90, /C

McBRIDE & CO.; Lisburn, 90, /C
McCABE S ; Wexford, 60, /PSI
McCANN Robert; Belfast, 90, 00/A
McCLEERY J ; Belfast, 80, /C
McCONNELL J M ;Cork, 60, /C
McCREA W ; Dublin, 90, /C
McCURDY J ; Dublin, 50, /DPS
McDERMOTT J ; Cork, 70, 80, /C
McDONNELL L ; Dublin, 50, /DPS
McDONNELL BROS.; Dublin, 60, /C
McDOWELL C ; Dublin, 90, /PSI
McFARLAND James ; Dublin, 80, /C
McGANLEY J W ; Dublin, 50, /DPS
McGEE Robert; Derry/Itinerant, 40, /C
McGWIRE-GULES (?) ;
    Dungannon, 50, /DPS
McKAY T ; Banbridge/Newry, 70, /C
McKEE W C ; Dublin, 80, /C
McMAHON J ; Dublin, 50, /DPS
McMILLAN E & J ; Belfast, 50, 60, /C
MACNEE-OLIVER J ; Athlone, 00, /C
M.J.B. (?) ; Dublin, 40, /A
MACK John ; Belfast/Coleraine, 60, /C
MACK W ; Coleraine, 60, /C
MAHONY Mrs.; Dalkey, 00, /PSI
MAGILL J ; Belfast, 60, 70, 80, /C
MAGUIRE R F ; Dublin, 90, /PSI
MALLERY J ; Dublin, 50, /DPS

MANNING (?) ; Ballinasloe, 60, /C

MANSFIELD George ;
    Dublin/Naas, 50 to 00, /C, PSI

MANSFIELD A B ; Dublin, 90, /PSI

MARCUS WARD & CO;
    Belfast, 60, 70, 80, /C

MARES Frederick H ;
    Dublin, 50, 60, 70, 80, /C, DPS

MARTIN Francis ; Dublin, 50, /C

MASON Thomas H ;
    Dublin, 90, 00, /PSI, C

MASSEY A G ; Belfast, 80, /C

MASSEY H ; Portrush, 70, /C

MATTHEWS C E ; Dublin, 90, / PSI

MATTHEWS C H ; Dublin, 90, / PSI

MAUNSELL George; Dublin, 50, /DPS

MAVIUS & VIVASH ; Belfast, 80, /C

MAXWELL Thomas ; Dublin, 00, / PSI

MEYER Rudolph ; Belfast, 60, 70, /C

MAYNE Alex ; Belfast, 50, / C

MAYNE Thomas;
    Dublin, 50 to 90,/ DPS, C

MEDCALF H B ;
    New Ross/Enniscorthy, 70, / C

MERCER Miss Blanche; Dublin, 00,/ PSI

MERCER Thomas ; Dublin, 70, 80, / C

MIDDLETON D ; Dublin, 90, / PSI

MILLARD & ROBINSON ;
    Dublin, 60, 70, / C

MILLARD R ; Waterford, 70, / C

MILLARD Thomas, Dublin, 70, / C

MILLER F ; Dublin, 90, / PSI

MILLER R C ; Dublin, 90, / PSI

MILLS A E ; Dublin, 90, / PSI

MILLS W C ; Dublin, 80, / C

MITCHELL George; Blackrock, 00,/ PSI

MITOFSKY (?) ; Dublin, 90, / C

MONNEY W H ; Dublin, 60, / C

MOORE H F S (Marq. Drogheda);
    Drogheda, 60, /APA

MOORE Rev. Ogle; Wicklow, 50,/ DPS

MOORE W G ; Dublin, 80, / C

MORGANTI M ; Dublin, 60, / C

MULRENNEN B ; Dublin, 50, / DPS

MULVANY George ; Dublin, 50, / DPS

MULVANY J S ; Dublin, 50, / DPS

MUNSTER PHOTO GALLERY;
    Limerick, 70/C

MURIEL Mrs. F M ; Dublin, 00, / PSI

MURPHY N D ; Kingstown, 90, / PSI

NEALE H ; Dublin, 60, / C

NEILL G W ; Drogheda, 80, / C

NEILSON Auguste ; 80, / C

NELSON Alfred ; Dublin, 50, / DPS

NELSON Horatio ; 40, 50, / C

NELSON & MARSHALL ;
    Dublin, 50, 60, 70, 80, / C

NEWCOMBE R ; Dublin, 60, / C

NEWTON D ;Dublin, 60, / C

NEWTON P J ; Carlow, 60, / A

NIXON W C ; Dublin, 70, / A

NOLAN J B ; Dublin, 90, / PSI

NOLAN Stephen ; Carlow, 00, / PSI

NORTH Thomas ; Dublin, 60, / C

NUGENT BROS.; Dublin, 60, / C

NUGENT S ; Dublin, 50, / DPS

O'CONNOR P T ; Clonmel, 70, / C

O'CONNOR T ; Limerick, 70, / C

O'CONNOR T J ; Dublin, 90, / PSI

OGLE T ; Grange, 60, 70, / C

O'GRADY S ; Waterford, 60, 70, / C

O'HALLORAN P J; Limerick. (?)

ORDE (?) ; Belfast, 80, / C

O'REILLY P ; Dublin, 90, / PSI

ORR A ; Derry, 70, / C

ORR F H ; Kingstown, 90, / C

ORR R D ; Dublin, 00, / PSI

O'SHAUGHNESSY Miss ;
    Dublin, 50, / DPS

O'SHEA Henry ; Limerick, 60, / C

O'TOOLE Fr. Hugh; Dublin, 00/A

OVANS Thomas ; Cork, 70, / C

PACKENHAM-BERESFORD D W ;
    Dublin, 50, / DPS

PARKES Alfred ; Dublin ; 90, / PSI

PARKES & GEDGE ; Belfast, 70, / C

PEARSON Charles W ;
    Kingstown, 00, / PSI

PENDER J ; Waterford, 60, / C

PENNY J ; Dublin, Dublin, 90, / PSI

PERCIVAL J; Cork, 00/A

PERRY Mrs. F ; Dublin, 00, / PSI

PETITT Rev. D ; Dublin, 90, / PSI

PHILLIPS I ; Belfast, 80, / C

PHILLIPS John ; Belfast, 70, 80, / C

PHOTOGRAPHIC STUDIO;
    Dublin, 60, / C

PHOTO NOVELTY CO; Dublin, 60, /C

PHOTO TRANSFER CO; Dublin, 60,/ C

PICCIONE J A ; Belfast, 60, 70, / C

PIGGOT Richard ; Dublin, 70, / C

PIKE Ebeniser ; Dublin, 50, / DPS

PIM John E; Belfast, 90, 00/A

PIM J ; Dublin, 50, / DPS

PIM Greenwood ; Co. Dublin, 90, / PSI

PINKNEY Joseph H; Dublin, 40, 50, /C

PLIMMER T ; Belfast, 60, 70, 80, / C

PLUNKETT W C ; Dublin, 50, / DPS

PLUNKETT Baron (?); Bray, 80, 90,/ A

POLLOCK Hugh ; Dublin, 00, / PSI

POLLOCK William; Belfast, 90, 00/A

POOLE A H; Waterford, 80,/ C

PORTE George; Dublin, 50, / DPS

POULTON & Son; G.B.(Eason) 00/C

POWELL E J ; Dundalk, 90, /C

POWELL F ; Dublin, 90, / PSI

PRIDEAUX F G ; Dublin, 00, / PSI

PRING Edward ; Dublin, 50, / DPS

PRING & WEBB ; Dublin, 60, /C

PROUDMAN W ; Mountmellick, 90, /C

QUEEN'S PHOTO ART STUDIO;
    Belfast, 90, / C

QUINN W H ; Belfast, 60, / C

RAMBAUT W J R ; Dublin, 90, / PSI

RATHBORNE James ;
    Dublin, 50, / DPS

RAWLINS Rev. J ; Cavan, 90, / PSI

REA S S ; Dublin, 00, /PSI

REAKS H W ; Dublin, 90, / PSI

REID BROS.; Belfast, 80, / C

REID (?); Dublin, 90, 00./A

REILLY Thomas H ;
    Dublin/Belfast, 60,/ C

REYNOLDS J Emerson;
    Dublin, 80,90,00, / PSI

RICHARDSON F J ; Dublin, 90, / PSI

RICKY (?); Dublin, 90, 00/A

RIGBY W ; Bray, 80, / A

RITCHIE D ; Belfast, 80, / C

ROBERTS F A; Dublin/Fermoy, 80,/ C

ROBERTSON John; Dublin, 60, 70,/ C

ROBINSON James ;
    Dublin/London,50 to 00,/DPS,C

ROBINSON J V; Dublin, 60 to 90,/PSI, C

ROBINSON J L; Dublin, 90,/ PSI

ROCHE A D ; Cork, 60, 70, / C

ROHU J L R ; Dublin, 80, / C

ROPER Edward ; Kingstown, 50, / DPS

ROSENTHAL L H ; Dublin, 00, / PSI

ROSSE Mary Countess of;
    Birr, 50, 60, / DPS

ROTUNDA GALLERY; Dublin, 40, / C

ROWE M W ; Carlow, 60, / C

ROWLAND John ; Dublin, 00, /PSI

ROYAL PANOPTICON etc.;
    Dublin, 69, /C

RUSSELL Charles ; Belfast, 90, /C

RUSSELL BROS.; (?), 80, /C

RUTHVEN J A C ; Dublin, 90, / PSI

W.H.S.(?) ; Dublin, 50, 60, /A

SAMUEL W B ; Dublin, 70, 80, / C

SANDYS H A ; Dublin, 00, /PSI

SARONY O F X ; Dublin, 60, / C

SAUNDERS Frederick; Dublin, 50, /DPS

SAUNDERS Gilbert; Dublin, 50, 60,/ DPS

SAUVY Adam; Cork/Dublin, 60, 70,/ C

SCHREODER Godfried ;
    Dublin, 60,70, /C

SCHREODER Auguste; Dublin 70,/C

SCOTT Prof. J Alfred;
    Dublin, 80,90,00, / PSI

SCOTT Augustine ; Dublin, 60, / C

SCOTT Charles ; Dublin, 69, /C

SCOTT BROS.; Dublin, 60, /C

SCOTT Walter ; Dublin, 00, / PSI

SCOULER J ; Dublin, 50, / DPS

SCRIVEN George ; Dublin, 00, / PSI

SCULLY Vincent ; Tipperary, 80, 00/A
SEAGRAVE H W ; Dublin, 90, 00, /PSI
SEATON M & S ; Dublin, 60, /C
SEGGONS (?) ; Belfast, 80, / C
SHACKLETON J ; Dundalk, 50, / DPS
SHACKLETON Mrs; Dublin, 80,90,00,/A
SHAPLAND Robert (Ld. Carew);
      Wexford, 60, /APA
SHARP George ; Dublin, 50, / DPS
SHARPE A P ; Dublin, 90, / PSI
SHAW Cecil ; Belfast, 80, / C
SHAW G B; G.B., 90, 00,/A
SHAW Sir Robert; Dublin, 50, 60, /A
SHAW Rose ; Co. Tyrone, 90, 00, /A
SHAW SMITH John ;
      Dublin/Co. Cork, 50, /DPS
SHAW T ; Dublin, 50, /DPS
SHEILS Gregory ; Dublin, 70, 80, / C
SHERIDAN Edward ; Dublin, 00, /PSI
SHERIDAN J P ; Dublin, 50, /DPS
SHERLOCK David ; Dublin, 90, / PSI
SILO Modesto & Sons; Belfast, 50, /C
SIBLEY W ; Dublin, 90, /PSI

SIMMONS R W
      Galway/Athlone,00,/C
SIMONTON James ;
      Dublin, 50, 60, 70, /C
SIMONTON & MILLARD ;
      Dublin, 50, 60, /C
SIMPSON James ; Kingstown, 90, /PSI
SINGLETON G J ; Dublin, 00, / PSi
SLATER Mrs; Cobh, 70, /C
SLATER & MASON ; Cork, 70, 80, / C
SLEATOR A ; Sligo, 70, / C
SLOAN C C ; England(?), 00, /PSI
SMELLIE John ; Dublin, 00, / PSI
SMITH E ; Dublin, 60, / C
SMITH E Webb ; Dublin, 00, /PSI
SMITH F R ; Dublin, 50, / DPSI
SMITH Vincent ; Dublin, 00, /PSI
SMYTH Victor ; Dublin, 90, 00, /PSI, C
SOLOMONS (?) ; Dublin, 70, /C
SOMERSET R (Viscount.Dunlo);
      Ballinasloe,60,/APA
SONE C ; Waterford, 70, / C
SPEAR R ; Dublin, 50, / DPS
SPEIRS H ; Dublin, 50, /DPS
SPILLANE (?); Co Cork, 00/A
STANLEY J & E ; Dublin, 00, / C
STANLEY W & O ; Dublin, 00, /C
STAPLETON W&O; Dublin, 50, /DPS
STARK BROS; Dublin, 70, /C
STAUNTON ?; Cavan, 60, /C
STEELE ? ; Dublin, 50, /DPS
STEELE C W ; Kingstown, 90, /PSI
STELFOX James; Belfast, 90/A
STEPHENS E R ; Dublin, 60, /C

STEPHEN'S GREEN PHOTO. C0.;
      Dublin, 70, /C
STEREO WAREROOMS; Dublin, 60, /C
STEVENS ?; Dublin, 80, /C
STEVENS ? ; Cork, 70, /C
STEWARD J J ; Belfast, 50, /C
STEWART (?); Dublin, 90, 00/A
STIRLING F ; Dublin, 70, /C
STRAIN William; Belfast, 90, 00/A
STRANGEWAYS Leonard;
      Dublin, 90, 00, /PSI
STREET W ; Waterford, 70, /C
STUBBS W C ; Dublin, 90, /PSI
STUTTARD John; Dublin, 00, /PSI
SULLIVAN D; Dublin, 90, /PSI
SURRIDGE F ; Dublin, 60, /C
SUTHERLAND Mrs ;
      Tipperary, 00, /PSI
SWANSON William; Belfast, 90, 00/A
SYNGE J M ; Dublin, 90, /A

TAAFFE J J ; Belfast, 00, /C
TALBOT A ; Belfast, 60, /C
TATE Alexander; Belfast, 90, 00/A
TAYLOR A&R ; Dublin, 80, /C
TELFORD W ; 50, /DPS
TEMPEST Harry; Dundalk, 00/A
TENISON Edward King;
      Co. Roscommon, 50, 60, /DPS
THOMAS C J ; Dublin, 50, /DPS
THOMSON J ; Fermoy, 70, 80, 90, /C
THOMPSON F ; Kingstown, 90, / PSI
THOMPSON J ; Belfast, 90, /C
THORNHILL F E ; Kildare, 90, /PSI
TICHBORNE T C; Dublin, 90, 00/A
TREFFRY ? ; Dublin, 40, /C
THWAITES Miss ; Dublin, 90, /PSI
TRIMBLE W J ; Dungannon, 70, 80, /C
TURNBULL & SONS ;
      Belfast, 70, 80, 90, /C
TYNDALL ? ; Dublin, 60, /C
TYRRELL J ; Maryboro, 00, / C

UNDERWOOD & UNDERWOOD;U.S.A.,
      (active in Ireland c1905)/C

VALENTINE James & Co; G.B., 00,/C
VANCE James ; Kingstown, 50, /DPS
VANCE M ; Dublin, 80, 90, /C
VERVEGA R ; Clonmel, 70, /C
VESEY T A ; Rostrevor, 60, 70, /A
VICKERS H T ; Dublin, 50, 60, /DPS
VICKERY ? ; Bantry, 90, /C
VIENNA ART STUDIO; Belfast, 80, 90, /C
VIENNA STUDIO ; Limerick, 80, /C
WAITE J R ; Youghal, 70, /C
WAKELEY Mrs ; Dublin, 00, /PSI

WALKER W J ; Co. Down, 90, /PSI
WALSH J ; Dublin, 60, 70, /C
WALSH R F ; Dublin, 00, /PSI
WALSH R W ; Dalkey, 90, /PSI
WARD Richard ; Cork, 70, /C
WATKIN C ; Ballymena, 70, /C
WATSON J&M ; Dublin, 00, /C
WEBB William P ; Dublin, 00, /PSI
WEBSTER J W ; Dublin, 90, /PSI
WELCH Alex; Enniskillen, 70,/C
WELCH D ; Newry/Bangor, 60,70,/C
WELCH Robert ; Belfast, 80, 90, 00, /C
WELLS Capt C C ; Mullingar, 50, /A
WERNER Augustine ;
      Dublin, 60, 70 80,/C
WERNER Alfred ;
      Dublin, 80, 90, 00, /C PSI
WERNER Louis ; Dublin, 50, 60,/ C
WERNER Mrs ; Dublin, 00, /PSI
WESTON BROS; Drogheda,(?)/C
WESTROPP T J ; Galway, 70, 80, / A
WHITE J ; Dublin, 00, /PSI
WHITE W ; Dublin, 50, /DPS
WHITTAKER T ; Kilkenny, 60, /C
WHITTAKER T ; Dublin, 60, /C
WIGHAM C ; Dublin, 90, /PSI
WILKINSON W ; Dublin, 50, /DPS
WILLIAMS John; Bangor, 60, /C
WILLIAMS John ; Athlone, 80, /C
WILLIAMS K. B; Cork, 90,00/A
WILLIAMS s ; Dublin, 60, /C
WILLIAMS T ; Belfast, 70, 80, /C
WILLIAMSON R ; Cork, 70, /C
WILLICK W A ; Enniskillen, 50, /C
WILSON William ; Dublin, 00, PSI
WILSON J L ; Dublin, 00, /PSI
WILSON & TALBOT ; Dublin, 70, /C
WINGFIELD Hon.;
      Powerscourt, Co. Wicklow, 60, /A
WINTER T ; Waterford, 70, 80, /C
WISE B D; Belfast, 90, 00/A
WOODS Dr. Thos.; Birr, 40, /A
WOODWORTH J H ; Dublin, 90, /PSI
WOOLFE & CO.; Dublin, 90, /C
WOOLLCOMBE R Lloyd;
      Dublin, 00, /PSI
WONFOR G H ; Dublin, 70, /C
WORKMAN R E; Belfast, 90, 00/A
WYNNE T A; Tipperary, 80, /C
WYNNE T J; Castlebar, 70, 80, 90, /C

YEATES George ; Dublin, 40, 50, 60, /C
YEATES S M ; Dublin, 90, /PSI
YELVERTON Hon.; Dublin, 50, /DPS
YOAKLEY Richard ; Dublin, 60, /C
YOUNG T H ; Dublin, 50, /DPS

APPENDIX VI

On the Mutual Relations of Photography and Art.

by Sir John Joscelyn Coghill, Bart.

This is the text of a lecture delivered on Friday, November 25, 1859 to the Combined Scientific and Artistic Societies of the R.D.S. of which the Photographic Society of Ireland was one. It was, in effect a reply to one of two lectures on art education which had been delivered to the same bodies in March and April of 1859 by Henry MacManus RHA. It is obvious from Coghill's text that he vehemently disagreed with MacManus's views on Photography and that a lively argument or discussion had taken place after the lecture.

MANY OF THE MEMBERS present will remember with pleasure two addresses delivered to the Fine Arts and Photographic Section of the Royal Dublin Society by my friend Mr. MacManus, on the subject of Art Education. Very practical and extremely lucid addresses they were; and if all Mr. MacManus's audience were as much interested, and found as much to instruct them as I did, I am sure he may be well satisfied with his success.

Perhaps while thus alluding to these two lectures, and so far as contributing my mite of thanks to Mr. MacManus, I may be allowed for a few minutes to revert to the only point in which I felt obliged to disagree with him on that occasion – not with the intention of renewing the discussion which followed his remarks, interesting as such a discussion would be – but with the view of bringing before your notice, as far as I am able, a renewed consideration of the topic, in order to convince members of the Photographic brotherhood, that Art and Photography have mutual relations of a very intimate character and that, while it is impossible to raise the status of the latter beyond that of a mere science, without a practical acquaintance with the principles of the former; so in like manner can Photography repay with interest the services which she has received from her elder sister, and an alliance be formed which must result in mutual benefit.

To accomplish this object, it will be necessary for me, in the first place, to define, as precisely as possible, how far the practical photographer may advance into the kingdom of Art; secondly, to inquire if there are any rules or land-marks which may serve to direct his progress, so far as progress is possible to him; and, thirdly, to review, as briefly as I can, the various ways in which Photography can be made available as an Art assistant.

One of the best results of Mr. MacManus's paper (to me at least) was, that it led me to pay a closer attention to the subject; and an implied challenge was thrown out to Photography to prove herself worthy of the association with the Fine Arts; which the Council of this Society has, I think, wisely effected; at that time I was persuaded, that although many of us were free to admit that there were some canons and rules of Art which must be observed in the formation of a picture, most of us were under the idea that the power of rendering objects and views in an artistic way was a sort of impalpable innate gift, incommunicable, and born with a person as much as Poetry, of which we know it has been said, *"Poeta nacitur non fit"*. Now a little study and reflection will go far to modify this rather hopeless view of the matter; and it will be found, that although study and adherence to rule will never of themselves make men into Landseers and Stanfields, a moderate but very satisfactory, amount of Art perfection is perfectly attainable by all in whom a love of the beautiful exists, and who will bring to its attainment steady, well directed practice, common sense, and a close adherence to certain tangible, practical, and invariable rules of Art, without which neither Stanfield nor Landseer could have ever brought their individual genius to bear. This gave me, as a photographer, some little encouragement, and I began to think that with regard to that evening's discussion, both sides were a good deal in the right, and some little in the wrong. Mr. MacManus was a little too hard upon Photography as a high Art-candidate, and I was a little arrogant in claiming too high a place for her. As usual, I think that truth exists somewhere between the two extremes; and that, while it is perfectly possible for the photographer to produce a picture from nature, in every respect fulfilling the requirements of Art, it is only rarely that nature is sufficiently good-natured to place at his disposal both accurate composition and artistic chiaro-oscuro, and that, therefore, an approximate amount of perfection is all that can be obtained as a general rule.

Perhaps it will be as well for me, in approaching the question of how far the practical photographer has it in his power to imbue his performances with artistic merit, to say a few a words as to the causes which lead to the unhappy prevalence of mediocre photographic compositions; for, unless we go to the root of the disease, we cannot hope for a radical cure, and the first of these causes lies in the naturally great difficulties with which even the best photographers have to contend. Art has many requirements – many component parts go to make up an artistic picture; and of but one of these has she been prodigal to the photographer – Form. There, indeed, has she blessed us with a lavish hand. Most writers upon Art, in utter hopelessness and despair, have warned beginners against too close an attention to detail, for they justly urge that the attempt can only result in labour at the expense of effect, and that, as the most microscopic handling can never rival the minutiae of nature, it is far better to content one's self with mere suggestive indications of detail, leaving it to the mind of the spectator to fill up the omissions.

As far as the brush or pencil is concerned, these authors have only done their duty in so speaking; but when the pencil of light is the instrument, the caution is unnecessary, and the reasons adduced inapplicable. As Moliere says, *"Nous avons change tout cela"*.

In Photographic Art we have infinite detail, without betraying any sign of labour, and therefore the eye is not offended by incompetency. It is in the finiteness of the draughtsman and the colourist's skill, that defeat lies, and not in the infinite variety of nature. We shall find, I think, that while it is quite possible for an unskilful photographer to parade detail to the injury of composition, it is quite within his power, by judicious selection, to subordinate this great gift of form to its proper use; so that, instead of his picture becoming an offensive mass of spottiness, broken lights, and flat and breadthless composition, each detail becomes an individual gem, harmonizing with the whole, and increasing rather than diminishing artistic effect. But by far the most prevalent cause of photographic art mediocrity is to be found in the ignorance of its practitioners; and of this, no better proof is needed than the walls of any photographic exhibition. There you will see the works of one man quite equal to those of another in manipulation, yet as far asunder as the poles in artistic merit. Two men can represent the same subject with equal skill, yet one man be little better than a mechanic, while the other is an artist. And this very discrepancy between the artistic merits of two photographers is a clear proof, that to a certain extent, photography is not the mere servile copyist that some think, but possesses scope for the development of artistic feeling. But the cause of this difference is clear: one man availed himself of his opportunities, with a perception of the requirements of Art: the other, though perhaps, as alive to the beauties of nature, goes to the work

without the Art-education which should have preceded his attempt upon nature, and which would have supplied him with those general rules and principles which he should bring to bear upon his practice, without which an artistic photograph is the merest accident.

How is it with draughtsmen? Would they be able to claim the title of artist as soon as they were able to merely represent objects on paper honestly, as they see them? Surely not. This, though one of the most necessary, is only a preliminary step. Yet this is what an inexperienced photographer expects. A very slight acquaintance with chemistry, a little practice in manipulation and he goes forth full of confidence, and looks for good results; forgetting, like the young artist before mentioned, that he has only mastered the art of depicting what his lens observes, and that all the higher knowledge of Art – that which brings the brain, the taste, the judgement, into play, is still a sealed book to him. Is it any wonder if he fails?

On the other hand, when the young draughtsman has graduated as an Art-student, when he has become familiar with the practice and principles of Art – so familiar that his hand and mind come to work together with such freedom that he is scarcely cognizant that he is exerting either one or the other – what bar is there to his Art-ambition? And so in like manner, may the photographer, up to a certain point, become, by the study and practice of these very same rules, as free from restraint, as unconscious of guiding principle, and will infallibly exhibit the traces of artistic thought and feeling, though it is but a photograph! It is the same in every branch of learning. The mind and fingers of the musician by rule and practice become so much in unison, that his performance becomes in one sense nearly intuitive. The student of a foreign language begins with the alphabet, plods wearily through the grammar, and by slow degrees only masters the idiom; but the moment at length comes for emancipation, and he finds he can speak and write this new language fluently, and without effort. Does he then ever trouble himself to think of either alphabet, grammar, or idiom? No, he can walk without such assistance, and may safely throw away his crutches; but remember, without the crutches he never could have walked at all; and without a knowledge of the elements and principles of Art, photographers will never give their favourite pursuit a fair chance, or raise it from that second-rate position in the kingdom of Art to which it has very naturally, but not altogether fairly, been consigned by many of the best theoretic artists.

And this brings me to consider how far photographers can avail themselves of the means at their disposal of obeying these great and universal laws.

This is neither the time nor place for entering systematically into a recapitulation and explanation of all the various rules of Art. It would require many a lecture, and a much more competent lecturer than I am, to do justice to such a subject. If I can cull a few such laws as are more especially applicable to the photographer, it is as much as I can do, leaving it to those who may agree with me to read and think for themselves. If my very rudimentary remarks do no more than point towards the path that leads to a full knowledge of Art and her requirements, I shall be more than satisfied. The road is a long and hilly one, I know, but I am sure there is no other. The royal road has not as yet been opened in this or any other science.

Up to the point, then, where a judicious artist leaves nature. and inserts into his picture that which is not in reality present, or subtracts that which does really exist in the scene before him, the photographer and the draughtsman are upon somewhat even terms, the photographer having the advantage as far as accuracy of delineation goes, and the draughtsman surpassing him in his ability of representing all the beautiful forms of clouds which enrich the sky, and which in the present (orthochromatic monochrome) state of Photography, can only partially, and under peculiarly favourable circumstances, accomplish.

We cannot, however, substitute one foreground for another which may be more suitable. We cannot throw effective but imaginary shadow over super-abundant detail. We cannot very conveniently make away with an obnoxious tree or house – though in Switzerland, where timber is plentiful, and few questions asked, I have made free with a pine or two! We are restricted (and this is a great drawback) to certain positions with regard to the light, and cannot take views directly in the sun's eye. Mountains for us are not elastic; and we cannot squeeze them into a smaller space than they really occupy, or enlarge them by a single cubit – all of which liberties our brethren of the brush can and do take. We must take things as we find them, and be content. Where, then, have we room for the exhibition of judgement and feeling?

I answer, that in the selection and treatment of our subjects, and in the careful watch for happy accidents, can this alone be effected. The means may seem small, but they include much. Let us consider a few of the laws of composition, as laid down by perhaps, the most characteristic artist that our country possesses, Mr. Harding, which are all, more or less, applicable to the photographer (I speak more particularly with regard to landscape composition, though the rules hold good through all branches of art). Harding tells us that it is necessary to avoid a repetition of forms in our pictures; and when the photographer, looking through his muffed glass, becomes conscious of monotony and dullness of interest, when he considers a little, he will probably find that it arises from a neglect of this very rule. It may happen that the removal of his camera some few yards to the right or left will remedy this defect, but, if not, the site is unsuited for the artist; and if he consider it merely from that point of view, he need not waste his time. Again, he tells us, that it is poor

composition to have any of the leading features of a view perpendicularly over or horizontally level with each other. Thus, let us suppose that in taking a view we find a man fishing in a stream; he is standing upright in such a position that the key-stone of a pointed arch of a bridge is immediately over his head; standing on the very centre of the bridge, over the man, is placed a woman, with a basket on her head, and immediately over the basket rises the principal tower of an old ruin, which crowns a pointed hill: this is an extreme instance of bad composition; but a much less amount of this fault would render the composition of the picture faulty. This would represent the perpendicular error – the horizontal one may be easily conceived. A third, bit of advice that he gives us is, to leave no part of the picture from which a perpendicular strip could be cut without losing some object of interest. This is an excellent rule, and particularly useful to photographers, who are often at a loss to know where to place a living figure, a cart, or a group of any kind, and generally manage to select the very worst spot. In another place he explains the meaning of the term "a well-balanced picture", which it is generally in the power of the photographer to attend to. He says, that where it is possible, the principal object of your subject should be placed near, but not exactly in the centre of the picture; but where there may be reasons why this cannot be effected, the balance of the picture should be preserved by some object of sufficient importance to catch the eye, though in subordination to the principal object, and oc-cupying a somewhat similar position on the other side of the picture. He illustrates this by the view of a fine castle crowning a rugged hill on the right. The left of his picture being a line of low, swampy-looking land, would of itself be insufficient to balance the castle, so he has thrown into the foreground a group of harvestmen returning with their carts and horses from their work; this breaks up the dead level of the flat country, and the eye is satisfied. This necessary manoeuvre can most often and best be effected by the distribution of foreground figures, which is precisely what the photographer has best at his disposal; a stranded boat, a group of peasants, a cart and horse, anything that he can lead or drag into the proper place for his compostion, will suffice, only taking care that in so doing he preserves an accurate focus; because his foreground should represent the sharpest and brightest bit of his whole composition.

Again: bring, where it is possible, the near objects in the foreground into abrupt opposition with the most distant portions of the picture, making them pass across all the different planes of distance. If this rule were better observed, we should not hear so much about the want of air and distance in photographs. Another rule to be observed is to contrive, if possible, that there shall be one principal light, and one principal shadow in your picture, to which all other lights and shades shall be subordinate; and, if possible, that the principal light shall include the chief object of interest where this is impossible, and the principal object is in shade, it should be made to contrast with some broad light, such as the sky. While on the subject of light and shade, I may add, that it is as well, in order to give transparency to shadows, to place some object darker than the original shadow, within its range – the general rule with regard to light and shade being that shadow should always be transparent, but lights mostly opaque. As a last advice I may suggest the necessity of caution in the employment of all that great variety which nature affords. Anything that detracts from the principal object of interest is destructive of breadth, and fatigues the eye. Often this very boon becomes the bane of photographers; a pet sin, from which he finds it hard to refrain. A little bit of well-focused detail is so tempting, that the composition of a whole picture has often been destroyed, in order to introduce it; whereas, it mostly happens, that even if it occurred within the range of the best possible point of view, it would be judicious to have concealed it. A great author once gave a young writer advice to read over his MSS. carefully before going to press, and wherever he found anything that he thought particularly good, to cut it out remorselessly. So I say to the photographer of detail. He has it, and to spare; do not let him be stingy of it. Sacrifice everything to the effect of the whole. Do not let your eye be attracted to that or this little portion of the picture; get into the habit of taking your first look into the muffed glass from a little distance, so that your eye may not be struck by the individual items which go to make up the picture, but by its general appearance as an entire composition; when that strikes you as good, and in accordance with the rules of Art, then, and not till then, begin to focus as sharply as you please. By proceeding in this manner, detail will rarely be found injurious. The variety which should be striven for in a picture is not to be found in this or that spray of foliage, the readableness of a poster on a dead wall, the accuracy of each link in a watch-chain, or any such puerilities. The variety that an artist seeks for is the variety of contrast. The contrast of action with repose; of round forms with angular; of the rugged with the smooth; of the flexible with the firm; of the curved with the straight; of the regular with the irregular.

Before leaving the subject of composition, I have a few words to say of the present want of progress among photographers in the delineation of clouds, to which I made a passing allusion. It is certainly a great drawback to the perfection of photographs, that our best subjects have to appear stripped of the beautiful forms which adorn our sky, and that in exchange, we have nothing but a dreary, dead level of white, from the horizon to the zenith. *(because photographic plates in use at this time were over sensitive to blue they tended to record that colour as white, hence the absence of clouds in many early photographs)*

Many attempts have been made, as you are all well aware, to take the clouds in a photograph as well as the other portions of the view, but up to the present, with the exception of Le Gray's celebrated pictures, and an occasional success, like the stereograph which I hold in my hands and which is evidently more the result of some happy accident than anything else, the problem has received but little solution. Even the case of Le Gray is hardly an exception, in as much as he only exhibits his powers in marine views, where all land is carefully excluded and, beautiful as his pictures undoubtedly are, they are such untrue exponents of nature, that his daylight productions have often been mistaken by the uninitiated for night scenes. The late Mr. Archer, always in the van of discoverers, was, I believe, the first to avail himself of the peculiar construction of his camera to obtain a partial, but not a satisfactory success in this matter. As his camera was both camera and dark tent combined, he was enabled, as it were to be present during the photographic exposure, and by means of a piece of card-board or wood, with an uneven wavy edge, which he moved slowly over the sky until within a few seconds of the time of closing the lens, he certainly, obtained a true copy of the clouds, without leaving a hard outline at the horizon. The objection to this, was two-fold. First, you had, unavoidably, a certain soft horizon light, running unevenly across the whole extent of the picture, which at once betrayed the contrivance, and was besides, eminently inartistic; and, secondly, he was tied down to whatever clouds might happen to be floating about in his field of vision at the precise moment, and which were not always such as one could have wished either from form or position.

Feeling greatly the want of some improvement in this respect, I have also made some trials to introduce natural clouds into photographs and have, I think, struck out a plan which promises very excellent results. I am not aware that I have brought my method before your notice at any of our previous meetings; and indeed I should not be surprised if some of my photographic brethren have, independently employed the same method, for it is a very obvious and simple one. I, every now and then, when the weather is favourable for such an expedition, betake myself to the sea-side, or any other place where a tolerably unbroken horizon line can be found, and from this place I take a series of negatives of clouds alone, by an exposure as nearly instantaneous as possible, and in this way become possessed of a stock of skies of vast variety of forms and significance. Whenever I wish to add clouds to any photograph, I first take a print in the ordinary way, from which I cut away all the sky with a scissors, following the outline tolerably accurately: this forms a shield to be used hereafter. I then take a second print, and when it is finished, I remove the negative, fit the shield over the print, taking care that none of it encroaches on the sky (it is of very little importance if it is a little below the outline), and, having selected my cloud negative,

109

place it in contact with the print in the pressure frame and re-expose it for a few minutes or seconds, until the clouds are sufficiently printed. I regret much that in consequence of my being about to leave Dublin shortly, all my apparatus; and prints have been sent away before me, so that I have no specimen of this method to produce; and you will have either to take my word for it, or try it yourselves. I should much prefer the latter method.

I have thus endeavoured to show that many of the most important requirements of Art can be fulfilled by the photographer in the simple matter of selection of subject, and in skilfully availing ourselves of such happy accidents as may be at our command. We cannot invent or adopt a foreground which does not exist, but nature often presents us with an excellent, or, at least, a sufficient one, if we will but learn what is sufficient. We cannot force nature to change her forms by the power of our imagination, but we can almost always insure that none of her principal features offend against the laws of composition or taste. We cannot throw a mantle of shadow over excessive detail, but we will know when to refuse such a point of view as is rendered inartistic by such detail, and will know when to take advantage of shadow when it suits our purpose – an advantage which we would have been slow to perceive in the days of our ignorance.

But, gentlemen, I have reserved for my last consideration one other point from which to view Photography in its relations to Art, and this is when it appears as an assistant, and not as a rival; and, perhaps, it is in this light that her services will appear most valuable and attractive. My own original intention in embracing photographic pursuits was to make them assistants to painting. I had then the false idea that photography was the short cut to fame as an artist, and so I threw away the brush, and took to the camera. I do not regret having done so. In the science of Photography I have passed many of the happiest hours of my life, and hope to pass many more in the same way; but, having said so much, I must confess that, so far from making an artist of me all at once, as I had fondly expected, I have every day since been confirming the truth of the old saying, " the longest way round is the shortest way home," and have, consequently, gone humbly back to the pot-hooks and hangers of art. No; Photography is a splendid assistant to the educated artist, but she will spare no one a single jot of the routine through which it is necessary to pass.

To one who has made the study of art his delight, and has the ambition not only to produce good photographs, but artistic drawings, Photography is an inestimable boon. What she has accomplished in the department of portrait painting is too well known and appreciated to need any remark from me, but it is as a companion to the sketchbook that I think the camera is most invaluable. To make a finished portrait of any spot requires a length of time which tourists can rarely bestow, and hurried sketches they take are but bad guides to memory, when they come to convert them in after days into finished drawings; but the man who makes Photography his sketching medium need have no fear of a treacherous memory; a few minutes secures to him a faithful representation in black and white, and as for colour, he can either enter into his note book such remarks as may guide him in that respect, or, if he has time, he can also make a rough sketch, embodying the leading features of the colour he wishes to remember, and no more. I have brought with me to-night a few water-colour drawings by a Dublin artist, taken from my Swiss photographs. The gentleman has never seen the places in question, and can, therefore, have but a conventional idea of the local colouring; nevertheless, I think they are very excellent proofs of the truth of what I have been saying. Of course, if he could have, as I before said, jotted down the correct colouring at the time and place, the effect would have been still better.

In conclusion, I hope I have proved that much of the artistic mediocrity which is set down and charged against Photography is the fault of the individual; and I feel sure that if the photographers in this country would accord an equal share of attention to acquiring a knowledge of Art as they do to the chemistry and manipulation of the science, they would go far to improve taste in Ireland, and remove much of the stigma which at present rests upon the handiwork of the sun.

Proceedings of Evening Meetings, 1859, Royal Dublin Society

APPENDIX VII

On a New Patent Compound View Lens for Photographic Cameras

by Thomas Grubb

This is the text of a paper which was read to the Combined Scientific and Artistic Societies of the Royal Dublin Society by Thomas Grubb on March 26, 1858

THE COMPOUND lens which I have the honour of submitting to the Meeting this evening is intended as a substitute and improvement on that lens well known to photographers as the view or landscape lens.

The lenses in general use with photographers are of two very different constructions. There is, first, the portrait lens, consisting of four single lenses, in which a moderate extent (or angle) of field is combined with a large angular aperture, and a good correction for both spherical aberration and dispersion of the compound, and consequently affording the means of taking a picture with corresponding sharpness and quickness of action; and, secondly, we have the view lens, consisting of a double convex lens of crown-glass combined with a nearly plano-concave lens of flint, the general outward form being that of a meniscus, and the lens placed (for the purpose of obtaining what is termed a flat field) in that position in which it has most spherical aberration.

So much indeed has it of this, that it is impossible to use any but a very small aperture in respect of focal length, if a picture sharp in its details be required. This circumstance is, however, of much less moment than might be supposed; for it commonly happens in taking photographs of views, that the differing distances of the objects included necessitates the use of but a small aperture of the lens as the only means of rendering the images of those objects not in focus (more especially those in the foreground) moderately distinct.

On the contrary, however, it often happens that the aberration of the ordinary view lens is that which limits the aperture, while, even if a small aperture is used, the image would be improved if the lens had less aberration. The improved lens accomplishes this. A reference to figs, 1 and 2, which are sectional representations of the old and new lenses, will suffice to show that, while the same general outward form is retained, the inner or connecting curve is (by an inversion of the places which the crown flint lenses occupy in the compound, and the consequent total change in the forms of these) about trebled in its depth of curvature, the same kinds of crown flint being supposed to be used as in the old lens; and hence it follows that the spherical aberration, left almost untouched in the old form, can be altogether or even overcorrected in the new.

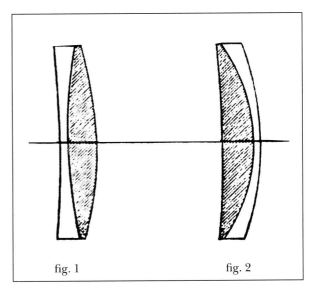

fig. 1   fig. 2

The patent lens is, however, not designed to take the place of the portrait combination although it may in some cases be used advantageously as such, but rather to afford a more distinct image, with moderately increased aperture, and therefore quicker action than the ordinary view lens; and that it accomplishes this I have ample proof in comparative trials with the improved lens, and lenses of the ordinary kind, as manufactured by first-rate English opticians.

APPENDIX VII

The Dublin Industrial Exhibition 1853

Extract from the Report on the Photographic Section

PHOTOGRAPHY was well represented in the Exhibition, although there were no remarkable specimens illustrative of the recent improvements in the art. There were twelve exhibitors representing the daguerreotype, the calotype, and the collodion processes. Among the daguerreotypes, the large portraits of Claudet, of London, deserved especial mention, not alone from their excellence as portraits, but as proofs of the numerous difficulties which M. Claudet has succeeded in overcoming in the construction of his cameras.

We have already mentioned the name of M. Claudet several times as connected with some of the earliest improvements in the art; but it is not merely in a technical point of view that his portraits are remarkable – they are equally so in the artistic grouping and disposition of the backgrounds, which in most photographic portraits is delineated in the same minute detail as the principal figure, and consequently diminishes very considerably the importance which the latter should hold in the picture. Another characteristic of all Claudet's photographs is the absence of all violent contrast of light and shade, and that disagreeable undefinedness of outline produced by a strong glaring sunshine. Among his collection we noticed one of Heinrich Rose, the celebrated chemist of Berlin, which, technically and artistically, we consider to have been unrivalled. The portraits of Mr. Glukman, of Dublin, were equally worthy of commendation; and although all were of a small size, and hence were not so difficult of execution as those of M. Claudet, they possessed many of the

qualities mentioned above. Mr. Pinkney, of Dublin, also exhibited some good daguerreotypes, among which "A View of Upper Sackville Street" was exceedingly good. Mr. Mayall who has been so eminently successful in the production of large daguerreotype views, exhibited some good ones of the interior of the Great Exhibition of 1851.

There were several exhibitors of pictures produced by the talbotype process. Two portraits exhibited by Messrs. Moran & Quinn, of London, and made by the Messrs. Henneman & Malone, who are, we believe, in immediate connection with Mr. Fox Talbot, were very beautiful and truthful, and showed the immense progress which the kalotype *(sic.)* process has recently made, and its Superiority, even for portraits, over the usual daguerreotype, by its warmer tint, greater vitality, and the absence of all reflection at their non-inversion, a property not possessed by daguerreotypes, except those made by Claudet, and, to a great extent, by those of Glukman also.

Mr. E. King Tenison, of Kilbonan *(sic. Kilronan)* Castle, exhibited a number of photographs of very large size, representing views of Spain. Although we have seen some French photographs, especially those of M. Martens, of Paris, far superior to those views, yet, when we take their great size into account, they were certainly remarkable examples, and showed what may be expected from this branch of the art, when fully perfected.

The finest and most effective specimen in the whole collection was a view of the city of Toledo; the view of the East end of Burgos Cathedral was also admirable; as were those of the Church of San Pablo, at Valladolid; and the Royal Palace of Madrid. There were two examples of the effects of treating the pictures with solutions of certain substances. One was a charming view of Cordova, of a peculiar and exceedingly agreeable warm yellow tint, produced by immersing the positive picture in extremely dilute muriatic acid.

There was another example of this fine sunny, sepia-like tint, in a pretty view of the Gate of Cordova. The second example of the effect of certain solutions was a view of the Palio de los Reyes, or Escurial, which had a curious violet tint, produced by immersing the picture in a solution of chloride of gold in aqua regia. It was, in fact, to some extent, an example of the chrysotype of Herschel, above alluded to. Several of these photographs exhibited great inequality of tints, such as the Portal of Leon cathedral, which was too black in the doorways; and the Congresso de los Deputados, or Chamber of Deputies, at Madrid, the foreground of which was absolutely black.

It is probable that had the negatives of these pictures been weakened by the process of Blanquart-Evrard, they would have been excellent. This defect is most likely to occur in taking views of buildings where there is great contrast of light and shade, and hence the process alluded to for weakening the negative is worthy of attention.

Mr. Robinson, of Grafton Street, exhibited a great number of French photographs, principally representing views of Paris, most of which were exquisite. One represented the facade of Notre Dame and the place in front of it covered with an intense concourse of people, and with a procession on the occasion of the marriage of the Emperor. This beautiful photograph, when seen through the stereoscope, was truly wonderful; the whole could not have been more fully realised by an actual spectator, than by looking at this little picture. We have, indeed, seen nothing which more forcibly impressed us with the extraordinary phenomenon of the action of light, or the future value of photography, than this sketch. Mr. Robinson also exhibited some portraits and sketches taken by the collodion

process, which he has helped very much to popularise in Dublin. Several very beautiful photographs taken by this process were exhibited by P. H. de la Motte, *(sic.)* of London. The peculiarity of the photographs taken in this manner is their extraordinary delicacy, which is quite equal, if it does not exceed, that of daguerreotypes, and an agreeable softness of tint, whilst the harshness and mirror effect of the latter are perfectly obviated. Hitherto the kalotype process has made but little progress in these countries in consequence of being protected by a patent; the collodion process has, therefore, opened up a new field which, being free to all, is receiving the most rapid development.

There were several exhibitors of cameras, and other apparatus connected with photography. Mr. Robinson exhibited a number of cameras of French make, which, being very portable and cheap, and giving very satisfactory results, have had, we believe, an extensive sale among amateurs throughout various parts of Ireland; a fact of considerable importance, as experiments of this kind are sure to be fertile in creating a taste for experimental science. In most of these cameras a glass containing zinc instead of lead, has, we believe, been used for the lenses; a great advantage which this glass possesses over the ordinary crystal or optical glass is, that while it has remarkable refractive powers, its dispersive powers are very small. This quality is of the greatest importance in photography. Messrs. Horne, Thornwaite, & Co., of London, exhibited complete apparatus for the daguerreotype, kalotype *(sic. calotype)*, and collodion processes, which were finished in the first style of workmanship; but as the most important point in a camera is the quality of the lenses, and as of these we had no opportunity of judging, we offer no opinion upon them. The same remark will apply to the lenses and accelerators of Mr. R. Beaufort. Mr. T. A. Dillon exhibited a very simple and ingeniously contrived portable camera, which would, we think, be very convenient for excursions. Mr. Glukman exhibited a machine for polishing daguerreotypes, which appeared to possess some very considerable advantages over those which we have seen in common use. Our limited space and the great length to which we have already extended the subject, forbid us from describing this, or any of the other photographic apparatus exhibited at more length. Indeed, it would be of very little use to do so, unless we could establish points of comparison, by describing all the contrivances hitherto invented, which, it is almost needless to observe, would occupy many pages; and which would be in some degree foreign to the object contemplated in the preparation of the materials for the present volume.

W. K. S.

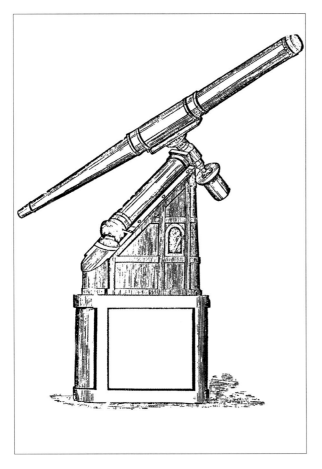

The large astronomical telescope, made by Thomas Grubb in Rathmines for the observatory at Melbourne, which was on show at the Dublin Industrial Exhibition

The official opening by Queen Victoria in 1853 of the Dublin Industrial Exhibition on Leinster Lawn, on the site of the present-day National Gallery

APPENDIX IX

On a Method of Photography in Natural Colours

by Professor John Joly, M.A. Sc.D. F.R.S.

Professor John Joly of Trinity College Dublin is internationally accepted as being the inventor of one of the first practical colour processes (see pp.84-85 of main text).
This is the text of a paper which he read to the Royal Dublin Society on June 26, 1895

IN 1861 Clerk Maxwell read a Paper before the Royal Institution of Great Britain, *"On the Theory of Three Primary Colours."* In this Paper he announced very briefly his discovery of a method whereby the colours of nature could be photographically reproduced by the superimposition by optical projection of three coloured images. How far the method then described by Maxwell embodies the theory and practice of recent efforts in this direction must be judged from his own words.

After displaying upon the screen the three primary colours by passing a beam of white light through three suitably coloured solutions he proceeds to show the synthesis of the spectrum by projection: "The graduated intensity of the primary colours in different parts of the spectrum was exhibited by three coloured images, which when superimposed on the screen gave an artificial representation of the spectrum." Then follows:

"Three photographs of a coloured ribbon taken through the three coloured solutions respectively were introduced into the camera, giving images representing the red, the green and the blue parts separately as they would be seen by each of Young's three sets of nerves separately. When these were superimposed a coloured image was seen which, if the red and green images had been as fully photographed as the blue, would have been a truly coloured image of the ribbon. By finding photographic materials more sensitive to the less refrangible rays, the representation of the colours of objects might be greatly improved."

In this description not only is the method of colour synthesis by triple projection described, but in the words defining the mode in which the three photographic images are to be secured, "as they would be seen by each of Young's three sets of nerves separately," the complete theory of composite colour

photography is specified. While this definition of the theory is clear, the wording of the report of his lecture leaves some doubt as to the actual nature of the light filters used by Maxwell. There is evident confusion in the wording of the report, as appears in the reference to the "three photographs introduced into the camera."

I cannot but think, however, that the three solutions referred to are those used by Maxwell to transmit the three primary colour sensations. This view is strengthened by his previous statement that the red sensation is stimulated most by the red wavelengths, but also by the orange and yellow wave-lengths, &c. This mistake would quite explain his use of the solutions transmitting the primary colours.

It is further of interest to note that at a yet earlier date Maxwell describes his idea of using our knowledge of the colour sensations for obtaining photographs in natural colours. As early as 1855, in a paper read before the Royal Society of Edinburgh, *"On Experiments on Colour as perceived by the Eye,"* he describes how by triple projection of three photographs, one taken through a red glass, a second through a green glass, a third through a blue glass, the final positives being backed respectively by red, green and blue, an image in natural colours could be obtained. In this case also he expresses the view that the several colour sensations are most stimulated by the wavelength, which most nearly represents the sensations, a statement which is, as we will presently see, erroneous.

I think, therefore, that Maxwell, while correctly defining the theoretical conditions governing the choice of light filters for obtaining the negatives, yet having himself an erroneous notion as to the rays which cause the maximum stimulation of the primary colour sensations, fell into a logical error in practising his own invention.

For many years after Maxwell's time triple, quadruple, or even more manifold projection were suggested by various writers; notably by Collen, Ducos du Hauron, and von Ransonnet. Maxwell's correct theoretical ideas seem to have been entirely unknown to these writers, and were not indeed revived till 1886, when Mr. Ives

115

of Philadelphia proposed just such a method, and applying modern resources showed how fully justified was Maxwell's prediction that, with improved plates, the representation of colours could be greatly improved. To Mr. Ives is also due the credit of clearly defining how the "taking" screen should be chosen. It must be observed that to Professor H. W. Vogel's great discovery in 1873, of the action of certain analine dyes in remedying the colour blindness of the salts of silver, the possibility of advance in this direction is entirely due.

As what follows involves an application of Maxwell's principles in a new manner, it is requisite here to describe, briefly, Maxwell's method of composite colour photography as developed by Mr. Ives.

Composite colour photography deals with the subjective reproduction of all visible wavelengths in two stages; a photographic analysis and an optical thesis. In the first operation the several wave-lengths are caused to produce three separate photographic images according to their physiological activity in exciting the supposed fundamental red, green, and violet sensations. Suppose, as a simple example, that we are photographing the yellow of the spectrum near the D line. One of the plates must record an image of the spectrum at this point having a density of silver deposit corresponding to the degree in which this wave-length can excite the red-seeing nerve, and a second must acquire a density corresponding to the degree in which this same wave-length can excite the green-seeing nerve. The third plate records no impression, for the wave-lengths near D excite no violet sensation; but this yellow sensation is the resultant of two physiological effects only, a red and a green sensation in certain proportions. The nature of these proportions can be ascertained by colour measurements effected upon colour sight. We have now obtained three negatives possessing densities of silver deposit corresponding to the degrees which the three several fundamental colour sensations are excited. These degrees of density will be interpreted as degrees of transparency in the positives. The first positive, if backed with a red glass, will transmit a quantity of red light corresponding to the intensity of the physiological excitation of redness in the 'red' nerves; the second, backed with green, similarly presents the stimulation of the 'green' nerves by the yellow colour of the object; the third positive is backed with blue-violet glass, but is quite opaque, and no violet light is transmitted through it. The projection now of all three images superimposed upon the screen forms the second stage of the procedure; the optical synthesis of the original colours. The eye, regarding the

superimposed image, receives in fact the same amounts of red and green sensation, and experiences the same absence of violet sensation which would have attended the formation of the image of this part of the spectrum upon the retina.

This process, if accurate reproduction of colour is sought, necessitates the use of two distinct sets of colour selective screens; for the analysing screens will by no means possess the tints ultimately required in the optical synthesis. This will be evident when it is considered that the wave-lengths which most strongly stimulate the several fundamental sensations are not those which most nearly represent those sensations to the normal eye. The C red for example, is not the wave-length which most strongly stimulates the red sensation; a wave-length which appears orange to the eye possessed of both red and green vision, will far more effectively excite the red sensation. Hence, in order to photograph the wave-lengths of the spectrum, according as they excite the red sensation, we require to produce a greater photographic effect by the D wave-lengths than by the C wave-lengths. To effect this analysis of the light, a screen transmitting as a predominant wavelength, a wavelength near D, must be used for obtaining the image which is to represent the appreciation of light peculiar to the 'red' nerves. Such a screen has a yellow-orange colour, which is not the sensation excited in or transmitted by the 'red' nerves. In the optical synthesis this must afterwards be represented by a C red colour. The same remarks apply to the other screens.

In the foregoing description I have spoken of the method as if based directly on actual colour sensation curves. Upon the revival of Maxwell's method, writers quoting from Maxwell fell into this mistake. Although supplying a convenient terminology in

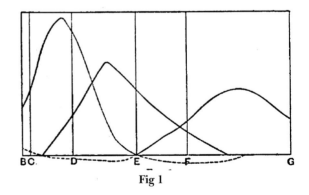

Fig 1

conveying a general idea as to the nature of the procedure, it is necessary now to be more precise.

Maxwell's curves (fig. 1) are not true colour sensation curves, but represent the subjective synthesis of the prismatic spectrum out of three chosen wave-lengths – a red, a green and a blue-violet. The question as to how far one or all these chosen wave-lengths may excite more than the one set of nerves remains however, and indeed can only be gone into by examination of abnormal colour

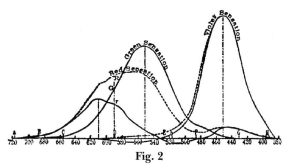

Fig. 2

vision. In Koenig's curves of colour vision, colour sensations are plotted to the normal spectrum. These are shown in the named curves of fig. 2.

If, from the knowledge afforded by Koenig's curves of the compound nature of the green sensation, Maxwell's curves be examined with reference to their suitability to serve the purposes of the photographic method, it will be found that assuming Maxwell's E green to excite the proportionate amounts of red and violet sensation revealed by Koenig's curves, a correct synthesis of the F green by Maxwell's curves is impossible. Although such a comparison is not strictly allowable owing to the red and violet curves of Maxwell being based on different wave-lengths to those used by Koenig, the fact of some inaccuracy is certain. This fact will appear if the spectrum is photographed according to Maxwell's curves. The blue-green will then be found to be reproduced too yellow in tone.

In order to apply the colour sensation curves of Koenig to the photographic method, we have to find by trial examinations of his curves the green most suitable for backing the 'green' positive; for we see that the several green wave-lengths excite very different amounts of red and violet sensation. We find as suitable a wave-length a little to the left side of the E line, about 550μμ. If we take this colour to back the green positive, we must, in order to find the correct red and violet curves which are to control the densities of the red and violet images, replot the red and violet curves with allowance for the proportionate mounts of red and violet which will be carried to all those points where in the image of the spectrum the green curve operates. The red and violet curves must be lowered by amounts obtained by ascertaining from the height of the green curve at any point the amount of red and violet sensations excited by the

amount our selected green is present at that point.

The necessity for the alteration of the curves will, perhaps, be more clearly understood if it be considered what consequences would ensue if we take three negatives of the normal spectrum through light filters, selecting according to the unaltered Koenig's Colour Vision curves.

In the process of synthesis we would, in this case, have upon the screen, at the point D (suppose) of the projected image a quantity of fundamental red represented by the height DR, and of green represented by the height DG. Now, whatever wave-length we make choice of to excite the fundamental green sensation in the optical synthesis, we inevitably excite both the red and violet sensations by the chosen wave-lengtlh. If we adopt the E green, we see by the curve that this wave-length excites the large amount of red sensation shown by the vertical height of the red sensation curve at the point E, and the small amount of violot sensation measured to the violet sensation curve at this point. In projecting then at the point D of the image a quantity of the E green, according to the height DG, we excite amounts of red and violet sensation which can be ascertained by comparing the height DG with the height of the green sensation curve at E. At D we are, in fact, not only projecting the amount of red sensation DR, but adding the large quantity of red sensation involved in the quantity DG of E green, as well as adding some violet. The image of the spectrum will, accordingly, be much too orange at this point. It is evident that the error arises from the compound nature of the sensations attending the excitation of the green sensation, over which we have no control. Hence it is that deductions from the red and violet curves are necessitated whenever green light is required in the synthesis; that is, wherever the green-sensation curve overlies the red or the violet sensation curves. Maxwell constructed curves to which the red and violet constituents are diminished by the amount of red and violet sensations conveyed in the green chosen by him as the fundamental green, and by him assumed to excite only the green sensation.

As the results of trials on Koenig's curves made with the object of ascertaining the green wavelength involving least negative red and violet, the accompanying figure 2 shows in the full lines derived curves which, in their general location, resemble Maxwell's, but are based on a more correct choice of the fundamental colours, and connect our photographic process directly with the colour sensation curves. It is seen that the violet curve is but little altered, and the red considerably altered.

The amount of negative colour (which cannot be realised) is inconsiderable. The outcrop of the red-sensitive curve in the violet is not difficult to realise in the use of orange dyes for the red-taking light filter, which in most cases show some transmission of the violet wave-lengths.

Although it is possible that the compound nature of our green sensations may deny absolute accuracy to this method of colour photography, still my own results on the curves just described, and the results of Ives and others on modified Maxwell curves, appear to show that a degree of accuracy baffling the criticism of the ordinary untrained eye may be attained, and that in the reproduction of the most complex tints.

The symmetry of the derived curves renders their application easy. The transmission of light through a pigment is not limited generally to a small group of predominant wave-lengths, but falls off uniformly at either side in the directions of longer and shorter waves. If we choose the pigments used on the analysing screens so that their predominant transmissions are at three points in the spectrum indicated by the axis of symmetry in the three curves, these being, nearly symmetrical, very accurate results are obtained. The positions of these axes of symmetry are shown by the vertical dotted lines. Accordingly, I make the colour of the red taking screen that of the spectrum at a point displaced to the red side of D by about one-sixth the interval D to C; for the green and violet taking screens the correct tints are found in the same manner by scaling from the figure. Good results are thus obtained, but I do not assert that these details of procedure are final.

Although referred to in what has preceded, the necessity of the separate screens, according to Maxwell's theory, cannot be too clearly understood. The necessity will be evident if the effects of photographing, and viewing the spectrum through the same screens be considered. Evidently, if these are the fundamental colours, the final result will show colour at three separated regions of the spectrum only. The red, green, and violet wave-lengths would alone affect the plate, and the purer we choose the fundamental colours the more restricted would the action be, and the less the action of the intermediate wavelength. On the other hand, if the negatives are taken through the 'taking' colours, and the positives subsequently viewed through the same, we can of course, have no pure red or violet upon the screen, for, in fact, these colours are entirely absent from our individual images. In short, the three primary colours by which correct synthesis of all colours of the spectrum can be alone made are indispensable to the final projection, but are quite unsuited to serve as the taking colour, as they will transmit to the plate only a limited selection of the various wave-lengths of nature, and that not at all according to the decree which these excite "Young's three sets of nerves separately." The use of the same screens for taking and viewing having intermediate tints can, of course, only mitigate the evils referred to.

It is further necessary to observe that, as no photographic plate has as yet been prepared which is uniformly colour sensitive, allowance must be made for this in the choice of pigments to act as light filters, and only by careful photo-spectroscopic work can these be selected.

Had we a plate possessing a uniform distribution of colour sensitiveness the curves could be directly applied to the choice of colours, and these be selected simply by eye observation of their effects upon the solar spectrum.

Any method of photography in natural colours must possess the characteristics not only of accuracy of colour rendering, but also of convenience of application and permanency of colour, if it is to possess value as a scientific method. For use under the various circumstances of travel the naturalist requires a method no more cumbersome than the present dry plate. In the method of positive colour photography, as described, the ordinary camera will not serve. The cumbersome necessity of obtaining three images remains, and subsequently no concrete image in natural colours is actually obtained. One can only be realised by triple projection upon a screen, or by using, some optical contrivance which, by the aid of reflectors, enables all three images to be simultaneously projected upon the retina.

I now proceed to describe a mode of applying the foregoing principles which is free of the objection of cumbersomeness, and which enables us to realise a concrete image in transparent colours. A plate is finally produced which may be held in the hand, regarded against the light, and which bears an image of the object in natural colours, or such as are so nearly accurate as to seem so to the eye. In this new method there is but the one image photographed. The ordinary camera, lens, and backs, &c., are used without modification. The first-class isochromatic plates on the market, which are sensitised down to the C red, will give very good results.

In the new method the idea is to carry the application of physiological principles still further, and divide up the plate like a hypothetical subdivision of the retina, so that all over the plate there should be minute regions uniformly distributed wherein the sensitive silver salt is excited to become reduced to the 'photogenic', material in the same degree in which the sensations of redness, greenness, violetness, would have been actually excited in the several nerves of the retina had the image been formed upon it. Development builds upon this photogenic material the denser silver deposit, and ultimately in the positive the amounts of the sensations are registered in the degrees of transparency of the successive regions. The lined screen which can bring about this will only show its individual colours when placed under the microscope. It is then seen to consist of closely ruled adjacent lines in reddish-orange, yellowish-green, and blue tints. This screen, applied closely to the sensitive surface, analyses the image in the camera. The screens I have used hitherto are coarse, about 200 lines to the inch, and even with this coarseness will show plainly, I regret to say, the imperfections of the only apparatus at my command in preparing these screens. I may observe, in passing, that the colours are ruled on in pigments made up as inks in gelatine and gum arabic or dextrine, and upon plates coated with a preliminary layer of gelatine. Such lines may be put on so close as 800 or 1000 to the inch. With between 300 and 400 to the inch, however, the eye is no longer annoyed by the structure of the plates. The lines may also be ruled on celluloid or on translucent paper.

Recalling now that the lines upon the positive register in their degrees of transparency, the degrees in which the three-colour sensations would have been excited, it becomes apparent that to complete the physiological parallel we must convert these degrees of transparency to quantities of the red, blue, and violet colour sensations. This is done by a second screen which carries red, green and violet lines to the same gauge as the taking screen. We apply this to the positive, and as we move it over the image, waves of every tint of colour appear till that position is reached where the red lines fall over the lined areas recording red sensation, and also for the others. The picture now suddenly appears in vivid colour and with all the realism and relief conferred by colour and colour perspective.

It is to be remembered that these results are attained by no new photographic operations. It is necessary to use good ortho-chromatic plates sensitised into the red, and also to have affixed in the lens an orthochromatic screen cutting off the ultra-violet light in the usual manner. The exposure is longer than the ordinary exposure, for we can of course only use visible light, and of this a part is stopped by the taking screen. The ordinary backs may be used. The displacement of the sensitive film from accurate register with the ground-glass camera screen, owing to the presence of the taking screen in front of it may be corrected (if thought necessary) by, simply reversing the surface of the ground-glass camera screen, turning the muffled side outward. This secures that the image will be accurately focussed in the plane of the sensitive surface. Negatives and positives may be used as ordinary negatives or positives till it is desired to recall the original colours. Thus, for those who wander with the camera, the possession of but the one seeing screen to test results is sufficient, and of course the one taking screen suffices to take an indefinite number of plates.

These considerations lead us naturally to observe that the registration of colour being really carried in the silver image, which with very little care in manipulation may be made permanent, secures that the colours are permanent. A faded screen may at any time be made good by a fresh screen; the colours in all cases being spectroscopically chosen, we are assured of the reproduction of the original colour. In this aspect the necessity of the detached colour screen is no disadvantage, but rather a necessary safeguard against the inevitable fading attending most pigment colours.

The question of course naturally suggests itself if results on paper, that is results seen by reflected light, are not also possible on the principles described. My early experiments in this direction were not encouraging. The difficulties of correctly superimposing the viewing colours upon a paper positive are considerable. For book illustration, the correct and sufficiently rapid register of printing surfaces, having the required minuteness, presents grave difficulties, and in all such printing processes the truth of colour vanishes with the uncertainty attending the amount of colour transferred to the paper. Again, if any fixed combination of the colours and the sensitive salt is sought for, the difficulties of preserving these colours during development or toning &c, present themselves. Finally, perhaps the gravest difficulty resides in the enfeeblement of the reflected light, already enfeebled by the inevitable loss due to absorption in the reflecting material.

Note added later (June 3, 1896.) I have recently ascertained that Ducos du Hauron 30 years ago, at the conclusion of a lengthy French patent for colour reproduction by triple projection, suggested the use of a screen lined in colours for combining the three images in one. The fact that his theoretical colour principles were erroneous and that consequently no practical result is possible on the procedure he suggests, probably accounts for the absence of any record of anything actually accomplished in this direction.

Transactions, Royal Dublin Society, vol.vi, 1895, part v.

APPENDIX X

On Instantaneous Photography

by Henry T. Vickers, B.A.

The text of a paper read to the Fine Arts Section of the R.D.S and the Photographic Society on February 21, 1859. Henry T. Vickers was Secretary of the Dublin Photographic Society and later the Photographic Society of Ireland during the late 1850s.

SEVERAL MONTHS ago at a conversation which took place among the members of the Photographic Society, at one of its meetings, in which the subject of instantaneous pictures was started, I stated that "I had taken photographs in what I believed to be the one-tenth part of a second."

The statement was at the time doubted by a professional photographer present; and, in order to test the matter, I set to work to construct the necessary apparatus for accurate experiment. What I stated was as a matter of belief; but now I am prepared to prove, as a matter of certainty, that I have taken photographs in the one-tenth of a second; and I am prepared also to prove that I have obtained a negative photographic impression in the one-hundreth part of a second.

Now I have not obtained this result by attempting to count the time (as the gentleman in question, being accustomed to the beating of his own metronome, may have supposed), but by taking a photographic impression of an object in motion, and moving at a known rate.

Before, however, more particularly alluding to the experiment, I must introduce to your notice the instrument which I have used for admitting the light on, and shutting it off from, the sensitive plate. The opening takes place at the centre of the lens by means of two perforated shutters, and the closing takes place by a continuance of the movement which is given to those shutters or disks for the purpose of opening. The only peculiarity or originality to which I lay claim on this part of the matter is, that the movement of both disks takes place, and must take place, simultaneously.

There is no jerk from the commencement to the end of the operation, the trigger being so constructed that it can be drawn out without the least disturbance of the camera; and there is a spring which prevents any secondary exposure after the shutters have once closed.

Now while the moving force of the spring is constant, and the resistance to that force, consisting of the *vis inertiae* of the disks, and the friction, is also constant, it follows that the times of the passage of the disks over the given space must be constant. If, therefore, I once can ascertain the time that one picture can be taken in, I know the time of all taken with the same instrument. When I stated my belief that the operation was performed in the tenth of a second, it was from observing as accurately as the eye can, the space that the image on the ground glass of a pendulum beating seconds travels while the machine is worked. But as an observation of such a short duration cannot be anything more than an approximation, and as the velocity of the pendulum at different points varies, it was my intention to construct a clock with a conical pendulum and a revolving dial, which could be photographed while in motion. On mentioning the matter, however, to my friend, Mr. Grubb, he very kindly lent me, the experimental clock which I now exhibit, and gave me permission to make such alterations as I might find necessary for my purpose. Accordingly, by regulating the flywheel or fan, and weight, I caused a hand to which there are two bright silvered beads attached, one in the centre, and one at the end, to revolve once in a second; and by placing the clock, while in motion, in the sun, I have succeeded in taking a photograph of the moving bead. I exhibit a positive proof of the original negative, and an enlarged drawing taken by measurement; and from them it will appear that, as near as possible from the commencement to the end of the exposure occupied but the one-tenth part of a second, the accurate numbers being, – entire exposure, 0.1; full aperture, 0.06; diameter of luminous body, 0.01, or 0.00855; and taking the diameter of the image of the moving luminous bead, and comparing it with the track which it made, it appears that each part of that track was produced by a luminous body, which moved over it in the one-hundreth part of a second.

Now having proved the proposition I started with, I would add a few words with regard to the difficulties to be encountered in taking instantaneous pictures, and I think these may be classed under two heads, viz., those arising from the peculiarity of the materials to be used, and those arising from the circumstances under which we have to use them.

With regard to the materials, in order to secure the utmost sensitiveness, the chemical affinities must be so nicely balanced that the faintest ray of light must be sufficient to change those chemical affinities, but when this is the case, other objects besides light produce that change, and dust and dirt here work mischief to their hearts' content; besides, it is necessary that the alcohol and ether should be most highly rectified; no water must be present, and this involves the consequence of speedy drying of the plates. This brings me to the circumstances under which we have to use them.

Now before anyone commences to practice taking instantaneous pictures, particularly in this climate, I recommend him to arm himself with patience and perseverance. It is all very well to talk of a spring shutter and a pistol camera, but what satisfaction is it if, after waiting for the favourable moment to spring his shutter or fire his pistol camera, he finds after applying half the developer in his dark box and being half smothered in it to boot, that he has got nothing, and wherefore because his plate was too dry. No one, unless he has tried it, can know the feeling of a photographer as he stands with trigger in hand, after having exhausted all his skill and tact, and having succeeded in placing a perfect plate in his dark slide, watching, as he does, the passing cloud, while the plate goes on drying and the sportive gleam will not visit him to light up the view(*so-called wet plate negatives had to be exposed wet in the camera, if allowed to dry they became insensitive and useless*).

The celebrated instantaneous pictures of Le Gray have, all been taken in the full blaze of sunlight but by the uninitiated they are taken for moonlight scenes. They are taken in a climate superior to this for the purpose, and you may observe that he has not produced any with a very rough sea and clouds: the appearence of roughness of the water is such as would be produced by a swell. If it were produced by a gale, the clouds would have been moving fast, and the difficulty of hitting the proper moment for taking the picture would have been greater.

I exhibit two instantaneous pictures: in one the clouds will, I think, be admitted to be good, while the ripple of the sea is there too. The second is one of the Boyne Viaduct, and a little reasoning is necessary to find out that it is an instantaneous picture, as there are neither clouds nor sea. I exhibit also a picture of two horses and two men; though taken in a very short time, this picture is not an instantaneous one, but I exhibit it to show the advantage of instantaneous pictures, as part of it is imperfect from a slight motion of one of the animals. To the artist, I think, instantaneous pictures may be of the greatest use; there he can have the permanent and true representation of a moving object to study and copy from at his leisure, whether it be sea, clouds, or animals, or even likenesses of individuals.

And now with regard to the easiest mode of taking instantaneous pictures. For a long time I sought for a collodion of extreme sensibility, and the most sensitive which I ever used I made myself, and iodized with iodide of ammonium, but at the time of iodizing I put a small bit of fresh burnt lime, which had the effect of still further removing the water and entering into combination with the free iodine by forming iodide of calcium; but this I have given up, in consequence of the lime accumulating in the bath and making the pictures streaky.

The best plan that I know of is suggested by Mr. Barnes, viz., to use an ordinary sensitive collodion, and to develop with a strong iron developer, as if for a positive, and then to carry on the process with the pyrogallic developer; it was by this process that I obtained the negative of the revolving bead; the collodion had been mixed more than a fortnight, and the exposure took place under glass, and under circumstances where the angular aperture of the lens was much diminished.

The Photographic Convention of the United Kingdom

HELD IN DUBLIN, JULY 1894

THE PHOTOGRAPHIC CONVENTION of the United Kingdom was an annual event held each year in a different city in the "United Kingdom" or the British Isles as they were then. This was the first of only two occasions on which the event was held in Ireland, the second was in 1904 when it was again held in Dublin.

The contents of a small booklet, which was published in connection with the Convention held in 1894, are reproduced on the following three pages.

Essentially the Photographic Convention was a sort of federation of all the various photographic clubs and societies in Britain and was an opportunity for photographers from different parts to get to know each other better.

As these pages show, apart from a few serious talks on photographic subjects, the accent was on social matters.

Sir Howard Grubb, a past president of the Photographic Society of Ireland the host society, assumed the office of president of the Convention for its duration.

THE

Photographic Convention

OF THE

United Kingdom.

DUBLIN MEETING,

JULY 9th to 14th, 1894.

The Meetings and Exhibition

WILL BE HELD AT THE

ROOMS of the PHOTOGRAPHIC SOCIETY of IRELAND,

35 DAWSON STREET.

6

Photographic Convention of the United Kingdom.

PRESIDENT FOR THE YEAR

SIR HOWARD GRUBB, F.R.S.

COUNCIL.

APPLEBY, E. J., 8 Argyle Street, Bath.
BRIDGE, F. A., East Lodge, Dalston Lane, N.E.
BRIGINSHAW, J. J., 42 Albert Road, Walthamstow.
BOTHAMLEY, C. H., Fernleigh, Haines Hill, Taunton.
CARNELL, A. A., Bedford Villa, Plymouth.
COWAN, A., Chaseside, Southgate.
DRAGE, R. P., 95 Blenheim Crescent, W.
GIBSON, J. P., Hexham.
HARDING, M. J., 4 Lexden Gardens, Shrewsbury.
HASTINGS, H. M., 54 Edith Road, West Kensington.
HENDERSON, H. L., 277 Lewisham High Road.
HEPWORTH, T. C., 21 Furnival Street, Holborn.
KEENE, R., All Saints, Derby.
KIDD, R. L., Castlemaine, Hampton.
KING, J. AUSTIN, 19 Portland Place, Bath.
LANG, W., Jun., Cross Park, Partick, Glasgow.
LANGE, PAUL, Dodd's Buildings, 6 Chapel Street, Liverpool
LUCAS, C. PHIPPS, The Elms, Mottingham, Eltham, Kent.
LYSAGHT, Major, Camera Club, London.
MACKIE, A., 3 Upper Baker Street, N.W.
MASON, GEORGE, 180 Sauchiehall Street, Glasgow.
MAYNE, THOS., Lord Edward Street, Dublin.
NAUNTON, W. W., The Square, Shrewsbury.

7

PORRITT, J., 66 London Road, Leicester.
PRINGLE, A., Cromwell House, Bexley Heath, Kent.
SAYCE, B. J., Red Cross Chambers, Liverpool.
SEAMAN, A., Chesterfield.
SMITH, H. M., 5 Beatrice Road, Stroud Green.
STUART, J., Buchanan Street, Glasgow.
STURNEY, H., 19 Hertford Street, Coventry.
TAYLOR, J. TRAILL, 2 York Street, Covent Garden, W.C.
W. TAYLOR, Slate Street Works, Leicester.
TATE, A., Longwood, Belfast.
WARNERKE, LEON., Silverhowe, Champion Hill, S.E.
WEBSTER, G. W., 33 Bridge Street Row, Chester.
WELLINGTON, J. B. B., 18 Marriott Road, High Barnet.
WERNER, A., 39 Grafton Street, Dublin.
WORTH, R. HANSFORD, 42 George Street, Plymouth.

Hon. Sec.:

F. P. CEMBRANO, jun.,

10 Cambridge Gardens,

Richmond, Surrey.

A group of delegates attending the Photographic Convention in 1894 taken by Alfred Werner on Leinster Lawn

14

Notice to Members.

1. Members are requested to report themselves at the Council Room, 35 Dawson Street (opposite Mansion House) on Monday morning, or as soon after arrival as possible, when they will receive Badges of Membership, and Invitations to the Conversazione and the Lord Mayor's Reception.

2. They will also be presented with a specially-prepared Guide Book, which will give full particulars of excursions and details of programme arranged, places to see and photograph, and general information useful to visitors.

3. Members are requested to book their places for excursions AS EARLY AS POSSIBLE ON MONDAY. It is absolutely necessary this should be done to allow adequate arrangements for cars, &c., to be made.

4. Besides the excursions mentioned hereafter, arrangements have been made with the various Railway Companies to issue to all members of Convention, upon production of voucher to be obtained from Secretary, return tickets at single fares from Dublin to any stations on their lines, from 9th to 31st July, and, in addition, special rates will be offered to Killarney, Lough Erne, and Rostrevor.

This offers unusual and valuable facilities to any member who wishes to take his holidays on this occasion, and it is hoped that many will avail themselves of it.

15

Arrangements.

MONDAY, 9th JULY, 1894.

Small parties will be formed, under suitable leadership, to see the City, and visit and photograph places of interest therein.

Opening of the Convention, and Presidential address, in the Royal Dublin Society's Buildings, Kildare Street, at 7.30 p.m. Full Dress Conversazione, at 9 o'clock, will be held in the Museum Buildings adjoining, by the permission of the Lords of Committee of Council of Education. It is expected that His Excellency the Lord Lieutenant will be present.

EXCURSIONS.

TUESDAY, 10th JULY.

EXCURSION TO THE HILL OF HOWTH
Leader - Mr. JOHN A. C. RUTHVEN.

Will leave Amiens Street Station, about 11 o'clock, by special train. The Hill of Howth rises about 56oft., is situated on the North side of Dublin Bay, and from it magnificent views may be obtained. After visiting the Abbey, which dates from the 11th century, visitors will be taken through the demesne of the

16

Earl of Howth, celebrated for its Fine Walks, Ruins, and Cromlech; thence by the Cairn Hill, and round the high cliff shore, from whence views of Dublin Bay, Killiney, Dalkey, and the Sugarloaf can be obtained. If time permits, Ireland's Eye may be visited. Return to Dublin about 5 o'clock.

EXCURSION TO BLESSINGTON AND POUL-A-PHOUCA.
Leader - Mr. V. E. SMYTH.

Will leave Nelson's Pillar, about 11 o'clock, by tram to Terenure; thence by steam tram to Blessington, passing the picturesque remains of Tymon Castle and Tallaght Church; from Blessington by car to the Rocky Pool, on the Liffey and Burgage, with its ancient Stone Crosses; thence to the waterfall at Poul-a-phouca, returning about 6 o'clock.

PAPERS—At 8 p.m., at 35 DAWSON STREET.
"The uses of Photography in Medicine."—By Mr. ANDREW PRINGLE, F.R.M.S.
"Color Photography."—By Dr. JOLY.
"An Unexplored Field of Photography" (with Lantern Illustrations).—By Mr. T. C. HEPWORTH, F.C.S.

WEDNESDAY, 11th JULY.
General Meeting at 35, Dawson Street, at 10 a.m.
Meeting of General Committee, ditto „ 11 a.m.
Convention Group on Duke's Lawn „ noon.
Annual Dinner and Smoking Concert „ 6.30 p.m.

17

THURSDAY, 12th JULY.
Leaders - Mr. J. L. ROBINSON and Dr. COSGRAVE.
EXCURSION TO VALLEY OF THE BOYNE.

Special train from Amiens Street Station, about 9 o'clock, to Drogheda, situated at the mouth of the river Boyne, visit St. Lawrence Gate and Old Walls, the Magdalen Steeple and West Gate, passing the Boyne Bridge and King William's Glen, where the great battle was fought, and continuing along the river, visit the celebrated Tumuli of Dowth and New Grange, the monastic remains of Mellifont, and the round tower and Celtic crosses of Monasterboice, returning via Drogheda to Dublin about 7 o'clock.

PAPERS—At 35, DAWSON STREET.
At 8.30 p.m.
"On the Effect of Temperature on Photographic Sensitiveness."—By Dr. JOLY.
"On a Photographic Sextant."—By Dr. JOLY.

FRIDAY, 13th JULY.
Leader - Mr. J. H. HARGRAVE.
EXCURSION TO ENNISKERRY, THE DARGLE AND POWERSCOURT.

By train from Westland Row or Harcourt Street Station, about 10 o'clock, to Bray; thence by car through the Dargle to Enniskerry; thence to Powerscourt Demesne and the Waterfall, returning to Dublin about 6 o'clock.

18

EXCURSION TO TRIM AND BECTIVE.

Leader - Mr. J. L. ROBINSON.

By train from Broadstone Station, visit the yellow steeple part of an Abbey founded by St. Patrick, the Castle, the Old Walls, the Watergate and Sheepgate, Newtown Abbey and the Priory of St. John, the Ruins of Bective Abbey, &c., returning to Dublin about 6 o'clock.

———

Full Dress Reception at the Mansion House, by the Rt. Hon. THE LORD MAYOR.

———

SATURDAY, 14th JULY.

Leaders - Dr. SCOTT and Mr. WERNER.

EXCURSION TO GLENDALOUGH AND THE SEVEN CHURCHES.

By train from Harcourt Street, about 9 o'clock, passing the rocky scenery of Brayhead to Rathdrum, thence by cars to Glendalough (glen of the lakes), visit the Round Tower, the Lakes, St. Kevin's Bed, and the Seven Churches, many interesting relics of early Christian times, returning through lovely scenery to Rathnew, and from thence by train to Dublin.

This excursion has been arranged for Saturday, in order that members wishing to visit the Vale of Ovoca or other parts of Wicklow, and able to stay over

19

Sunday, may do so, and it is arranged that the tickets will be available for this purpose.

———

Arrangements will be made to enable those returning to England on Saturday night to reach Dublin in time for the steamer.

20

Places of Interest in and around Dublin.

———

Permission to photograph the following places of interest in the City has been obtained :—

Christ Church and St. Patrick's Cathedral.

———

Trinity College, the Castle and Courtyard, the House of Lords, National Gallery, Science and Art Museum, the Zoological and Botanical Gardens, Prospect and Mount Jerome Cemeteries, St. Audoen's Arch, St. Stephen's Green, Royal Hospital, Pro Cathedral, Guinness and Co.'s Brewery, Inchicore Works, and the Phœnix Park.

———

Amongst the places worth visiting in the vicinity may be mentioned :—

THE PHŒNIX PARK, with the Vice-Regal Lodge, the Furry Glen, the lakes, deer, &c.

———

THE STRAWBERRY BEDS and the river scenery of the Liffey Valley.

———

LUCAN, with its Spa, Leixlip, and the Salmon Leap Waterfalls.

———

KINGSTOWN, with its magnificient Harbour, mail boats, and yachting scenes.

———

KILLINEY and its beautiful bay, Strand and Hill, from which grand and far-reaching views are to be obtained.

21

General Information.

———

MEMBERSHIP.

Application for Membership should be made to the Hon. Sec. or to the Hon. Local Sec. The subscription is 5s. per annum, and is due on the 1st of January of each year.

Ladies are eligible for Membership.

———

AN EXHIBITION OF PHOTOGRAPHS AND PHOTOGRAPHIC APPARATUS

Will be held in the Rooms of the Photographic Society of Ireland, 35 Dawson Street, from July 9th to 14th inclusive, between the hours of 10 a.m. and 6 p.m. Members must produce their badge on entering.

The public will be admitted by ticket, obtainable at the door, price sixpence.

———

ANNUAL MEETING.

The Annual Meeting will take place at 35 Dawson Street, on Wednesday, July 11th, at 10 a.m.

———

GROUP.

The Group will be taken, weather permitting, on Duke's Lawn, by Mr. A. Werner, on Wednesday, July 11th, at noon ; size, 18in. by 15in. Price, in silver or platinotype, mounted, 5s.

———

HOTELS.

A list of suitable Hotels and Tariffs will be found on pages 23-24.

(Booklet in the Chandler Private Collection)

Documentation Consulted

The National Library of Ireland:
The Clonbrock House Papers
The Lawrence and other photographic collections
The Griffith Valuation
Thom's and other streets directories, (1850–1900)
Catalogues of R.D.S. Exhibitions, (1840s–60s)
Report and Catalogue of the Irish Industrial Exhibition, (1854)
Official Catalogue of the Dublin International Exhibition, (1865)
NEWSPAPERS: (1850S TO 1900)
The Irish Times, The Freeman's Journal,
Saunder's Newsletter, Dublin Advertising Gazette, The Advocate
The Belfast News Letter,
The Dublin Correspondent (1864),
Banner of Ulster, (1841)
The Dublin Journal (1858-9),
PERIODICALS:
The Dublin Builder (1850s–70s),
The Illustrograph, (1890s)
Illustrated London News (1860s)

Trinity College Library:
The Uses of Photography in Ireland, 1839-1900 —
Peader Slattery, Dublin (Unpublished thesis, 1991)

The National Archives, Dublin:
Archives relating to photographic activities and
photographic records of Fenian prisoners, 1850s to 1880s
Dublin Photographic Society/Photographic Society of Ireland—
List of members, 1854-59

The Public Record Office, Kew, London:
Photographic Copyright documents relating to
Irish photographers 1860s to 1900

The Royal Dublin Society:
Proceedings of Evening Meetings, 1851–1859
R.D.S. Journal, 1860
R.D.S. Scientific Transactions, 1896

The Royal Irish Academy:
Library and archives

The Royal Society of Antiquaries in Ireland
R.S.A.I. Journal, (1890s)
Photographic Collection

The Photographic Society of Ireland:
Minutes, records and collection

The Royal Photographic Society:
Historical Group News Letter 1985–95
The Photographic Journal, 1853–1859

The Science Museum Library, London:
The Photographic Art Journal, (1859–65)
Photographic News, (1879)
The Amateur Photographer, (1880–1900)

Select Bibliography

GENERAL

Bingham, Robert — *Photogenic Manipulation*, Part II: The Daguerreotype (London 1852)

Buckland, Gail — *Fox Talbot and the Invention of Photography* (Boston 1980)

Eder, Josef Maria — *History of Photography* (New York 1972)

Gernsheim, Helmut — *The History of Photography* (London 1968)

Gernsheim, Helmut — *L. J. M. Daguerre: The History of the Daguerreotype etc.* (London 1956)

Greenough, Sarah etc. — *On the Art of Fixing a Shadow* (Washington 1989)

Harker, Margaret — *The Linked Ring* (London 1979)

Haworth-Booth, Mark — *The Golden Age of British Photography* (London 1984)

Hershkowitz, Robert — *The British Photographer Abroad* (London 1980)

Moholy, Lucia — *100 Years of Photography: 1839–1939* (London 1939)

Newhall, Beaumont — *Photography, Essays and Images* (Boston 1980)

Newhall, Beaumont — *The History of Photography from 1839 to the Present*, (New York 1982)

Pepper, Terence —*High Society Photographs, 1897-1914* (London 1998)

Piazzi Smyth, Charles — *An Astronomer's Experiment* (London1859)

Picknett, Lynn and Prince, Clive — *Turin Shroud–In Whose Image etc.*, (London 1994)

The Photographic Society, London — *The Photographic Journal*, (London 1853–59)

Pritchard, Michael — *A Directory of London Photographers, 1841-1908*, (Watford 1986)

Scharf, Aaron — *Art and Photography* (London 1968)

Shaw, Eglon — *Incunabula of British Photographic Literature 1839-75* (London 1984)

Ward, John etc. — *Printed Light* (Edinburgh 1986)

Stevenson, Sara — *D.A. Hill & Robert Adamson* (Edinburgh 1981)

Stevenson, Sara — *The Photographs of John Muir Wood* (Edinburgh 1988)

Time-Life Series — *Caring for Old Photographs* (1972)

Werge, John — *The Evolution of Photography* (London 1890)

Witkin, C. & Embree, A. — *The Photograph Collector's Guide* (London1979)

The History of Photography (periodical)

Miscellaneous Other Photographic Periodicals (1839–1900)

IRELAND

Chandler, Edward — *Photography in Victorian Dublin* (Dublin 1980)

Chandler, Edward — *Ireland: A Cultural Encyclopaedia*, Photography Section (London 1983)

Chandler, Edward/Walsh, Peter — *Through the Brass Lidded Eye* (Dublin 1989)

Coghill, Sir John Joscelyn — *Catalogue of the Irish International Exhibition*, Photography section (Dublin 1865)

Davison, David — *Impressions of an Irish Countess* (Dublin 1989)

Gorham, Maurice — *Dublin From Old Photographs* (London 1971)

Gorham, Maurice — *Ireland From Old Photographs* (London 1971)

Hemphill, William Despard — *The Abbeys Castles and Scenery of Clonmel etc.* (Dublin 1860)

Hickey, Kieran — *The Light of Other Days* (London 1973)

Kissane, Noel (Ed) — *Ex Camera, Photographs from the National Library of Ireland* (Dublin 1990)

Kissane, Noel (Ed) — *Treasures from the National Library of Ireland* (Dublin 1994)

William Lawrence (publisher) — Emerald Isle Albums (Dublin 1890–1910)

Maguire W. A.— *A Century in Focus, Photography in Northern Ireland,1840-1940* (Belfast 2000)

Merne, Oscar — *The History of the Photographic Society of Ireland* (Dublin 1954)

Royal Dublin Society — *Proceedings* (1848-1861, 1895)

Sexton, Sean — *Ireland, Photographs 1840-1930* (London 1994)

Shaw, Henry — *Dublin Pictorial Guide and Directory* (Dublin 1850, Reprint 1988)

Slattery, Peader — *The Uses of Photography in Ireland, 1839-1900* (Unpublished doctoral thesis, TCD, 1991)

Wyndham-Quin, Edwin, Earl of Dunraven — *Notes on Irish Architecture* (1875)

The Camera — periodical, (Dublin 1922-c1937)

Cinema Ireland 1895-1976 — exhibition catalogue, (Dublin 1976)

The Industries of Dublin (Dublin 1889)

The Photographic Convention of the U.K.— booklet (Dublin 1894)

Notes

1. Helmut Gernsheim—*L. J. M. Daguerre: The History of the Daguerreotype and the Diorama*, 1956

2. The process described in *Turin Shroud–In Whose Image?* leaves a scorch type brown image on a fabric base with no chemical residue. It may, in fact, have been a process commonly used by artists for transferring drawings to canvas for subsequent painting over and because of this no examples have survived.

3. Gernsheim— History (1).

4. S. Greenough — *On the Fixing of a Shadow*, 1989

5. Alfred Werner — Text of lecture delivered to the Dublin Camera Club in *The Camera*, Dublin. December 1922

6. Gernsheim — History (1).

7. T, H. Fielding,*The Art of Engraving etc.* — 1839 (a copy of this book is in the N.L.I.)

8. F. S. Beatty, *The Photographic News* — London, August 8, 1879, pp.362-3

9. ibid.

10. Alexander S. Wollcot, (1804-1844)

11. J. T. Cooper, a chemist who lectured and demonstrated the daguerreotype process at the Polytechnic Institution in London in 1841

12. John Frederick Goddard, (1795-1866)

13. 25 May, 1842

14. *The Dublin Journal*, January 30,1858

15. National Archives, Dublin

16. Mount Jerome Cemetary Records

17. Gernsheim — History (1) etc

18. Allison Morrison-Low — *Sir David Brewster and Photography* in *Review of Scottish Culture*, p. 71

19. ibid.

20. ibid.

21. ibid.

22. ibid.

23. The late Harold White A.R.P.S. c1970

24. ibid.

25. ibid.

26. Maurice Gorham — *Dublin in Old Photographs*, 1971

27. Helmut Gernsheim — *History of Photography* 1968

28. Royal Irish Academy — Transactions

29. Royal Dublin Society — Minutes

30. Peter Walsh — *Through the Brass Lidded Eye*, 1989

31. Helmut Gernsheim — *History* (27)

32. F. S. Beatty — (8)

33. Maria Edgeworth — *Letters from England*, 1873

34. Dubreuil's full name is given in a directory entry as Alexander Doussin Dubreuil, he may also have been Belgian, a photographer with this name operated in Brussels in the 1890s, and may have been related.

35. Peader Slattery — *The Uses of Photography in Ireland*, 1839-1900, Thesis, T.C.D. 1991.

36. Glasshouse Street off Regent Street in London and numerous other streets and roads with "glasshouse" in their names is a reminder that photogrphers operated there.

37. Horatio Nelson's bizarre first name possably means that he was born close to the date of the Battle of Trafalgar.

38. Slattery — (35)

39. Marriage records of old St. Thomas's parish church.

40. Glukman/Constable Correspondence.

41. Walsh — (30)

42. ibid.

43. It is not surprising that photographers would be interested in an alternative to natural light for studio photography, bearing in mind the vageries of natural light in Ireland, particularly during Winter months.

44. Foster's name will be familier to older readers for the series of headline copybooks which bore his name and were the bane of school-children's lives in the 1930s and 1940s.

45. Morrison-Low — (18)

46. Walsh — (30)

47. Oscar Merne — *The History of the Photographic Society of Ireland*, 1854

48. Robert Herschkowitz — *The British Photographer Abroad*, 1980, p.80

49. Merne — (47)

50. Slattery — (35)

51. ibid.

52. Patent Office Records, Dublin and *Photographic Journal*, May 21, 1858, p.220

53. David Davison

54. Sean Sexton — I*reland, Photographs 1840-1940*, 1994

55. Gernsheim — (1)

56. David Davison — *Impressions of a Countess*, 1994

57. List of Exhibits

58. Clonbrock Papers, N.L.I.

59. Charles Piazzi Smyth — *Teneriffe, an Astromomer's Experiment*, 1859

60. The most complete copy of this book in public hands appears to be that in the library of Trinity College Dublin

61. *Photographic Journal*, 1856

62. Greenough — (4)

63. Patent Office Records, Dublin

64. Merne — (47)

65. W. A. Maguire — *A Century in Focus*

66. Glukman/Constable correspondence.

67. ibid.

68. ibid.

69. Another indication of Glukman's wealth is the fact that he left Clair Grece £1000 in his will, the equivalent of at least £100, 000 today.

70. *Westmeath Independent*, 1864

71. Various newspaper reports

72. List of Exhibits

73. Newspaper reports

74. There are copies of most of these books in the N.L.I.

75. Kieran Hickey — *The Light of Other Days*, 1973

76. The Lawrence Collection is available on microfilm at the Photographic Archive

77. *The Mason Family Busines, (*Booklet), Dublin, 1980

78. Alfred Werner, lecture text in *The Camera*, 1922 (5)

79. Transcribed from Merne (47)

80. Calotype Club was founded in London in 1847 with Roger Fenton as secretary.

81. Merne — (47)

82. ditto

83. *The Photographic Journal*, 1854-1859

84. ibid.

85. List of Members, P.R.O., Dublin

86. David Davison — (56)

87. Greenough — (4)

88. Gernsheim —(1)

89. Merne — (47)

90. ibid.

91. Gordon L. Davies — *The Story of Science in Trinity College Dublin*, (1977) p. 16-17

92. T.C.D. Archives

93. The late Mr. Louis Werner, nephew of Alfred Werner, c1980

94. Terence Pepper — *High Society Photography*, 1998

95. ibid.

96. Merne — (47)

97. Roderick O'Moore — *Cinema Ireland 1895-1976*, pp. 4-5. A booklet published in connection with an exhibition held at T.C.D. as part of the Dublin Arts Festival.

98. Liam O'Leary — *Cinema Ireland 1895-1976*, p. 21

General Index